D0383945

Multicultural Manners

Multicultural Manners

Essential Rules of Etiquette for the 21st Century

REVISED EDITION

Norine Dresser

WILEY

John Wiley & Sons, Inc.

Copyright © 1996, 2005 by Norine Dresser. All rights reserved

Published by John Wiley & Sons, Inc., Hoboken, New Jersey
Published simultaneously in Canada

No part of this publication may be reproduced, stored in a retrieval system, or transmitted in any form or by any means, electronic, mechanical, photocopying, recording, scanning, or otherwise, except as permitted under Section 107 or 108 of the 1976 United States Copyright Act, without either the prior written permission of the Publisher, or authorization through payment of the appropriate per-copy fee to the Copyright Clearance Center, 222 Rosewood Drive, Danvers, MA 01923, (978) 750-8400, fax (978) 646-8600, or on the web at www.copyright.com. Requests to the Publisher for permission should be addressed to the Permissions Department, John Wiley & Sons, Inc., 111 River Street, Hoboken, NJ 07030, (201) 748-6011, fax (201) 748-6008, or online at http://www.wiley.com/go/permissions.

Limit of Liability/Disclaimer of Warranty: While the publisher and the author have used their best efforts in preparing this book, they make no representations or warranties with respect to the accuracy or completeness of the contents of this book and specifically disclaim any implied warranties of merchantability or fitness for a particular purpose. No warranty may be created or extended by sales representatives or written sales materials. The advice and strategies contained herein may not be suitable for your situation. You should consult with a professional where appropriate. Neither the publisher nor the author shall be liable for any loss of profit or any other commercial damages, including but not limited to special, incidental, consequential, or other damages.

For general information about our other products and services, please contact our Customer Care Department within the United States at (800) 762-2974, outside the United States at (317) 572-3993 or fax (317) 572-4002.

Wiley also publishes its books in a variety of electronic formats. Some content that appears in print may not be available in electronic books. For more information about Wiley products, visit our web site at www.wiley.com.

Library of Congress Cataloging-in-Publication Data:

Dresser, Norine, date.
    Multicultural manners: essential rules of etiquette for the 21st century/ Norine Dresser.—Rev. ed.
        p. cm.
    Includes bibliographical references and index.
    ISBN-13 978-0-471-68428-2 (pbk.)
    ISBN-10 0-471-68428-7 (pbk.)
        1. Etiquette—United States. 2. Multiculturalism—United States.
    I. Title.
    BJ1854.D75 2005
    395—dc22

                                                            2004027079

Printed in the United States of America

10 9 8 7 6 5

To
El Pueblo de Nuestra Señora La Reina
de
Los Angeles
for providing me with the most exciting journey—
without need of passport or luggage.

Contents

Acknowledgments   xvii

Introduction   1

1

The New Rules of Communication

Body Language   11

Heads Up, Down, or Sideways?   11
High Five   12
Giving Change   12
Physical Contact   13
Sign of the Cross   14
Hands off the Head   15
Greetings   15
Signs of Affection   18
Thumbs-Up   19
Crooked Finger   20
Smiling   20
Eye Contact   22
Lining Up   24
One at a Time   25
Smell   26

Child-Rearing Practices   29

Lazy New Mom   29
Sharing the Bed   29
Breast Milk   31
Independence   32
Chaperone   33
Coining   34

Classroom Behavior   37

Testing   37
Enrichment Activities   38
Special Education   38
Fear of Authority   39
Student Participation   40
"Stupid!"   41
Left-handed   42
Corporal Punishment   43
Cheating   44
Respect for Teachers   46
Teacher Knows Best   47
Absenteeism   49

Clothing and Jewelry   51

Hats Off—Not!   51
Camouflage   52
Six-Pointed Stars   52
Swastika   53
Shoes   54
Boutique Boo-boos   55
Unsoulful Soles   56
Donkey Beads   56

Glass-Bead Necklaces 57
Modesty 59
Kirpan 60
Dress for Respect 62

Colors 63

Green Hats 63
Red Ink as Death Sign 64
Light Blue 65
White Bonnets 65
Wedding Guests Wearing White 66
Black at a Chinese Wedding 67
Yellow Tags 68

Foodways 71

Cracked Eggs 71
Refusing Food 72
Changing Food Habits 72
Offering Food 73
Milk Intolerance 74
Potluck 75
What Makes a Meal? 76
Food Taboos 77
Utensils 79
Making Eating Noises 80
Cleaning Your Plate 81
Boxes of Food 83
Food and Politics 83
Fast-Food Bags 84
Food as Medicine 85
Hot/Cold 87

Gifts   91

Yellow Flowers   91
White Flowers   92
Funeral Flowers   93
Bribery   94
Gift Taboos   95
White Envelopes   96
Refusing a Gift   98
Birthday Cake   99

Health Practices   101

AIDS   101
Misunderstanding the Doctor's Orders   102
Heart Transplants and Licorice   103
Hospital Accommodations   105
Ignoring the Baby   106
Alternative Healers   107
Sacrificing a Rooster   108
Physical Examinations   109
Birth Attendants   110
Prayer Position   110
Birth Control   111
No Heroic Measures?   112

Holidays   115

Ramadan   115
Thanksgiving   116
Halloween   116
Jumping over Fires   117
New Year's Offerings   118
First Foot   119
Sweeping Away the Luck   120

Luck and Supernatural Forces

Gris-Gris	123
Ashes	124
Permanent Wave	125
Hot Rocks	126
The Voodoo Squad	127
Eclipse	128
Feng Shui	129
Moving and the Almanac	131
Numbers	132
Numbers in Photos	134
Odd or Even?	135
Black Magic	136
Red Envelopes	136
Baby Furniture Delivery	137
Evil Eye	138
Rocks	139

Male/Female Relations and Gender Issues

Gender Expectations	141
Lesbian Bridesmaid	142
AIDS Education	143
Spousal Abuse	143
Romantic Implications	145
Hospital Roommates	146
Chastity	147
Inequality	148
Child Custody	149
Home Alone Together	149

Miscellany

Traffic Violations	151
Points of View	152

The *Qur'an* (Koran) 153

Generosity 153

Temples 154

Japanese Business Cards 155

Temporary Nuns 156

Business Practices 156

Sealing a Deal 158

Welcoming Home Ceremonies 158

Birthday Dates 160

Friendship 161

Hospitality 162

Political Differences 163

Shoveling Dirt on the Coffin 164

Menstruation 164

Prejudice 167

Post–September 11 167

Race Manners 169

Green Card 170

Mosque Phobia 171

Bridge Builders of Anchorage 171

Math Skills 172

False Assumptions 173

Time 177

Urgency 177

Being on Time 178

Dropping In 179

Taboo Times 180

Verbal Expressions 183

Complimenting a Baby 183

Beating around the Bush 183

"Hello!"   184

Giving Praise   185

Too Friendly   186

Accent   187

Forms of Address   188

Naming Traditions   189

Idioms   191

"No Molesta"   192

Compliments about Appearance   193

Yes or No?   193

Can't Say No   194

Bargaining   195

Believing What They Say   197

2

Clearing Cultural Confusions

A Quick Reference Guide   **201**

Map   **202**

Africans   **204**

Algerians   204

Egyptians   205

Eritreans   206

Ethiopians   206

Ghanaians   207

Kenyans   208

Liberians   209

Libyans   210

Malians   210

Moroccans   211

Nigerians   211

Rwandans   212

Somalis   213

Sudanese   214

Tunisians   214

Ugandans   215

Asians   **216**

Bhutanese   216

Chinese   217

Japanese   218

Koreans, North   218

Koreans, South   219

Taiwanese   220

South Asians   **220**

Afghans   220

Bangladeshis   221

Indians   222

Myanmar/Burmese   223

Nepalese   224

Pakistanis   224

Sri Lankans   225

Southeast Asians   **226**

Cambodians   226

East Timorese   227

Filipinos   227

Indonesians   228

Lao   229

Malaysians   230

Singaporeans 231
Thai 231
Vietnamese 232

The Balkans **233**
Albanians 233
Bosnians and Herzegovinans 234
Croats 234
Macedonians 235
Serbians and Montenegrans 236
Slovenians/Slovenes 237

Independent Members of the Former USSR **238**
Armenians 238
Azerbaijanis 239
Belarusians 239
Estonians 240
Georgians 241
Kazakhs 242
Kyrgyz 243
Latvians 243
Lithuanians 244
Moldovans 245
Russians 245
Tajiks 246
Turkmens 247
Ukrainians 247
Uzbeks 248

Middle Easterners **249**
Iranians 249
Iraqis 250

Israelis	251
Jordanians	251
Kuwaitis	252
Lebanese	253
Saudis	254
Syrians	254
Turks	255
United Arab Emirates	256
Yemenis	256
Bibliography	259
Index	271

Acknowledgments

This list is long with names of colleagues, students, friends, relatives, and readers of my *Los Angeles Times* column, in short, all those folks who gave me wonderful stories for this book or reactions to particular issues. I thank you all:

Elizabeth Adams, Ph.D.; Jesus R. Aguillon; Chelo Alvarez; Navneet S. Arora; John Aventino; Ana Balzer; Abot Bensusan; Andrea Berne, R.N.; Sharon Birnkrant; Betty Blair; Linda Burns Bolton, Ph.D., Director of Nursing Education, Cedars-Sinai Medical Center, Los Angeles; Stephen V. Bomse; LuAnn Boylan; Judy Bravard; Milada Broukal; Lise Buranen; Darcel Linh Cao; Amy Catlin, Ph.D.; Susan Daniels; Esther De Haro; Sgt. Mark Dallezotte, San Diego Police Department; Linh M. Diep; Shirlee Dresser; Hoa Duong; Minh Duc; Isabel Elac; Robin Evanchuk, Ph.D.; Susan Fein; Terry Flores; Ysamur Flores-Peña, Ph.D.; Natalie Flyer; Kathleen Flynn, Ph.D.; Yvonne Freeman; Frank Heron of the *Syracuse (NY) Herald Journal*; Yolanda Galvan; William L. Garrett; Julia Gavilanes; Jeanne Gee; Mary Georges; Ingo Giani; Clarice Gillis; Sandy Glickman; Dale Gluckman; Lorenzo Gonzalez; Lin Griffith; Anahid Grigorian; Nelson Gutierrez; Alice Thuc Ha; Janice Nghi Nha Ha; Stephanie Hang; Jayasri Hart, Ph.D.; Judith Haut, Ph.D.; Alan Hedman, Ph.D.; Carole and Isaac Haile Selassie; Officer Abdiweli Heibeh, San Diego Police Department; Jeff K. H. Hsu; Detective Paul Jean-Louis, Miami-Dade Police Department; Marjorie Keyes, R.N.; Ann Kiuchi; Venida Korda; Carolyn Krueger; John Kusmiss, Ph.D.; Han Lam; Ceci Ledezma; Kuang-Hua Liu; Ada Lopez; Emma Louie; Letty Maravilla; Roobina Markarbabrood; Joanne Marshall; Richard E. Marshall; Mika Matsui; Quinn McDonald; Rabbi Levi Meier, Cedars-Sinai Medical Center, Los Angeles; Doug Metz; Robert A. Miller; Rosa Montes De Oca; Vivian Moore; Patricia Morales; Anna María Wong Mota; Than Ha Nguyen; Raihana Niazi; Seung-Young Oh; Michi Okano; Nanelle Oropez; June Parris-Miller; Alberto Perez; Joel T. Pham;

Tony Phuong; Sheila M. Pickwell, Ph.D., CFNP; Brin Pime; Dorothy Pittel; Morris Polan; Patrick Polk, Ph.D.; Bunny Rabiroff; Buddy Roberts; Malcolm Roberts; Alice Roy, Ph.D.; Arpi Sarafian, Ph.D.; Richard Seltzer; Dong-Jin Seo; Kathy Shannon; Stan Sherer; Linda Wong Smith, President, the Chinese Historical Society of Southern California; Mark Stehle; Bill Sterling; Theresa Sterling; Yale Strom; Edward Sun; Frances Tally, Ph.D., and the UCLA Archive of Popular Beliefs and Superstitions; Satoshi Tanaka; Rosemarie Taylor, R.N., North Dade County Florida Health Center; Leilei Thein; Teresa Toribio; Linh Tran; Tai Truong; Lucia van Ruiten; Scarlet Vartanian; Celín Vasquez; Marie Vester; Denh Voong; Alan Voun; Jennifer Warren; Sammy Tone-Kei White; Christiana Wise; Dolores Wong; Pat Wong; Tong Yin; Wilhelmina Ramos York; Fay Zachary; Magda Zelinska-Ferl, Ph.D.

Special words of gratitude go to my medical consultants and dear friends Karl Seligman, M.D.; and Rachel Spector, R.N., Ph.D. I am also fortunate to have other knowledgeable buddies on whom I depend: Virginia Crane; Marilyn Elkins, Ph.D.; and Montserrat Fontes. Their consultations and checking of the manuscript often rescued me from myself. Jan Steward gets a special nod for being the ever-present voice on the other end of the phone line (for over 50 years), to discuss myriad issues. Cheryl Rilly and Janice Garey were there for me, too, offering ideas and support. Additionally, Phyllis Roberts, graphic artist, receives my applause for her wonderful map. I am indebted to all of you.

And what would I do without the family? I pay tribute to Harold, sweetheart of a husband, eager to make a last-minute library trip or to bring in take-out dinners; to "the kids," Mark, Carol, Andrea, Amy, Julio, and Leila—suppliers of leads, anecdotes, and advice; to my brother Mickey, who jumps in to assist no matter what the venture.

Here's a toast to Sheree Bykofsky, capable agent and enthusiastic ally, alongside her terrific associates, Janet Rosen and Megan Buckley. Thanks also to Tom Miller, executive editor at John Wiley & Sons, who encouraged me to write this second edition. And a special note of appreciation goes to editor Teryn Johnson, who patiently dealt with my time compulsions and responded ably and quickly to my concerns.

To everyone: *gracias, danke, merci, arigato.*

Introduction

Introduction to the Revised Edition

While in a hospital cafeteria, I looked for tea to go with my sandwich. I tapped the shoulder of a man standing in front of me in the checkout line. "Excuse me. Can you please tell me where the tea is?"

He wheeled around. He was Chinese and clearly offended by my question. Emphatically he answered, "*I don't drink tea.*"

I felt embarrassed. Of course, by only seeing his back I had no clue that he was Chinese. By asking him about tea it seemed as if I was making a stereotypical assumption about his foodways. Obviously, that irritated him. Despite my innocence, I felt guilty. What irony! I'm supposed to have heightened sensitivity about avoiding cross-cultural blunders, but in this situation nothing could rescue me.

Nonetheless, as important as it is to be cross-culturally savvy, equally important is the ability to laugh at oneself. Blunders don't have to turn into world wars. As long as we maintain a sense of humor, mistakes may even serve to strengthen bonds, as they did in the following situation.

I arranged to interview a Hmong family for my *Multicultural Celebrations* book. I had read that they remove their shoes indoors, and when I arrived at their home I saw a pile of shoes outside the front door. Feeling smug about having prepared for the visit, I took off my sandals. Lia stood at the door protesting that it was unnecessary, but I wanted to show her I knew about Hmong customs. To my chagrin, when I entered her living room filled with family, no one was barefoot except me. They thought it was comical. I did, too.

I was also able to turn it around and make fun of myself, breaking the ice as I interviewed them about Hmong weddings.

How Is *Multicultural Manners, Revised Edition,* the Same as the First Edition?

Basically, this is still a how-to book—how to get along with others who are culturally different. As before, it is not targeted just to those who travel or conduct international business. Cultural information has many applications: To help interact more effectively with new populations from East Africa, the San Diego Police Department has created a videotape for officers about the customs and folkways of these recent residents; the U.S. Marine Corps offers cultural information to its occupational forces in Iraq, counseling them on do's and don'ts for their own safety and to increase rapport with the locals. Moreover, Lt. Col. Michael T. Mahoney, the U.S. Army commanding officer of Forward Operating Base Thunder in Iraq, has worked hard to absorb Iraqi customs and etiquette. His motivation? To win the peace.

So, my goal is still to demystify the behaviors of people of different cultural backgrounds. Holocausts and ethnic cleansings are monstrous results of people who refuse to accept those unlike themselves in religious practice, language, or color. Instead, I'd like to increase appreciation for all peoples and emphasize that showing respect for differences usually creates respect in return.

Mainly, however, the information is relevant to ordinary Americans, for we all deal daily with those who are culturally different: in the workplace, the neighborhood, and perhaps even our own families. Since one in nine U.S. residents was born in another country, and the total foreign-born population now exceeds 33 million with an estimated 1.3 million immigrants arriving annually, we regularly encounter people who are culturally different more frequently than in the past. In 2004, more than 70 percent of the residents of Elmhurst, Queens, New York, were foreign born. The U.S. Census Bureau projects that by 2050 the Hispanic and Asian American populations will triple.

My own awareness of multicultural issues developed over more than twenty-five years as a folklorist teaching at various colleges in the Los Angeles area, later collecting first-person stories about cross-cultural miscommunication, particularly from non-native English speakers. For eight years I wrote a twice-monthly "Multicultural Manners" column for the *Los Angeles Times* about the ways that cultural differences sabotage effective communication, emphasizing the "what went wrong?" in each situation. In 1998, the column and the original *Multicultural Manners* book received an award from the Los Angeles County Department of Human Relations for contributions toward promoting intergroup harmony. For me as a folklorist, this award acknowledges the importance of knowing about others' customs and beliefs.

This knowledge and this book do not venture to cure racism, nor is the book intended as a finger-pointing book of "shoulds." Rather, it points to cross-cultural hot spots and suggests methods of creating respect for diversity. The goal is to help identify what went wrong in cross-cultural interactions that failed and to help avoid future blunders.

Every part of our planet today is multicultural. Even the most isolated, such as North Korea, has a small Chinese community and a few ethnic Japanese. Yet for some, the word "multiculturalism" has become a dirty word—the "M" word. Diana Eck, Harvard Professor of Comparative Religion and Indian Studies, illuminates the bias against multiculturalism: "Some people mistake it for a political platform rather than a social reality." Readers of my *Los Angeles Times* column occasionally protested that reality: "They're in *our* country now. Let them adapt to *our* ways. Why should *we* have to adjust to *them*?"

Of course, no one *has to* adjust to newcomers in a society, but those who do are more likely to reap rewards. It's all quite pragmatic. Having information about other people's folkways can improve human relations—as those who work in the business world have known for some time. In California, Rose Hills Memorial Park provides incinerators for bereaved Chinese families who burn paper money to ensure a happy afterlife. To honor the Chinese/Vietnamese Lunar New Year 2000, Year of the Dragon, certain J.C. Penney's distributed beautifully illustrated dragon posters. Western Union and State Farm Insurance gave out traditional good-luck red envelopes to Lunar New Year celebrants. Responding to cultural differences of customers, clients, employees, patients, students, neighbors, and family pays off!

Increasingly, in more and more parts of this country, there is an overwhelming quantity of cultural information to absorb and accept. Pity the latest immigrants who, in order to get along, must become accustomed not only to mainstream rules but also to those of other newcomers as well. Think about the Mexican cook in a Pakistani restaurant who must learn English and master Muslim food taboos at the same time.

According to Eck, "It's one thing to be unconcerned about or ignorant of Muslim or Buddhist neighbors on the other side of the world, but when Buddhists are our next-door neighbors, when our children are best friends with Muslim classmates, when a Hindu is running for a seat on the school committee, all of us have a new vested interest in our neighbors, both as citizens and as people of faith."

As a folklorist, I delight in learning about cultural differences in customs and beliefs. Nonetheless, I know that these differences sometimes cause people who are unacquainted with the significance of particular acts to respond negatively. Therefore, I wanted to use my expertise to explain unfamiliar practices. However, I hope that I have not inadvertently created or reinforced stereotypes. Moreover, I have tried to avoid generalizations, yet some were necessary to make the book useful. Accordingly, based on my research, the guidelines apply to the majority of the people to whom they refer. Treat these rules as general principles, but remember that there will be exceptions. No blanket statement can apply to everyone.

I have also tried to be sensitive to sexist issues, but I have had to be forthright in differences in gender issues that exist for people coming from many countries outside the United States. In addition, I have strived throughout to use non-value-laden language. I have avoided the use of the word *superstition*, for one person's superstition is another person's belief.

Academic training in anthropology and folklore has influenced my emphasis on cultural relativity—attempting to see the validity and function of cultures without value judgment. I would like readers also to avoid being judgmental. Despite this desire to be objective, I know it is more an ideal than a reality. The outlooks of all of us have been shaped by our backgrounds and have given us particular lenses through which we view the world.

One of my greatest apprehensions is that I will appear patronizing by encouraging others to bend over backwards to understand the behavior of newcomers. This deliberate attempt to comprehend unfamiliar behavior is never intended to be insulting. I only want to cast some illumination upon cultural rules and traditions. Be that as it may, my concern is that these good intentions may boomerang.

I wrote *Multicultural Manners* because I wanted to ease the conflicts and misunderstandings that happen to all of us every day. My experience as a teacher has convinced me that we really want to understand and accept one another; most of our failures to do so stem from ignorance rather than from bad intentions. Finally, this book is my attempt to guide well-meaning people such as you through the increasingly complicated labyrinth of modern life.

How Does *Multicultural Manners, Revised Edition,* Differ from the First Edition?

In the first *Multicultural Manners*, most cultural mishaps occurred in the United States. The emphasis was on groups of immigrants who arrived in the last three decades of the twentieth century, with many Asian and Latino examples. This time, I have broadened the scope to include some of the newer arrivals from Ethiopia, Kosovo, and Bosnia, as well as incidents occurring in Albania, Azerbaijan, Albania, Nepal, and Spain. To make the book more timely, I have added stories about reactions post–September 11 as well as misunderstandings about lesbian relationships, children with autism, and people with AIDS.

Because I discovered that readers savored the stories of the original book, I have added many more true-life anecdotes. In order to accommodate this expansion, I eliminated other sections on rules for holidays, worship, and multicultural health practices.

Our world has changed dramatically since the first edition. September 11, 2001, turned our lives upside down. Until then, Al Qaeda and the Taliban were not part of our vocabulary. Today,

Baghdad, Kabul, and Islamabad are commonplace names, yet most of us know little about the people who live there. For this reason I have created a new section: Part 2, Clearing Cultural Confusions. It gives easy-to-understand information about the international players affecting our daily lives, such as Africans, Asians, the Balkans, independent members of the former USSR, and Middle Easterners. The section has two functions: an overview of native cultures and customs as well as the numbers living in the United States.

How This Book Is Structured

Part 1, The New Rules of Communication, organizes miscommunications according to major issues, for example, Body Language, Child-Rearing Practices, Classroom Behavior, Clothing and Jewelry, and so on. Examples follow each heading. Guidelines or generalizations are marked with bullets. Throughout the book, topics are consistently cross-referenced.

Guidelines are not absolutes. You may read parts of this book and say, "That's not true. My brother-in-law *never* does that." There will be exceptions to every rule because conduct differs with individuals. Furthermore, the acculturation process is not completely predictable. Many variables influence how quickly a person replaces traditional behavior with the new country's customs and values. Much depends on the length of time a person has been residing in the United States. Naturally, the longer people have been here, the more likely they will be affected by American culture, but even that is not inevitable.

Part 2, Clearing Cultural Confusions, is a handy reference guide and brief overview of people about whom we need to know more. Within each designated geographical area, populations are broken down into ethnicities, languages, religions, customs, and numbers from that area who are now living in the United States. More specific information is given in the introduction to that section, and a map is included.

Bibliography

While the majority of the information has been taken from my personal archives and field research, other books, pamphlets, and articles from newspapers, magazines, and journals were consulted. All are documented in the bibliography.

Invitation

If you discover that I have omitted an issue of importance to you or if you wish to share your experiences with me, I would be delighted to hear from you. Contact me in care of Teryn Johnson, editor, John Wiley & Sons, Inc., 111 River Street, Hoboken, NJ 07030, or you can contact me through my Web site: www.norinedresser .com.

1
The New Rules of Communication

Body Language

Heads Up, Down, or Sideways?

(See also: Yes or No?, p. 193; Albanians, p. 233.)

Covering a 1997 Albanian uprising, American reporters in the capital, Tirana, ask a driver if he can take them to the airport. The driver shakes his head from side to side, so they look for another driver and receive the same response. After several negative encounters, they discover that the drivers were available, after all.

- In Albania, shaking the head from side to side means "yes" and nodding the head up and down means "no."

Pity the poor American husband taking his visiting Albanian in-laws to the airport for their return home. When the attendant checked their luggage, she asked the usual questions: Did you pack your own bags? Have you left your bags unattended at any time? Did anyone ask you to carry something on board for them? Imagine the attendant's alarm as the Albanians nodded their heads up and down. Picture the son-in-law's panic trying to convince her that Albanians shake their heads in the opposite direction from Americans.

While in a Bulgarian restaurant, American tourists asked if stuffed cabbage was available. The waiter nodded "yes," but the stuffed cabbage never appeared. The disappointed diners learned that when the waiter shook his head "yes," he meant that they had none.

- Reversal of meaning of yes/no head gestures occurs in Bulgaria, too.

11

- People from Southern India tilt their heads to one side or both to indicate agreement.
- On many South Pacific Islands, they signal yes by raising their eyebrows.

High Five

Community leaders arrive for a meeting in Las Vegas. Karl, an African American director of an educational institution, attends and is greeted by Henry, the white chairperson. Henry slips into a mock African dialect and says, "Hey, bro, how's it going?" He follows with a high-five hand slap and walks away. Karl is aghast.

Angrily, Karl explains to a colleague, "This is supposed to be a professional organization and Henry assumes that because I'm African American, I come from the ghetto. I'm not, and in my home, I was never allowed to do that handshake or to speak jive."

Karl had an upper-class background, had attended the best schools, and had worked in high-level positions at blue-chip corporations. Although Karl recognized that Henry acted from ignorance, not malice, it did not lessen the insult. Henry's stereotypical assumption may have cost him an important business contact.

- Be careful when appropriating the jargon or gestures of other ethnicities, lest it be considered patronizing. These actions can sabotage a relationship.

Giving Change

Cheryl regularly shops for cleaning supplies at a local Michigan Dollar Store. Usually the manager, Mr. Hakim, puts her change on the counter instead of in her hand. One day, she has the exact amount for her purchase. She hands him a five-dollar bill and while dropping eighteen cents into his hand, her fingers accidentally touch his palm. Mr. Hakim recoils. Thinking she has accidentally scratched him, she says, "Whoops, sorry!" Looking back on the incident, she realizes that Mr. Hakim didn't want to be touched.

The next time Cheryl shops there, she places her money on the counter. Mr. Hakim smiles, something he has never done before, as he takes her money and in return places her change on the counter.

- Mr. Hakim is a Muslim, and it is taboo for unrelated males and females to have body contact. (See also: Greetings, p. 15.)
- Unrelated Orthodox Jewish men and women cannot touch.
- Koreans avoid touching strangers, particularly between members of the opposite sex but between the same sex as well.
- The avoidance of body contact does not necessarily signify rejection or discrimination. It may be customary or even a sign of respect.

Physical Contact

(See also: Japanese, p. 218.)

When Brin travels to Japan, she meets Kenji, who invites her for a motorbike ride through the countryside. Instead of climbing into the side seat, Brin sits behind Kenji. As soon as she puts her arms around him, he abruptly announces, "Let's get in the car."

This exemplifies how uncomfortable Japanese are with public physical contact. It not only applies to male/female contact but to same-sex contact as well. When Dorothy hugged her neighbor, Mrs. Yamashita, at the wedding of Mrs. Yamashita's son, the groom's mother stiffened. Even at such a joyous occasion as a wedding, Japanese customs about physical contact are not relaxed.

- Avoid body contact with Japanese people.
- At Japanese special occasions, offer verbal felicitations and nod the head slightly forward.
- Most Asian cultures frown on heterosexual touching. (See also: Signs of Affection, p. 18.)

Sign of the Cross

The California audience sits raptly engaged in the opera. Suddenly an earthquake strikes. The singers drop to their knees, cross themselves, then, with regained composure, stand up and resume singing.

The performers were Roman Catholics from Spain. Making the Sign of the Cross is an automatic gesture for the faithful when experiencing fear or as a sign of respect to their religion.

Roman Catholics make the sign by using two fingers of their right hand joined with the thumb to touch their foreheads, the center of the chest, then the left side over the heart and then the right side of the chest. Members of the Orthodox Church make the Sign of the Cross in reverse direction: After touching the forehead and center of the chest, they move to the right side of the chest, then to the left.

An Eastern Orthodox Church member explains the difference. When Christ was on the cross, he was between two thieves, also on crosses. Because only the thief on the right asked for forgiveness, he was labeled the "good thief." For that reason, the Eastern Orthodox cross from right to left.

The number of fingers used can be controversial. During the mid-seventeenth century Great Church Schism in the Russian Orthodox Church, Nikon, the new patriarch, undertook reforms including one that required the Sign of the Cross to be made with two fingers instead of three, the customary number up to this time. Those who refused, the Old Believers, were so adamant about maintaining their traditions that they left Russia and emigrated. Some came to the United States and now live in the Alaskan Kenai Peninsula and near Portland, Oregon.

- Regardless of direction of the gesture, the Sign of the Cross reflects a person's relationship to a higher power. It expresses reverence and/or a need for protection.

Hands off the Head

In a class that helps primary-school children improve their English-language skills, Alma, a new teacher, distributes worksheets with outlines of human figures. She asks the children to identify different body parts by coloring them with assigned colors. They comply until asked to color noses, ears, or any other parts located on the head. Then they refuse to follow her instructions.

The children were Hmong, from the hill country of Laos. The Hmong believe the spirit resides in the head; thus the head is sacred. The children refused to color the heads because by touching them, even in drawings, they might bring harm to the persons the pictures represented. The head must not be touched in reality, either. Previously, Alma and many other teachers had been accustomed to patting youngsters on their heads as a sign of affection. However, after distressed reactions from the children and their parents, the instructors discontinued the patting.

- Many Southeast Asians believe that touching their heads places them in jeopardy because that is where their spirit resides.

Greetings

(See also: Romantic Implications, p. 145.)

Hoa has just arrived from Vietnam. Her cousin Phuong and some of his American friends are waiting at the airport to greet her. Hoa and Phuong are both excited about this meeting because they have been separated for seven years. As soon as Hoa enters the passenger terminal, Phuong introduces her to his friends Tom, Don, and Charles. Tom steps forward and hugs and kisses Hoa. She pushes him away and bursts into tears.

Among Chinese from Vietnam, if a boy hugs and kisses a girl in public, he insults her. Chinese culture in Vietnam is very strict about this, especially in the rural areas where Hoa grew up. She described her village: "After children are ten years old, boys and girls cannot play together. A boy and girl cannot date without their parents' approval. A man and woman cannot hug or kiss if they're not married." (See also: Signs of Affection, p. 18.)

In Hoa's village, if anyone violated these rules, the villagers punished the girl by forcing her to kneel on the ground so they could spit at her and throw rocks at her. No wonder Phuong's American friends frightened Hoa. She did not know what punishment for public hugging and kissing might be meted out to her in this country. She confused Tom, who by American standards was doing the right thing.

Eventually Hoa learned to be comfortable when greeted with hugs and kisses, accepting them as merely perfunctory acts.

Analogous to this situation is another in which Duane, a Chinese American employee, invited his non-Chinese boss, Mr. Keck, to a large family celebration. When Mr. Keck arrived, he shook hands with Duane and, when introduced to Duane's grandmother, leaned over and kissed her on the cheek. This shocked the older woman, yet Mr. Keck was totally unaware that he had committed a social blunder. What he considered a respectful act, Grandmother considered disrespectful. Instead, Mr. Keck should have nodded to the older woman and offered her a verbal greeting.

- When establishing relations with Asians, avoid body contact. The safest form is to nod and give a verbal salutation. Follow their lead as the relationship changes.

Increased cross-cultural interaction brings about changes in customs; many Asian businesspeople have accommodated to the American handshaking tradition. On the other hand, in a situation where it seems as if bowing would still be the only polite move to make—especially to the Japanese—following these guidelines should make it easier:

- When bowing to people from Japan, the hands should slide down toward the knees or remain at the side.
- The back and neck should be held in a rigid position, while the eyes look downward.

- The person in the inferior position always bows longer and lower.

Those from India, Sri Lanka, and Bangladesh use the *namaste* for both greetings and farewells and as a sign of respect. They do this by holding their hands chest-high in a prayerlike position, then slightly nod the head, but they do not bow. American students of yoga who are taught by Asian teachers become familiar with this gesture that heralds the beginning of each session. Thais have a similar greeting, but they call it a *wai*.

While body contact is generally taboo in most Asian countries, elsewhere body contact is expected; shying away from contact gives off negative signals.

- When greeting, people from India, Sri Lanka, Bangladesh, and Thailand hold their hands together in front of their chins in a prayerlike position and nod their heads.
- When greeting, most Latinos expect body contact. Hugging and kissing on the cheek are acceptable for both the same sex and the opposite sex. The *abrazo* is commonplace—friends embrace and simultaneously pat each other on the back.
- When greeting, most people from France, Spain, Italy, Portugal, and other Mediterranean countries expect to be kissed on both cheeks.
- When greeting, most Middle Easterners, especially Muslims, avoid body contact with the opposite sex (see also: Giving Change, p. 12), but men may embrace and kiss one another. Women may do the same. When shaking hands, men should avoid pulling their hands away too quickly.
- When greeting most Armenians, expect some body contact. Women kiss once on each cheek and hug; men shake hands. Men may also hug and kiss women on the cheek if they are close friends.
- When greeting Orthodox Jews, avoid body contact with the opposite sex.
- Muslims, especially older ones, make the *salaam* greeting by using the right hand to touch the heart and move the hand upward to touch the forehead. They may say "*Salaam alaykum*" (Peace be with you).

Signs of Affection

(See also: Physical Contact, p. 13; Greetings, p. 15.)

Sheree Bykofsky, an American writer, is thrilled when a cruise ship line purchases copies of her new romantic travel guide, *The Best Places to Kiss in and around New York City*. The cruise line plans to give the books as dinner favors during their special Valentine's cruise.

They invite Sheree on board to greet the passengers and autograph their copies. The Americans and Europeans delight in meeting the author and having her sign their books. However, when Sheree visits the tables of the Japanese passengers, most of them refuse to acknowledge her.

Japanese people do not approve of public body contact and, thus, have developed a complex system of bowing to express relationships. Touching a member of the opposite sex is particularly repugnant to their sensitivities; consequently, kissing in public is considered a disgraceful act.

The Japanese snubbed Sheree because the title of her book suggested behavior that did not conform to their standards of respect. They would not acknowledge her because in their eyes she promoted vulgarity.

Asians from countries other than Japan are equally disapproving when they see American men and women openly displaying affection in public. In their own countries, women are thought of as "easy" if they act this way. Even husbands and wives avoid body contact in public.

Conversely, in Asian countries, it is perfectly acceptable for two women or two men to walk in public holding hands. However, when they practice this sign of friendship here, they are frequently mistaken for homosexuals. This shocks them.

Same-sex hand-holding or walking arm-in-arm also occurs among Latinos, French, Spanish, Italians, Greeks, and Middle Easterners.

- Most Japanese people strongly disapprove of public expression of affection by males and females through kissing or any other form of body contact.

- Same-sex hand-holding between Asians, Middle Easterners, Latinos, or those from Mediterranean countries is a sign of friendship. Walking with arms on each other's shoulders or with hands or arms linked also equates with camaraderie.
- This taboo is changing with the younger generations in the United States, who have begun to adopt more open public expressions of affection.

Thumbs-Up

Caroline works in the administrative office of a community college. She informs students about how they have fared on the English as a Second Language Placement Test. She is very friendly and patient with these students who have limited English skills.

One day, Zitilla, a girl from Afghanistan, comes to inquire about the results of her exam. She has done very well, and Caroline wishes to communicate this to her. She gives her the thumbs-up gesture. When Zitilla sees this, she turns red and beads of sweat form on her forehead. She rushes out of the office without saying a word.

In Zitilla's Afghan culture, the thumbs-up sign has the same sexual connotation as the American middle-finger gesture. Other Middle Eastern countries, as well as Nigeria and Australia, also think of it as obscene. It does not have any meaning for Southeast Asian (Cambodian, Hmong, Laotian, Mien, Vietnamese) cultures.

During the 1992 Democratic Convention, presidential nominee Bill Clinton used that sign on national television to indicate his pleasure over being nominated. One can just envision the amazed reaction of global TV watchers whose interpretation of the thumbs-up gesture matched Zitilla's.

- Gestures do not have universal meaning. For people from many parts of the world, thumbs-up is obscene.
- Pointing with the index finger is considered rude to people from outside the United States, especially people from Asian countries.
- The American "bye-bye" gesture means "come here" to people from Southeast Asia.

Crooked Finger

A Japanese-owned corporation in the United States hires American office workers, including Helen Olson. All the top management executives are Japanese males with very limited English language skills.

On her second day at work, Helen needs to communicate with one of the big bosses about some paperwork on her desk. Because of the language barrier, she uses gestures to indicate that she would like her boss to come over to her desk to look at the problem.

After she catches his eye, she crooks her index finger and moves it in a "come here" motion.

The boss looks horrified.

Totally unaware of Japanese body language, Helen had made an obscene gesture. She felt humiliated when she found out what the boss thought she meant. Of course, Helen had no intention of insulting him, but as a result of this misunderstanding, she became so uncomfortable working in this office that she decided to quit. However, when she gave notice, the boss would not accept it. In Japan, employees usually don't quit. If Helen left the company, it would cause the boss to lose face. Because of this, Helen remained working there for a short time and then, in spite of her employer's protests, she quit.

Japan is not the only country where this gesture has negative connotations. In Yugoslavia and Malaysia, it is used to call animals; in Indonesia and Australia, the gesture beckons prostitutes; in Vietnam, this gesture is used to call animals or to beckon an inferior. Frequently, when used between persons of equal status, it becomes an act of hostility. Among other Southeast Asians, it is a threatening gesture to children and an insolent one to adults.

- Don't use the crooked-index-finger "come here" gesture with Japanese or other Asian people.

Smiling

People are lined up at the DMV to have their photos taken for their picture identification on new and renewed drivers' licenses.

Russ Conner is the man behind the camera. Most people give him a great big smile when he asks them to do so. However, one day, when he asks a Japanese man to smile, the man refuses.

The Japanese man didn't smile because the picture was for a government document. To smile would have meant that he did not take his driving responsibility seriously enough. Generally, in their native country, the Japanese do not smile for photo IDs. Equating smiling with frivolous behavior may also be the reason why so few Japanese government officials are photographed with smiles, except when they are coached to do so for photos taken with American dignitaries.

According to Hiroto Murasawa of the Pola Research Institute of Beauty and Culture in Tokyo, who studies faces for a living, it's not proper to move the face or body too much. Until the twentieth century, some Japanese women shaved their eyebrows and blackened their teeth to veil natural expression. Many Japanese women still hide their mouths behind a hand when they speak or laugh. Concealing emotions has been an ideal for men as well.

While Americans primarily associate smiling with friendliness, a smile can mean something different in another culture. In Japan, people smile when they are sad, happy, apologetic, angry, or confused. In Korean culture, smiling signals shallowness and thoughtlessness. The Korean attitude toward smiling is expressed in the proverb, "The man who smiles a lot is not a real man." Lack of smiling by Koreans has often been misinterpreted as hostility when Korean shopkeepers interact with non-Korean customers. After the 1992 Los Angeles riots, Byung Sik Hong, a Korean American management expert, began coaching Korean immigrants in Los Angeles and Orange counties about the importance of smiling and other ways to convey friendliness to Americans.

For other Asians, smiling can mean disagreement, anger, frustration, confusion, or a substitute for "I'm sorry" or "Thank you." When Puerto Ricans smile, the message may be "Please," "Thank you," "You're welcome," "Yes, what can I do for you?", or "Excuse me, please. May I see you for a moment?" For Puerto Ricans, the variation in meaning depends on eye expression and forehead movements.

- Americans smile primarily as an expression of friendliness. People from other places may attach other meanings to it.

A summary of results of 134 Japanese medical students revealed that 69 percent interpreted smiling as a sign of happiness, 10.6 percent as a sign of disgust, 8.9 percent as sadness, 6.2 percent as contempt, and 2.5 percent as fear.

As of August 15, 2003, the government of Canada issued new specifications for passport photos. Canadians must now send in two photos with a neutral expression, meaning a closed-mouth, straight-ahead gaze. No more smiles. The purpose is to make it easier for security personnel to recognize the passport holder.

Eye Contact

Mr. Hayes, the manager of a chain drugstore, prides himself on the way he runs his business. Customers seem happy to shop there, and he believes it is because of the *esprit de corps* he has created among the employees.

One day while helping Isabela unpack a new shipment of toiletries, he invites her to take a break and sit down and have a cup of coffee with him. Shyly, she accepts. Mr. Hayes chats with her casually but notices that when he speaks to her, Isabela looks down at the floor and seems uninterested. He believes she is being disrespectful and reprimands her for this.

She is surprised at his anger.

In his typically American open style of communication, Mr. Hayes confronted Isabela about not looking at him. Reluctantly, she explained why. As a newcomer from Mexico, she had been taught to avoid eye contact as a mark of respect to authority figures—teachers, employers, parents. Mr. Hayes did not know this. He then informed her that most Americans interpret lack of eye contact as disrespect and deviousness. Ultimately, he convinced Isabela to try and change her habit, which she slowly did.

People from many Asian, Latino, and Caribbean cultures also avoid eye contact as a sign of respect. Many African Americans, especially from the South, observe this custom, too. A master's thesis by Samuel Avoian, a graduate student at Central Missouri State University, tells how misinterpreting eye contact customs can have a negative impact when white football coaches recruit African American players for their teams.

He reports that when speaking, white communicators usually look away from the listeners, only periodically glancing at them. They do the opposite when listening—they are expected to look at the speaker all the time.

Many African Americans communicate in an opposite way. When speaking, they tend to constantly stare at the listener; when listening, they mostly look away. Therefore, if white sports recruiters are not informed about these significant differences, they can be misled about interest and attentiveness when interviewing prospective African American ballplayers.

- Avoidance of eye contact may be a sign of respect. Cultural differences affect how people use their eyes to speak and listen.

In multicultural America, issues of eye contact have brought about social conflicts of two different kinds: In many urban centers, non-Korean customers became angry when Korean shopkeepers did not look at them directly. The customers translated the lack of eye contact as a sign of disrespect, a habit blamed for contributing to the open confrontation taking place between some Asians and African Americans in New York, Texas, and California. Many teachers, too, have provided stories about classroom conflicts based on their misunderstanding Asian and Latin American children's lack of eye contact as being disrespectful.

On the other hand, direct eye contact has now taken on a new meaning among the younger generation and across ethnic borders. Particularly in urban centers, when one teenager looks directly at another, this is considered a provocation, sometimes called mad-dogging, and can lead to physical conflict.

Mad-dogging has become the source of many campus conflicts. In one high school, it resulted in a fight between Cambodian newcomers and African American students. The Cambodians had been staring at the other students merely to learn how Americans behave, yet the others misinterpreted the Cambodians' intentions and the fight began.

Mad-dogging seems to be connected with the avoidance of eye contact as a sign of respect. Thus, in the urban contemporary youth scene, if one looks directly at another, this disrespects, or "disses," that person. Much like the archaic phrase "I demand satisfaction," which became the overture to a duel, mad-dogging may become a prelude to a physical encounter.

At the entrances to Universal Studios' "City Walk" attraction in Los Angeles, they have posted Code of Conduct signs. The second rule warns against "physically or verbally threatening any person, fighting, annoying others through noisy or boisterous activities or by *unnecessary staring*. . . ."

- Direct eye contact among urban youths can signal an invitation to a fight.

Lining Up

The usual long line confronts Judith Smartt as she steps up to her window at the DMV to begin taking pictures for drivers' licenses. After snapping several photos, the next person in line, a woman, moves forward, at the same time signaling four other people to join her.

Annoyed, Judith asks, "How many persons are you?" In halting English, the Armenian woman answers, "Five." Judith calls over a translator, who informs the woman that she cannot hold four extra places. Disappointed, the rest of her family goes to the end of the line and waits one more hour until they each reach their place in front of Judith's camera.

Lining up in Armenia had different rules. There, what this woman did would have been acceptable. Emigrés from other former Soviet dominated societies react similarly. A social service agency handling Soviet immigrants had difficulty because applicants would not line up in an orderly fashion. The clients were used to pushing and fighting to win the attention of the staff, a tactic that worked well in their former countries. To avoid this contest, the administrator switched to an appointment-only service and avoided lining-up problems.

Americans are particular about rules for standing in line. As children, they learn that no one can cut in, that each person must wait in line, and "first come, first served." No one has special privileges. Ideas about the correct way to line up exemplify values of democracy and efficiency.

- Many new immigrants don't understand the American rules for standing in line. For situations that require lines, an appointment-only system can be used to avoid lining-up problems.

One at a Time

Harold needs to buy a new TV and goes to an appliance store that has a very large stock. Ed, the eager salesman, shows Harold the different models and features. In the middle of doing so, he abandons Harold to attend to another customer who has just walked into the department. This offends Harold. In spite of the lure of the good prices, he leaves the store in a huff.

Harold believed that once a salesperson began working with a customer he should stay with that customer until the interaction was consummated—sale or no sale. That was the way he had run his own small business for fifty years and that was how he had always been treated before.

In contrast, Ed—actually Eduardo—came from Puerto Rico, where the concept of one customer at a time did not apply. In Puerto Rico and other Latin American countries, a salesperson takes care of up to four people at a time. Not only that, a newcomer has priority over the previous customer, so according to Ed's background, he was behaving courteously when he left Harold. To have given his attention only to Harold would have been rude to the new customer.

This system often baffles American tourists overseas, particularly when banking in Asia or Latin America. However, while the tourists may expect to find differences while traveling, they don't expect them here at home. That presents a challenge to both sides.

Ed was not trying to be discourteous. He just didn't know that business practices here are different, and he had not been trained otherwise by management. On the other hand, Harold was unaware of the possibility that styles of doing business are not universal. He had interpreted Ed's behavior as a discourtesy and a personal slight.

Because of these cultural differences, Harold bought his television at a store where he received the personal attention he felt was due him, and Eduardo lost the sale.

- While most Americans expect to be waited on one at a time, those from Latin American and Asian countries might have learned an opposite system.
- When training new retail employees from other countries, managers should alert the newcomers to the customary American salesperson/customer relationship of one at a time.

In social science terms, one-at-a-time interactions, typical of the United States, are called monochronic. Arabic, Asian, and Latin American interactions tend to be polychronic—more than one person or one thing is taken care of at a time. This difference explains why there is more interrupting in conversations carried on by people from Arabic, Asian, and Latin American cultures. Additionally, it can account for classroom behavior differences in interruption patterns and explain why some children from some cultures expect attention from the teacher while the teacher is taking care of others.

Smell

(See also: Child-Rearing Practices, p. 29.)

Bunny loves teaching this particular college class in Early Childhood Development because her students are so lively and outspoken. Now she has assigned a reading by psychoanalyst Erik Erikson about parents creating trust in their children. When American parents go out for the evening, they believe that telling the child a story beforehand and assuring them that Mommy and Daddy will be back is enough to make the child feel secure.

Wilhelmina, a Filipino student, objects and says that method's "too limited and upper middle class."

Wilhelmina gave an alternative method for building trust, one that she learned in the Philippines. Whenever she went out and the baby stayed at home with a sitter, Wilhelmina always left a piece of clothing that she had just removed on the child's pillow or in the baby's crib. That way, her scent remained with the child, offering reassurance that, indeed, the mother hadn't gone; part of her remained.

Nowadays, that technique is being adopted here, especially by working moms who have to return to the job soon after childbirth. Each day before going to work, they leave a recently worn article of clothing with the baby. Mommy's odor on the garment is a constant reminder of her presence.

Smell seems to play a bigger part in sensory-information gathering among Filipinos. One Filipina American reported that when she went back home to visit her relatives, her grandmother always sniffed her. While originally shocked by this act, she came to accept this behavior. Grandmother's sniffing was not a frivolous act; odors disclose information about health and hygiene.

- Different cultures place different emphasis on the senses. Some may stress smell, others sight, sound, or touch.
- When a mother tells a child, "I will be back," she's stressing sound. Another mother might convey the same message through her scent.
- The Maori of New Zealand ritually greet each other with the *hongi*. They press their noses and foreheads together and share the same breath—a kind of smelling. In ancient Hawaii, traditional Hawaiians inhaled one another, too. Although many people today consider *haole* (outsider) a derogatory word, in Hawaiian it originally meant "not of the same breath." There is a connection between these smelling habits and the Inuit greeting of rubbing noses.

Child–Rearing Practices

Lazy New Mom

Evelyn resents it when her Filipina daughter-in-law, Zen, has a baby and assumes that everyone should wait on her, especially Evelyn. Zen expects Evelyn to bathe and change the baby, clean the house, and prepare all meals. Despite adoring her first grand-child, Evelyn is offended.

Evelyn was unaware that her daughter-in-law was observing common Asian postpartum behavior: the new mom goes to bed for a month while everyone pampers her. Family members, and some-times neighbors, take over cooking and cleaning; when the baby needs to be fed, they bring a freshly changed infant to the mother.

In China, this practice is called *zuo yuezi* (sitting through the month). The woman must stay in bed behind closed windows, cover her head, and take many precautions to insure that she not damage her ability to produce breast milk.

Once Evelyn discovered that her daughter-in-law was behaving in a customary postpartum manner, she relaxed her attitude.

- Sometimes what we perceive as negative behavior has roots in another paradigm.
- Other cultures give more physical support to new mothers, where family and friends assume household obligations so that the new mom can rebuild her strength for at least one month after delivery.

Sharing the Bed

Working mom Jeanne has a surprise when she leaves her ten-week-old son Zachary with the Mexican babysitter, who lives with

29

her husband, children, and parents. The family falls in love with little Zachary and calls him Santo (the holy one).

Jeanne is Jewish, and even though she realizes that this refers to a saintly child, she knows it is a compliment and she is not offended. In fact, she is touched by the way the entire family loves and fusses over the child. However, one day when she goes to pick up her son, she finds him sleeping in bed with Grandma.

This upsets Jeanne.

Nowadays, many middle-class Americans expect to have not only a private bed but a private room for each child. This is in part tied to American notions about independence and individuality. However, in places where space has been a limited resource, children are expected to share beds with family members, just as they did in the early days of this country.

Many Asian, Middle Eastern, and Latin American families accept bed-sharing matter-of-factly. Sharing of beds demonstrates family closeness. Latinos use a colloquialism, *agusto*, to describe the coziness felt when snuggling with a relative. To be *agusto* is to be completely relaxed.

In the United States, cuddling up with one's parents or grandparents is relegated to special occasions. It gives children safe harbor and feelings of comfort. Nonetheless, no one expects to see their own children cuddling up with someone else's family members. This was a foreign concept for Jeanne—but one she eventually got used to because of all the love showered upon *Santo*.

Joni, another American mother, had a similar start when she discovered that her thirteen-year-old daughter who had gone to spend the night with a Filipino friend had shared the bed with both the girlfriend and the girlfriend's grandmother. In that household, it was not a matter of limited space, but rather a preferred sleeping arrangement.

- People from Latin American, Asian, and Middle Eastern cultures often share sleeping space with family members.
- As children become closer with friends from other cultures, they will experience new customs that they may easily adopt but that may be difficult for parents to accept.

Breast Milk

(See also: Hot/Cold, p. 87.)

The community health clinic treats mothers from mostly Latino backgrounds. The clinic hires Andrea as their lactation consultant to encourage the women to breast-feed their babies and to hold classes to provide appropriate information.

Andrea knows that the women have never received formal instruction about breast-feeding and have misconceptions about the process. At the first class meeting, she asks what they already know about breast-feeding. The first woman responds, "If someone hits you on the back, it will spoil your milk."

Andrea is dumbfounded.

The women shared their other beliefs:

If your milk spills on the floor, none of it will be any good.
If you get upset or angry, you will spoil your milk.
After a year, it's bad for babies to breast-feed because the milk
    is no good.
Smoking, drinking, or taking medication doesn't affect the
    baby.
Formula is as good as breast milk.
If you eat beans, the baby will get too much mucous.
If you don't cover your back, all the milk will dry up.
Beans or chiles will ruin the taste of the milk.

None of these beliefs is true, and Andrea had a difficult time reeducating the mothers. To add to the misconceptions, many new Latina moms believe the colostrum (the first fluid secreted after birth) is unclean. Accordingly, they do not breast-feed their babies until the third day when the true milk arrives. This is unfortunate because the colostrum contains vital immunity-building substances for the newborn.

Andrea discovered an additional negative attitude about breast-feeding. Immigrant mothers from a variety of backgrounds think it is more American and more modern, and thus more desirable, to bottle-feed their babies. They needlessly spend money on formula, a commodity that cannot match the quality of milk they naturally produce. Breast milk won't cause intestinal infections because it is pure. In addition, it is always at the proper temperature, and it costs nothing.

- Many immigrant mothers have misconceptions about breast-feeding.
- Younger Cambodian, Chinese, and Vietnamese women are more reluctant about breast-feeding than older women.
- Lactation education is important for immigrant mothers, particularly those who are away from their own mothers, who would ordinarily provide breast-feeding encouragement.

Independence

Robert and Greta Lyons are a very friendly couple, so when they meet eighteen-year-old Paulino from Colombia, South America, they invite him to live with them until he gets settled here. After a short time, Paulino tells them he would like to go to school and look for a job to pay for his school expenses. He asks his new friends if it would be all right if he continues to live with them.

Robert and Greta say yes, but they ask him how he will cover his living expenses. Paulino is shocked. He becomes cold and silent.

Where Paulino grew up, one offers a friend or relative a helping hand with no questions asked and no strings attached. That's the Colombian way. Colombian hosts would never expect their guests to pay for their own expenses.

While at first Paulino resented their questions, his hosts finally convinced him that the request for money was not a negative commentary on how they felt about him. They explained that they would request the same of their own children who remained at home past the age of eighteen. Paulino eventually accepted their point of view. He cheerfully contributed toward his living costs and felt like a full member of the Lyons family.

When they are old enough to work, children from other ethnic groups contribute to household expenses; however, parents do not charge for their offspring's living costs. Rather, children give a portion of their earnings to help the family. The difference is semantics and attitude.

- American attitudes regarding an offspring's independence and responsibility may be misinterpreted as being stingy and unloving.

Chaperone

(See also: Home Alone Together, p. 149.)

Two girls from different Latin American countries meet in an American high school. Luisa was born in Costa Rica but raised in the Dominican Republic, while Viviana is from Ecuador. The girls agree to see a movie together on Saturday night. After Luisa arrives at Viviana's door that night, Viviana's mother answers and looks at the girl strangely.

Luisa steps into the house while the mother leaves to notify her daughter of Luisa's arrival. Fifteen minutes pass before Viviana comes into the room, her eyes red from crying. Viviana explains that she won't be able to go out. She tells Luisa she will see her at school on Monday, but, in fact, their friendship ends that night.

In Ecuador, girls between the ages of sixteen and twenty don't go out unaccompanied. If they do, people assume them to be loose women. In giving permission for her daughter to go to the movies, Viviana's mother assumed that Luisa would be bringing along her family. In Ecuador, that would have been the only acceptable way that a respectable girl could go out. If Viviana's mother had allowed her daughter to go out without a chaperone, even in this country, her reputation would have been ruined. She could not undertake such a risk.

On the other hand, even though Luisa also came from a Latin American culture, the customs were different, and no stigma was attached to her going out without a chaperone. That is why the reaction of Viviana's mother caught her off-guard.

- Latin American cultures are complex. Although they share a language, they have a wide diversity of customs, such as child-rearing practices.

Coining

(See also: Alternative Healers, p. 107.)

One day as Mr. Hart walks from desk to desk in his sixth-grade class, he notices strange-looking red marks on Jenny Truong's neck and forehead. Alarmed, he informs her that she needs to be seen by a doctor right away.

Without giving her a chance to explain, he notifies the principal that Jenny is a probable victim of child abuse. In spite of Jenny's protests, the teacher and the principal notify the authorities and accuse Jenny's father of physically abusing his child.

People from a number of different Asian countries believe that internal bad winds cause illness. However, by bringing the wind to the surface, the illness can leave and the person will be healed. The home remedy for making the wind or illness leave the body is called "scratch the wind" or "coining."

When a person has a backache, cold, upper respiratory problem, or headache, the symptoms are alleviated by rubbing a coin rigorously against the back, neck, or forehead. In the United States, Asian immigrants first dip the coin into an oil or mentholatum. Then they rub very hard with the coin until the skin turns red. Unfortunately, the resulting red marks have frequently been misinterpreted by school officials who are vigilant about indications of child abuse.

After contacting Jenny's parents, who spoke only Vietnamese, the school officials found a translator who convinced authorities that Jenny was not a victim of child abuse, but rather a recipient of a folk remedy. Although school officials eventually accepted this explanation, they warned that the next time Jenny was sick she should see a doctor.

Coining is similar in concept to the old-fashioned American mustard plaster, which when placed on the chest becomes hot, breaking up respiratory congestion. It is also related to the Middle Eastern and Mediterranean practice of cupping, in which heated inverted cups are placed on the patient's back to create a suction to draw the "poison" to the surface. These different home treatments share a similar belief: if the source of the physical problem is brought to the surface, it can escape, and the patient will recover.

Officials have also been called in erroneously as a result of suspicion about other skin marks called *las manchas Mogolica* (Mongolian spots). These are bluish-gray or purple birthmarks that most often appear at the base of the spine of Asians, Native Americans, Latinos with Native American ancestry, and some people of Mediterranean background. Children are born with them, and they usually fade in time. They are not the result of parental abuse.

Unfortunately, one day-care worker in California assumed these Mongolian spots were signs of mistreatment on a Latino preschooler. Consequently, the child was placed in foster care for two weeks because California enforces mandatory reporting of child-abuse suspicions. The traumatized child was finally released to her parents.

- An immigrant child's bruises don't always mean child abuse. On the other hand, teachers should not be too quick to dismiss them as merely folk-medicine treatments.
- School workers and others should double-check with culturally aware consultants regarding suspicious marks and potential signs of abuse.

Classroom Behavior

(See also: Hands off the Head, p. 15; Modesty, p. 59; *Kirpan*, p. 60; Red Ink as Death Sign, p. 64; Bribery, p. 94; Eclipse, p. 128; AIDS Education, p. 143; Romantic Implications, p. 145.)

Testing

In Los Angeles, fourth-grade teacher Mr. Kennedy is dumbfounded by tests he must administer to his students. Among the many objects they must identify are scuba-diving equipment, a wading pool, and a pear.

At another school, Miss Dunn is equally disturbed by required reading materials. Her first-grade students must relate to nineteenth-century pushcarts in Brooklyn. On a second-grade test they need to comprehend what a father who is described as an investment banker does.

The students in these classrooms came from very poor Latin American countries, where some of their primary languages were Indian dialects, for example Konjobal, spoken in Guatemala. No one coming from a village could possibly identify scuba-diving equipment. A wading pool had no meaning, either. As for the pear, none grew locally; they would have to be imported from northern latitudes, but poverty prevented these children from ever seeing one. As for understanding what pushcarts in Brooklyn are or what investment banker fathers are, forget it!

No wonder test scores for schools like this are low. It is, of course, impossible to mass-produce culturally neutral tests. Nonetheless, more efforts should be made to create tests and reading materials that are relevant to newly arrived children from remote rural areas now living in low-socioeconomic-status urban environments.

- To accurately assess student capabilities, reading materials and tests are more appropriate if they bear some relation to children's backgrounds. Culturally biased tests lead to misleading results.

Enrichment Activities

Professional development experts from Australia and Rhode Island give workshops for teachers in New York City elementary schools. They make recommendations for the following activities for the children:

1. Have them go into their garages and look inside their father's tool kit and identify the objects.
2. Have them go into their backyards and collect materials.

So what's the problem? What garage? What tool kit? What backyard? All of these items were nonexistent in these children's lives.

- Experts should have at least a basic understanding of students' family variations and housing conditions.

Special Education

Inside a preschool special education class, the teacher walks holding hands with two students. In her left hand, she holds the right hand of a girl. In her right hand, she holds the right hand of a boy, but he is walking backwards.

These are children with autism, who best cope with their environment through repetition and structure. Deviations in routine throw them. The boy had been accustomed to holding his teacher's left hand in his right as he walked with her, but this time her left hand was not available. He could only function by continuing to hold her hand in his right, even if it meant walking backwards.

The teacher accepted his behavior. He had created a way to maintain his routine, albeit in a manner unusual to most of us.

- Autism is a spectrum developmental disorder of the brain that interferes with the brain's normal development.
- Children with autism are commonly misunderstood. They are of normal intelligence but perceive the world differently, and thus their output is different.
- There is a wide range of behavior. The most common traits are oversensitivity to certain stimuli and impairment in social interaction. Examples include a delay in or total lack of spoken language, little or no eye contact, and difficulty with motor skills.
- For parents, the most difficult task is accepting that their children will always have special needs.

Susan Sheehan reports on the parent of a child with autism who asks the school psychologist, "Are you telling me that Daniel won't be a quarterback at Harvard?" The psychologist answers, "Well, actually, he may not graduate from high school."

According to a 2004 *New York Times* article, autism cases are dramatically increasing. In California alone, the number of children receiving special services for autism tripled from 1987 to 1998 and doubled in the four years after that. National figures are similar. Although scientists have not yet agreed on the cause, autism has become such a recognized syndrome that Walt Disney World in Florida offers a tip sheet to parents of autistic children on how to accommodate to their children's special needs while visiting the theme park. Since mainstreaming of children with autism is becoming a popular strategy, we, our children, and our grandchildren will be interacting more with them on a daily basis.

Fear of Authority

Jackie, an educator, visits a fourth-grade class where most of the students are from Central America. Jackie speaks to the children individually. She interviews one girl and asks her name. Demonstrating typical Latino respect (see also: Eye Contact, p. 22), the child looks down at the floor and speaks so softly that Jackie cannot hear what she is saying, so Jackie asks her to write down her name: Amalia. Since this interaction succeeds, Jackie asks Amalia to write down the names of other family members. When the list is complete, Amalia looks up and worriedly asks, "Why do you want to know the names?"

Jackie quickly realized how her request for names had threatened Amalia. Regardless of status, immigrants fear authority, especially immigration officers. Although Jackie tried to convince the child that she was not from a government agency, Amalia looked frightened. In an attempt to reassure her, Jackie told her the names of her own brothers and children and grandchildren. Still, Amalia remained uneasy. Jackie felt remorse for having caused the child anxiety.

- Most immigrants fear authority representatives. They may have come from countries with corrupt government officials.
- They may lack trust in our system as well. They fear that by saying something wrong or revealing personal information, they might create negative consequences for their families.
- Teachers in schools with large immigrant populations generally reinforce that whatever is talked about in the classroom will remain in the classroom, that the information will not be used against the students or their families.
- In retrospect, Jackie recognized that she might have put Amalia more at ease if she had torn up the list in front of her. Alas! That realization came too late.

Student Participation

Mrs. Litt and Ms. Gollin compare notes in the faculty lounge. Mrs. Litt has new students from Ethiopia. They are very bright and do good work, but are too quiet, she says. They never raise their hands to ask questions or volunteer answers. This frustrates her.

Ms. Gollin has similar problems with Linh, a Vietnamese student who refuses to participate in class activities.

Mrs. Litt was unfamiliar with Ethiopian customs. From kindergarten on, children are taught the following proverb: "Speaking up is gold. Silence is diamonds." By remaining quiet, these children were paying the highest respect to their teacher and culture.

Ms. Gollin discovered that her student Linh didn't participate because it was an unfamiliar form of learning. In most Asian countries, the teacher is the complete source of knowledge. Students listen, take notes, memorize, recite, and follow directions. Students' ideas are not requested, nor are they valued. Students do not ask questions, argue, or challenge the teacher. To do so would be disrespectful.

- Because teachers are so highly regarded, students from Ethiopia and many Asian countries find it difficult to ask questions or share or challenge ideas.
- To avoid classroom lulls, use small-group activities among multicultural students who are reticent about participation.

"Stupid!"

(See also: *"No Molesta,"* p. 192.)

Miss Magrum is frustrated with her kindergartners. They have just spilled paint all over the floor while working on a mural for open house. Pepe dips his paintbrush into the spilled paint and draws a design on his arm. Angrily, Miss Magrum says, "Pepe, what a stupid thing to do."
The next day, the principal calls her aside.

While Americans use the word *stupid* to mean something done incorrectly or pointless, the meaning is benign, like *dummy*. In the United States, we actually purchase books bearing titles such as *Cooking for Dummies*. However, in Mexico, *estúpido* is the worst possible insult.

Pepe was so upset by Miss Magrum using that word about him that he informed his parents, who in turn complained to the principal. After Miss Magrum learned that she had grossly insulted Pepe, she apologized to the class and in the future avoided using this trigger word.

- Words in other languages that seem similar to English words may have far different connotations.
- Calling a Mexican "*stupid*" can lead to an altercation between students. Parents respond abruptly, too, as did Angela's mother, who took a belt to Angela for using that word.

Left-handed

Kosovar parents enroll their two-year-old daughter in a U.S. nursery school. The child shows left-handed tendencies, and the teachers accept her natural preference. But each time the child's parents visit the class and see her holding a crayon in her left hand, they switch the crayon to the right hand.

In part, the preference for right-handedness relates to the family's Muslim beliefs tied to the *Qur'an's* Order of Revelation 78, associating the right hand with believers and the left hand with disbelievers. Additionally, in some countries, they use the left hand for hygienic toileting practices.

Even when hygiene necessities are obsolete, the taboo against using the left hand remains. Depending on context, words for left-handed in other languages also reveal negativity: In Latin, *sinistra*, the word for left hand, can mean "stealing."

Disapproval of left-handedness used to prevail in the United States. Some left-handers recall their parents tying down their left hands. Sometimes teachers tried forcing students to switch merely for classroom convenience. Anti-left-hand attitudes changed in the mid-twentieth century when educators realized that switching hands might interfere with the learning process.

- Because of deeply embedded cultural or religious beliefs, it may be difficult or impossible to dissuade parents from switching their children from left hand to right hand use. Nonetheless, teachers should attempt to direct parents to information showing how this may be harmful to their children. They may also cite famous left-handers: Presidents Bill Clinton, Gerald Ford, Ronald Reagan, and Harry Truman; musicians Cole Porter, Paul McCartney, and Jimi Hendrix; and artist Leonardo da Vinci.

• When interacting with Muslims, avoid using the left hand for gesturing, touching objects, and handling foods and utensils.

Corporal Punishment

Teachers at an academically high-achieving private school meet individually with parents to discuss their children's progress. Since most of the students earn high grades, the teachers, rather than spend scarce time distributing praise, focus on the children's weaker skills.

Days later teachers notice bumps and bruises on some of the students.

The students with signs of physical abuse were recent arrivals from Asian countries, where it is acceptable for more traditional parents to physically discipline their children for lack of achievement. Once teachers realized the cause-and-effect relationship between their discussions and the physical abuse, they changed their methods. Since the weaknesses of these children would not be considered deficiencies in ordinary school settings, in subsequent parent/teacher conferences the teachers only talked about the academic achievements of the students.

Taiwanese college students reveal astonishment when learning that American teachers cannot treat them as their teachers did at home—by throwing erasers or pieces of chalk at misbehaving students. Likewise, Iranians describe the relationship of teachers and students at home like "dogs and cats," where teachers physically abuse students and an atmosphere of fear pervades the classroom. Most are pleasantly surprised when they discover that teachers do not and cannot physically punish them—it is illegal.

Susan, a classroom teacher in a Latino neighborhood, could easily spot children from Latin American parochial schools. As she approached them, they would cover their heads and bend forward to protect themselves from expected teacher's blows.

Corporal punishment in the classroom is acceptable in many Asian countries. Parents not only expect this, but appreciate it. Unaware that it is illegal here, some Latino parents encourage teachers to hit their children. One African American mother advised the teacher: "Just hit him on the backside." Parents use physical punishment as well. When Asian immigrant parents first learn that in the United States spanking their children too hard can get them into trouble with authorities, they are surprised. This confuses Asian parents over here, who believe that by giving up physical discipline they have lost control over their offspring. In their home countries, physical punishment is the norm, even when children are in their twenties.

Some children learn the rules of a new country faster than their parents and discover effective methods of intervention on their own. They threaten, "If you hit me, I'll call the police." Whether serious or bluffing, this often stops parents before they start hitting.

- Most newcomers believe that American forms of discipline at school and at home are too lenient. Corporal punishment is acceptable in Asia, the Middle East, and Latin America.

Cheating

Mrs. Fine is exasperated with her English as a Second Language class. Each time she gives a test, she must watch her students like a hawk. She patrols up and down the aisles. She warns them in advance that there will be no conferring with one another and that everyone's eyes must be on their own papers. Nonetheless, the students seem to take her threats lightly. They whisper answers to one another during exams and lean toward one another to allow friends to look at their papers.

Mrs. Fine had been warned when she took the job that cheating was rampant at this school. She discounted the warning because she had never had a problem with cheating at other institutions. At this school, however, certain differences in the student population were apparent. Students were always talking. They would rather confer with each other than ask the teacher for help. Mrs. Fine told them that their friends gave incorrect information, but she could not stifle them.

She tried the obvious solutions—separating pairs who were guilty of sharing work, moving the most talkative students to isolated seats. What puzzled her was that in their native countries, cheating was not tolerated. Why was this practice so prevalent here?

Mrs. Fine discovered that students felt obligated to help one another. They felt honor-bound to stick together while making their frightening and perilous journey of learning American language and culture. She overheard one student complaining about a friend, "I'm angry with her. She wouldn't even give me the answer to the first question."

The teacher tried to put the issue into a cultural context. She explained to the students that American nontolerance about cheating was tied to cultural values: competition over cooperation, emphasis on individuality, the importance of being number one.

Mrs. Fine told them that if a person wanted to be number one, they certainly would not tell their answers to others. That would lessen their chances for having the highest score. However, most of the students came from countries where cooperation and group values were primary.

The teacher eventually resolved her dilemma. She instigated small-group cooperative learning assignments. Then students dealt with each other within the group, and *they* could monitor the fairness of participation. She graded each group, and each person in it received the same grade. This avoided the issue of cheating. Instead of haranguing her students, she built a more positive learning environment.

- Cheating can be dealt with in several ways: make variations of a test; separate friends; isolate problem students; proctor carefully; create group projects.

Respect for Teachers

(See also: Teacher Knows Best, p. 47.)

As Professor Roberts leaves the faculty dining room, he runs into one of his Taiwanese students. The student bows to a startled Roberts, who doesn't know what to do in return.

In this situation, both parties felt embarrassed. However, the student was merely demonstrating how Asian students show their respect for teachers. They observe other customs of respect as well. In Taiwan, students rise when the teacher enters the room, and in chorus they say, "Good morning, teacher." They remain standing until the teacher gives them permission to be seated. When students hand papers to teachers, they use two hands, avoid looking them in the eye, and bow. Asian students bring these behaviors to the American classroom, and it is a while before they learn American ways of respect.

Asian students show esteem by calling the teacher "Teacher." American instructors sometimes misinterpret this and correct the students, advising them to call them by their family name instead of their title. This confuses the students. Moreover, students from most other countries are often shocked by the informality of U.S. teacher–student relationships. They describe American teachers as being more "like friends." Elsewhere, teachers are sometimes feared.

A student from Yerevan said, "At home, if I were to be outside the school and see a teacher walking by, I would run away and hide. I wouldn't want her to know I wasn't studying."

- If an Asian student bows to you, nod your head in response.
- In most other parts of the world, the teacher is an authority figure—one to be respected and feared. Thus, students are often misled and confused by American teachers' informality and friendliness.
- Students from many other countries expect more careful supervision by American teachers. The students are surprised that here responsibility for completing assignments and homework belongs to them.

- Those from educational systems outside the United States often consider informal, noisy classrooms as places of play, not learning.
- Students from outside the United States are often shocked by some teachers' behavior—sitting on desks, wearing casual clothing, encouraging students to call them by their first names, engaging in humorous banter. (See also: Dress for Respect, p. 62; Forms of Address, p. 188.)

In a related issue, a college writing professor felt very frustrated after reading so many unsatisfactory essays written by students from Armenia in the former Soviet Union. The students wrote only in generalities. They would not give examples from their own experience, even though he had told them to. Later he discovered why: Under the Soviet educational system, students could write *only* in generalities. They were not allowed to give their own opinions, only the opinions of famous people or officials. No individual ideas could be expressed. Once the professor understood the students' former educational writing conventions, he could then specifically address those issues and point out the differences in expectations here.

- Students from authoritarian educational systems have a difficult time expressing their own ideas and considering personal experience as valid support for their assertions.

Teacher Knows Best

Joyce's parents know their daughter is smart. She receives very good grades, so they are surprised when they meet with her high school counselor, Mr. Evans, on Career Night.

The counselor explains that Joyce needs to make a decision. She must choose between an academic and a vocational track for her high school curriculum. Mr. Evans urges that Joyce elect vocational courses and aim for a good job after high school.

Even though they silently disagree, the parents give approval to the counselor's recommendation.

Joyce and her family were from Jamaica, where teachers and school administrators are revered and rarely challenged. In spite of the counselor's recommendation being detrimental to their daughter's future, the parents accepted it. To question his advice would have been disrespectful.

Mr. Evans had assumed the family was poor. He based this on the low-paying jobs both parents held and Joyce's clothing. Mr. Evans believed they would prefer to have Joyce join the workforce as soon as possible. Besides, from his point of view, Joyce did not seem ready for college. In spite of her good grades, she seemed socially immature and not ready to handle being in an adult academic environment. She was shy and had difficulty in speaking up for herself.

Mr. Evans's decision about vocational training was based on misreading cultural cues. The family was not poor. In fact, the parents each held two jobs but listed only one on school forms, believing that how they supported their family was their own private business. Furthermore, from a Jamaican perspective, Joyce was not shy but respectful. (See also: Respect for Teachers, p. 46.) Speaking up for herself would have been considered uncouth. Finally, her wardrobe seemed out of step with the other students because most Jamaicans parents favor conservative school clothing over trendy outfits.

Fortunately, an administrator who also had a Caribbean background took Joyce under her wing and encouraged Joyce to go on to college. After high school graduation, Joyce went to a university, where she excelled in the field of education.

- School officials may be misled by incorrect cultural assumptions. What might be labeled as nonassertive from one cultural perspective might be called respectful by someone else. (See also: Student Participation, p. 40.)
- Don't assume that people are poor because of their clothes or their listed jobs. They may have more conservative ideas about school garb, and they may be holding down more than one job and not telling about it.
- In Jamaica and other parts of the Caribbean, teachers are respected and revered and rarely challenged.

- Most parents from the Caribbean will follow the teacher's directives to the letter. If a teacher recommends discipline, the parents unquestioningly carry out the request.

Absenteeism

(See also: Generosity, p. 153; Urgency, p. 177.)

On Monday morning after taking attendance, Mrs. Hale heaves a big sigh. She notes that Esperanza is absent again, the fifth time in the first three weeks of the new semester. When the child reappears on Wednesday, Mrs. Hale questions her about her absences.

Esperanza explains that her grandmother living in Nogales is ill and that she had to go with her family to visit and care for her. A skeptical Mrs. Hale gives the child a warning about attendance requirements—but to no avail. On Friday, Esperanza is once more missing from class.

Esperanza's Mexican family values dictate that when a family member needs help, one drops everything to assist, regardless of obligations outside the family, whether at work or school. Allegiance to the family is primary. Esperanza didn't show up on Friday because her grandmother had died and the family once more had to leave to prepare for the funeral.

American teachers, like Mrs. Hale, often become frustrated with the high absentee rate of their Latino students. Some families cross the border for four to six weeks during the Christmas fiestas, but parents are reluctant to notify teachers in advance, knowing well that the teachers will scold them. Sometimes even first graders will stay home to take care of younger siblings if their mother has to go to work or to see the doctor.

This confuses teachers. They don't understand why families would jeopardize the education of their children by taking them out of school so frequently. However, Latino families place higher priority on loyalty to the family than on anything else.

Another kind of absenteeism exists among children of migrant workers, who themselves may be field workers helping to contribute to the family economy by working to pick crops. Teenagers especially may be essential to the survival of their families. In one study, migrant teenagers contributed approximately 80 percent of the money they earned to the family. From the age of twelve years and on, these young people are as valuable as any other family worker in the amounts of produce they are able to take from the fields. Consequently, their status in the workplace has higher priority than in the classroom.

- Latino families give priority to family loyalty, even if it might negatively affect a child's standing in school.
- When Latino young adults miss school, they may be working to help support their families.

In an all-female adult class with a high Yemeni population, the teacher became frustrated when the students disappeared for two to three weeks at a time. The missing students later explained that either someone in the family had a baby, someone had died, or someone was getting married. All these major life events required their participation, regardless of personal consequences.

- For these Yemeni students and for many other immigrants and Native Americans, family comes first. They also know that when they are in need, their family will support them, too.

Clothing and Jewelry

Hats Off—Not!

(See also: *Kirpan*, p. 60; Post–September 11, p. 167.)

To celebrate his wife's birthday, Dr. Singh escorts her to a nightclub in Pittsburgh, Pennsylvania. A club employee advises that they won't be allowed in unless he removes his turban. When Dr. Singh explains that his turban is a sacred article of his Sikh faith and that he can't remove it, the manager refuses to make concessions. He claims that they wouldn't even let in a Jewish person unless he removed his *yarmulke* (skullcap). According to the manager, no exceptions can be made to the club's dress code.

Dr. and Mrs. Singh leave and inform the Sikh Mediawatch and Resource Task Force (SMART), a Sikh American advocacy group. SMART approaches the management team of a set of nightclubs in Pittsburgh and collaborates with them, and in 2003 they amend their dress code. Henceforth, certain Pittsburgh nightclubs will allow customers to wear turbans and other religious head coverings.

Elsewhere, religious hat conflicts have also found resolution. Accommodations have been made for Orthodox Jews who must wear *yarmulkes* (skullcaps) even when serving in the military. Despite the dangers, Amish construction workers are allowed to wear their black felt hats instead of hard hats when on the job.

- It is an act of discrimination to force people to remove items of clothing that have religious significance.
- When acts of religious discrimination occur, it is important to take action to preserve one's rights by informing company management, civil rights agencies, and, in extreme instances, an attorney.

Camouflage

Ira, the army surplus store manager, rings up charges for a customer purchasing camouflage-patterned pants, shirt, and cap. When the customer mentions that the new clothes are for a trip to South America, Ira tries to discourage the sale.

Wearing military clothing in politically unstable countries can be dangerous. The wearer might be perceived as part of the governing regime and thus the target of dissidents. Likewise, the person may be thought to be a member of a rebel faction and an enemy of the ruling party.

During the 2004 occupation of Iraq, when working with the Iraqi people, Marines were advised to wear dark green uniforms, rather than their desert camouflage outfits, to make them less visible as targets. They were also counseled to shed their sunglasses so that better rapport could be established with the locals. Direct eye contact is important for the Iraqis.

- When visiting African, Latin American, and Middle Eastern countries, avoid wearing military clothing to help ensure personal safety and to avoid being associated with an unpopular faction.

Six-Pointed Stars

Over the fence, Barbara's neighbor Jim calls out to her, "Happy Hanukkah, Barbara."

"Happy Hanukkah to you, too, Jim," she replies.

Jim says, "But I'm not Jewish."

Barbara says, "Well, neither am I."

"But you always wear that six-pointed star around your neck."

"That's because I work for the Sheriff's Department," she explains.

In antiquity, five- and six-pointed stars were used for protection against evil spirits. In contemporary times, the six-pointed star (*magen David*), star of David, has become a primary symbol of

Judaism. According to one legend, the relationship of the star to sheriff's badges dates back to a nineteenth-century governor of Texas who affixed his personal seal, a star-shaped ring, to some sheriff's department's papers.

• Don't jump to conclusions about the meaning of symbols.

Swastika

When the American bride-to-be came for a fitting of her Indian wedding sari, she panicked when noticing, for the first time, a swastika motif in the border design. Her groom was Jewish, and she could not wear it.

Although the swastika is commonly associated with Nazis, in Sanskrit *svastika* means something conducive to well-being. This equilateral cross, with arms bent at right angles, is the most widely used auspicious symbol of Hindus and Jains. For Buddhists, it symbolizes the feet or footprints of Buddha. Tibetan Buddhists frequently use it as a clothing decoration.

• Meanings of symbols change over time.

Hitler adapted the *svastika* for his own meaning, so for Jews the symbol evokes horror. The bride-to-be could never wear that dress with tragic implications to her wedding, so she switched to another fabric.

Sometimes misunderstanding symbols can become threatening, as happened with a high school teacher commenting on the comedy/tragedy dual mask necklace worn by her student. "Oh, I see that you're a thespian." The student became irate and threatened the teacher with bodily harm.

The teacher didn't know that the symbol for the theater had an alternative interpretation. It had become a gang symbol interpreted as, "First you laugh and then you cry." Likewise, the student didn't know the meaning of *thespian* and thought the teacher was commenting on her sexual orientation.

- It's easy to misinterpret symbols. Often they have multiple meanings and over time may develop an alternative interpretation.
- Symbols have emotional as well as logical associations.

Shoes

Before entering the homes of some of his customers, Mike, the Southern California Gas Co. serviceman, routinely covers his shoes with surgical booties.

Many of Mike's customers are Asians whose custom is to remove shoes before entering homes. However, OSHA regulations require service personnel to wear leather boots with metal toe covers while they work. The company wanted to fill both needs. Surgical booties, those disposable shoe cover-ups worn in operating rooms, became the solution. This pleased the customers and the service personnel, who felt that by wearing the booties they showed respect for their Asian clientele.

- Koreans, Filipinos, Thais, some Chinese, Iranians, Japanese, and Indian Buddhists remove their shoes when entering homes. If you notice that shoes have been placed outside your host's door, remove your shoes as well. This is a sign of respect and your hosts will be pleased. When visiting a Japanese home and taking off shoes, the toes of the shoes should face the door.
- In Japanese, Chinese, Korean, and Iranian homes, leave on your socks.
- In Indian and Pakistani homes, remove shoes and socks.
- Remove shoes before entering a Buddhist temple, Hindu temple, Muslim mosque, and Sikh gurdwara.
- If you notice that shoes have been placed outside your host's door, remove your shoes before entering. Your hosts will be pleased, but shoes outside the door can also be misleading.
- Sometimes a person may be reluctant to remove shoes because of extenuating circumstances, for example being embarrassed about having socks with holes in them. Even in such situations the guest should take off the shoes.

Boutique Boo-boos

The boutique features elaborate Indian designs on bikinis, T-shirts, shoes, lunch boxes, and toilet seats. Customers eagerly buy these decorative objects, but some of the items outrage the Hindu community.

To non-Hindus, the colorful illustrations are simply attractive artwork—an elephant's head on a man's body, a young man playing a flute—but to Hindus, they are manifestations of deities.

Commercialization and lack of reverence for a spiritual tradition offend them. Gods displayed on bikini bottoms are sacrilegious. Even worse is the appearance of the gods Krishna or Kali on toilet seats, which because of pressure from the Hindu community have been removed from the market.

Equally disrespectful is the appearance of deities on shoes. Shoes cover the lowliest part of the body and are not allowed inside Hindu temples. Wearing shoes adorned with deities and then walking on dirty streets besmirches the holy depictions.

Hindus are not the only ones to take offense at the inappropriate use of religious symbols. In July 2004, Victoria's Secret withdrew its Buddha-print bikini and apologized to Buddhists in Sri Lanka after a Buddhist monk, Daranaagama Kusaladhamma, petitioned the courts to ban the company's bikinis with pictures of a seated Buddha on the breast areas of the halter. The monk claimed that commercial exploitation of the Buddha image offended Buddhists, who constitute nearly 70 percent of the country's 19 million people.

Akin to this, on the 473rd anniversary of the appearance in Mexico of the Virgin of Guadalupe on December 12, 1531, Mexican Roman Catholics in Los Angeles voiced their objection to the Virgin's image on nonreligious items such as mouse pads, pens, air fresheners, belt buckles, hairspray cans, cowboy boots, and salsa bottles. For the faithful, the Virgin represents the beginning of the Mexican nation and the emergence of the mestizo people. Father Paul Sustaya of the Holy Spirit Church in Los Angeles says the Virgin should not be a marketing gimmick, complaining that they are using her image to make a buck. Another Mexican Catholic called the commercialism "outrageous. . . . It loses the message. It blurs what it all really means when you see it on a phone card."

• Avoid placing designs with religious connotations on utilitarian objects.

Unsoulful Soles

When the new graduate student arrives from Myanmar to study in the United States, she cannot believe her eyes. While listening to the professor's lecture, some students have propped their legs up on chairs. She is aghast.

The new student believed that it was extremely disrespectful for students to show the soles of their shoes to the professor. In her country teachers and parents are put on the same level as God. To show the bottoms of the feet to them is a grave insult.

This belief is related to the notion that the feet are the lowest part of the body, both physically and metaphysically. Consequently, it is impolite to point them at someone. This could happen intentionally, as in the college classroom, or inadvertently, for example, when persons cross their legs or sit in a recliner and the shoe soles point outward.

• It is insulting to show the soles of the shoes to people from the Middle East and Asia.

In April 2003, when the statue of Saddam Hussein came down, Iraqis paid him the greatest humiliation when they whacked his statue with their shoes.

Donkey Beads

Beautiful clothing and jewelry from ethnic groups often attract us, but wearing the garb in the company of those same people may bring unexpected reactions. Instead of putting ourselves in their good graces, we may be making ourselves look foolish; we may be offensive; we may be confounding them.

When bright cobalt blue ceramic beads from the Middle East become fashionable in the United States, Kathleen buys a strand with matching earrings and thinks she looks terrific in them. However, years later her Iranian brother-in-law has a fit of laughter when he sees her all dressed up and proudly wearing these beads. Kathleen can't understand what's so funny.

Kathleen knew that her beads were sometimes called "donkey beads," but until the moment the relative laughed at them, it had never occurred to her that they were actually worn by donkeys. She found out that Iranian peddlers decorated donkeys with these beads when they pulled their laden carts through the villages. When Kathleen wore these donkey beads, she was indeed making a jackass of herself. After that incident, she never enjoyed wearing the necklace and earrings again.

Wearing the donkey beads merely amused the Iranian fellow, yet other reactions can be more serious. Many American and European women enjoy wearing brilliant orange-colored Indian silk scarves with patterns. Non-Indian women don't realize that these are Hindu prayer scarves and that the patterns on them are actually words from prayers used for holy devotions. To a religious Hindu, having others wear the scarves in a secular way can only be disrespectful and offensive.

Similarly, *koufeih*, the black-and-white or red-and-white head coverings worn only by Arabic men (the kind worn by Yassir Arafat), have become a fashion accessory for European and American women and men. How disturbing this must be for traditional Palestinian males who undoubtedly see this as a violation of gender rules and a mockery of their political beliefs.

- Be careful when wearing clothing or jewelry from an ethnic group to which you do not belong. You may be creating an offense or making yourself look ridiculous.

Glass-Bead Necklaces

Lorenzo is president of his block association and tonight he is chairing a meeting. He warmly greets his mostly Latin American and African American neighbors as they enter the church meeting hall. The last person to arrive is Rudy, a Cuban American. The moment Rudy takes off his jacket, a hush sweeps the room.

Rudy is wearing several *collares* (glass-bead necklaces). As soon as they notice the necklaces, two participants hurriedly leave.

Glass-bead necklaces usually indicate that the wearer is a member of the Santería religion, also known as *Lucumi* or *Orisha* worship. Due to sensationalized and misleading media accounts, the public primarily associates Santería with animal sacrifice and involvement in illegal activities. Consequently, many people have erroneous and fearful ideas about this religion. In addition, the populace often confuses Santería with *voudun* (also known as voodoo), a religion practiced by Haitians. (See also: The Voodoo Squad, p. 127.)

In fact, Santería is a bona fide religion with roots among the Yoruba people of West Africa. During the slave trade, the Yoruba brought these ideas with them to the Caribbean. In Cuba, Roman Catholic influences merged with Yoruba beliefs, and today some people still make a link between the Santería *Orishas* (lesser deities) and Catholic saints. Approximately one hundred thousand Americans practice this religion.

While members do sacrifice chickens, doves, or goats on sacred occasions, such as the consecration of a priest, a curing ceremony, or celebrations of births and deaths, there is nothing illegal or unethical about it. In the 1993 case of the *Church of the Lukumi Babalu Aye v. Hialeah*, the U.S. Supreme Court upheld the rights of members to sacrifice small animals in religious ceremonies. Furthermore, the sacrificed animals become food for participants at such rites.

The glass-bead necklaces have particular meaning depending on their colors, each associated with a particular *Orisha*; for example, red-and-white beads refer to Shango, who presides over the fire of life and human energy; yellow beads embody qualities of Oshun, the goddess of love, fertility, and the beauty of life; white beads represent Obatala, everyone's father, the wisest and oldest Orisha, who created the human body.

Just because persons wear these beads doesn't mean that they are bona fide worshipers. The necklaces can be purchased in *botánicas* (shops selling religious and spiritual supplies), and anyone can buy them.

Whether or not Rudy was a follower of this religion or was merely wearing the necklaces for aesthetic value did not concern the people who fled. Unfounded fear motivated their departure.

- Glass-bead necklaces are associated with the Santería religion, the practices of which are legal and moral. There is nothing to be feared about this religion.

Modesty

A heat wave strikes, and Mrs. Elden, a fifth-grade teacher, is concerned about Kamchana, a newly arrived student from Thailand. In spite of the sizzling temperatures, she wears long-sleeved shirts and long pants, a practice that the teacher feels is unhealthy. Mrs. Elden suspects that perhaps the child is covering up bruises she has received at home.

Mrs. Elden sends a note home requesting to meet with Kamchana's English-speaking aunt. The aunt is stunned to learn of Mrs. Elden's suspicions.

Kamchana wore clothing that covered her arms and legs because of modesty, not child abuse. In Thailand, Kamchana had to cover as much of her body as possible. She could not wear anything that exposed her body, whether she was inside her home or outdoors. Particularly, she would never dare wear shorts in public, much less to school. However, after living in the United States for several years, she changed. Now she is comfortable wearing shorts on hot days and has plans to go to the beach and one day wear a bikini.

Rules of modesty also require Muslim girls to wear scarves covering their heads. At one grammar school, mischievous non-Muslim boys tormented the Muslim girls by pulling off their scarves. The rules affect physical education. Some Muslim girls are not allowed to participate in swimming classes because of the prohibitions against exposing their bodies. Often Asian newcomers have difficulty undressing in front of their classmates in the locker room. This affects both sexes. During a San Diego, California, heat wave, a Vietnamese college student would not remove his T-shirt during a tennis match because of the cultural ban on exposing his body. During a lifeguard strike in Israel in the late 1990s, some Orthodox Jews drowned. Because of their modesty rules, they went into the water fully dressed and their clothing pulled them under.

- People from other cultures have different rules—some stricter, some more lax—about keeping their bodies covered. It is best not to tamper with these practices.
- When others tease students about religious rules pertaining to clothing, teachers should intervene.

Kirpan

(See also: Hats Off—Not!, p. 51; Post–September 11, p. 167.)

Two boys are playing basketball on the school playground. As ten-year-old Rajinder leaps to make a basket, his shirt lifts, revealing a sheathed knife tied to his waist by a sash.

A classmate of Rajinder's asks about it, and Rajinder replies that he wears it because of his religion. Later, when the school discovers that Rajinder's seven-year-old brother and eight-year-old sister are also wearing knives, they suspend all three children from school.

The children belonged to the Khalsa Sikh religious community, which originated in the Punjab area of northwest India and has five hundred thousand members in the United States. The knife, or *kirpan*, is one of five holy symbols these followers must wear once they are formally initiated, a tradition going back three hundred years. This obligation is part of their vows to keep the five K's, which must be worn at all times, even while bathing or sleeping: long hair (*kesh*), a comb in the hair (*kangha*), a steel bracelet on the right wrist (*kara*), special cotton undershorts (*kachha*), and a sword (*kirpan*) held close to the body by means of a shoulder harness.

The *kirpan* has never been a threat to the public in either Britain or Canada, with Sikh populations of one million each. Likewise, there has never been an incident where children have used these knives as weapons on U.S. schoolgrounds; nonetheless, the Livingston Union School District in Merced County, California, was concerned about school safety. They claimed, "These *kirpans* are daggers, with steel blades. In the wrong hands, they could be very dangerous."

A dagger is a knife that is sharp on both sides of the blade, intended to do bodily harm. A *kirpan* has blunted sides and is not meant to give injury to another. In court, San Francisco attorney Stephen V. Bomse demonstrated that the *kirpan* was innocuous— short, with a blade of only 3 to 4 inches; difficult to retrieve because it is sewn into the sheath; and so blunt as to make it very difficult to pierce the skin with it. Moreover, he argued that the *kirpan* is simply a religious symbol and not a weapon. He likened it to the *yarmulke* (skullcap) that must be worn by religious Jews.

Bomse pointed to other potentially dangerous school implements, such as scissors used in art classes and baseball bats for sports. They are not viewed as weapons because their use is not intended to bring harm. Likewise, the *kirpan* is not meant to be harmful. It is a sacred symbol of commitment to defend the weak and oppressed.

Other school districts dealing with this Sikh religious practice have not suspended children wearing the *kirpan*. Instead, they have come to mutual agreements; for example, in Yuba City, California, the *kirpan* must have a blunted, enclosed tip and be riveted to its sheath. Such policies take into consideration fears about safety, as well as people's right to practice their religion.

Although the court originally upheld the decision of the Livingston, California, school to bar the children from attending while wearing their ceremonial knives, the decision was later overturned. In September 1994, the U.S. Ninth Circuit Court of Appeals upheld the Sikhs' right to wear the *kirpan*. The court agreed with the Sikh parents that the school's policy had placed an unlawful burden on their freedom of religion. Lawmakers ruled that the school must make all reasonable efforts to accommodate the religious beliefs and practices of the children in question. They suggested that the *kirpan* be blunted and sewn or locked into its sheath.

- Danger is in the eye of the beholder. An object that is threatening to one may be a decoration to another or a religious symbol to someone else.

Dress for Respect

(See also: Respect for Teachers, p. 46.)

Writer Erica Goode relates the following scenario.

Vladimir, newly arrived from Russia, anxiously waits with his interpreter in a doctor's examining room. Suddenly a woman dressed in casual clothes bursts into the room. She smiles at Vladimir and says, "Hi, nice to meet you. I'm a nurse practitioner. How are you today?"
  Vladimir scowls and asks the interpreter, "Who is this fool?"

Vladimir was put off by the nurse practitioner because of her lack of formality. She did not wear medical garb and was too friendly. This caused him to lose respect for her as a professional.

Newcomers, especially from authoritarian countries, expect to see symbols of power and status from those who are treating them. Patients anticipate that any medical professional will dress in a uniform. They expect authorities to act formally and to maintain social distance.

- Immigrant patients respond more positively to medical professionals who are formal in dress and demeanor. Ultimately, conduct and clothing affect patient compliance. This not only applies to health care environments, but extends to many places, including the classroom. (See also: Respect for Teachers, p. 46.)

Colors

(See also: Yellow Flowers, p. 91; White Flowers, p. 92; White Envelopes, p. 96; Red Envelopes, p. 136.)

Green Hats

Arthur entertains visiting English-speaking Taiwanese business connections. Because it is March, he and his wife Jean prepare a St. Patrick's Day celebration with corned beef and cabbage, green beer, and shamrock and shillelagh decorations. The hosts wear green hats and have their guests don them, too. The evening progresses with the hosts unaware of their guests' discomfiture and seeming reluctance to participate.

Unknown to Arthur and Jean, many Chinese believe that when a man wears a green hat, it means his wife or girlfriend has been cheating on him. Ordinarily, for Chinese people, green has positive connotations, as evidenced by the popularity of jade; green is associated with health, prosperity, and harmony. The exception is hats. The Taiwanese never mentioned the green hat connotations. Instead, they graciously accommodated to the St. Patrick's Day traditions of their hosts. Nonetheless, it made them uncomfortable, as they revealed a year later when they knew their hosts better.

- For many Chinese people, green hats are associated with infidelity.

Red Ink as Death Sign

(See also: Classroom Behavior, p. 37.)

Mrs. Gussman is one of the best English teachers in the school. She spends every weekend reading her immigrant students' compositions and making careful comments in red ink. To soften her criticisms, she says something positive before writing suggestions for improvement, using the students' names to make the comments more personable. "Jae Lee, these are fine ideas, but . . ."

These red-inked notes send shock waves through the families of her Korean students, but Mrs. Gussman is unaware of this until the principal calls her into the office.

Koreans, particularly those who are Buddhists, only write a person's name in red at the time of death or at the anniversary of a death. Therefore, to see the names of their children written in red terrified the Korean parents.

Once the principal of the school discovered how this upset the Korean parents, she requested that every teacher in the school refrain from using red ink on any student's paper. All the teachers switched to other colors.

Ordinarily, most Asian parents would not complain to school administrators about a teacher. This would be considered disrespectful. However, the principal of this school met regularly with her international parents to discuss school issues. She created such an environment of trust that parents felt free to reveal how much it disturbed them to see their children's names written in red.

The negative association of names written in red is not limited to religious Koreans. In parts of Mexico and among some Chinese, it is equally offensive to write one's name in red. A businessman working with a consortium of Asian companies told of the negative response he received to invitations printed in red ink. A print-shop owner confirms that her Asian customers never order red lettering on custom-printed stationery supplies, selecting blue or black instead; Korean employees refused to sign their time cards with red pens that had been provided for that purpose, and Korean college students were reluctant to sell their used texts to the bookstore because only red pens were available for filling out the refund forms.

- To avoid emotional upset for Korean children and parents, don't write students' names in red—this has death connotations.
- To avoid any potential problems, avoid red lettering on items targeted for an Asian audience.

Light Blue

In exchange for learning Russian, Lauren, an American student, travels to Russia to teach English to a Russian family with whom she lives. She speaks no Russian, and they speak a minimum of English. Their routine consists of pointing to an object, Lauren saying the word in English, and one of the family members saying the word in Russian. Then they write down the new words on their study sheets.

Lauren has been studying the names for colors all day, so when her Russian host "dad" enters the room wearing a light blue sweater, she points at him and with a big smile says the Russian word for light blue. He becomes angry.

Lauren didn't know that in Russian "light blue" has another connotation. It also means gay. The father assumed she was calling him gay, something that offended his masculinity. To calm the scene, the mother stepped in and straightened out the misunderstanding.

- Words can have connotations that can get the speaker into social straits. Misunderstanding occurs more frequently when speakers do not share the same native language.

White Bonnets

The hospital staff presents gift packets of white infant bonnets to mothers of newborns, but the Asian mothers refuse to place them on their babies' heads.

In many Asian cultures, wearing white signifies mourning. If a baby wears white, it means that its parent is dead. The parents didn't want to tempt fate. Similarly, when Angela, a new student from Vietnam, saw her classmate wearing a white headband, she said, "I'm sorry," believing that her classmate's parent had died.

- White is frequently a mourning color in Asian countries. This explains why a Chinese client rejected a float designed by a public relations company. The banners were of red satin but had white lettering. While the red banner was fortuitous, white letters would have doomed the entire year. (See also: First Foot, p. 119.)
- Because of the death connection, fishmongers and greengrocers in New York City's Chinatown avoid using white plastic bags for customers' purchases. Instead, plastic shopping bags are orange, red, or pink, all fortuitous colors for the Chinese.

Wedding Guests Wearing White

(See also: Black at a Chinese Wedding, p. 67.)

Arina is excited about attending the wedding of her Indian friend, Kamila Rajpoor. In keeping with her own Afghan tradition, Arina wears a white dress, a symbol of friendship for the bride and an omen of luck, harmony, and happiness for the wedding couple.

Ordinarily, Mrs. Rajpoor warmly welcomes Arina; but on her daughter's wedding day, Mrs. Rajpoor turns ashen when she sees Arina at her door. Mrs. Rajpoor greets her coldly, hands trembling. She orders Arina to follow her and leads her to the bedroom. On the way, others react strangely when they notice Arina.

When Arina and the mother reach the bedroom, Arina asks if she can see Kamila. "No!" retorts the bride's mother. "No way are you going to bring her bad luck and death!"

Kamila's mother explained that if someone wears white to an Indian wedding it can bring bad luck, even death, to the wedding couple. Only an enemy wears white to a wedding.

After accepting Arina's apology, Mrs. Rajpoor righted Arina's wrong. She brought out one of her daughter's red dresses for Arina to wear and finally permitted her to see the bride and join the other guests. However, Kamila's grandmother would not forgive Arina and tried all night to keep her away from her granddaughter.

- Some people believe that certain colors worn by wedding guests bring bad luck to the wedding couple. One should not wear white to an Indian wedding.

Black at a Chinese Wedding

(See also: Wedding Guests Wearing White, p. 66.)

Maynae is Chinese, born in Vietnam, and has been living in the United States for eleven years. Now friends of her mother have invited her to a wedding party at a Chinese restaurant. Maynae buys a new dress for the occasion—a black velvet dress with white pearls running around the neckline and down the length of the dress to the knees.

She is delighted with her purchase and thinks it's perfect for the event. However, when Maynae picks up her mother to take her to the wedding, her mother screams at her about the dress, shattering Maynae's elation. Now Maynae feels shame and embarrassment, but she doesn't have time to go home and change. Besides, she has nothing else nice to wear.

At the restaurant, all the other guests stare coldly at Maynae and her mom, who sit in a corner of the room, apart from everyone else. At the end of the party, when the newlyweds toast each guest individually, they completely ignore the two women. From that day forward, the family never has anything to do with Maynae and her mother.

When attending a Chinese wedding, female guests should not wear black or white. The wedding party will interpret this as a hostile act, for both black and white are associated with death. Yet black is not a universally negative wedding color. In nineteenth-century

California, Hispanic brides took their marriage vows wearing black wedding gowns. In the 1990s, black again became chic for some daring brides. At one wedding on Halloween, the entire wedding party dressed in black, except for the flower "ghoul," who wore white.

- Many Chinese people believe that guests should not wear black or white to weddings. Both colors have death connotations.

Yellow Tags

Richard works for an American company that ships refrigerated containers to Asia. Before exporting them, the company places yellow markers on the products to indicate that they have passed inspection. This makes customers in China suspicious of the products' quality.

Chinese use a yellow marker to identify a defective product. They use green markers to indicate products that have passed inspection. Even though the American supplier insisted that yellow markers meant the merchandise was up to industry standards, the Chinese customers still felt uneasy.

The American company grappled with the possibility of changing yellow to green, which the customers requested, but the American company's color symbolism was as deeply embedded as the Chinese, and they refused to change. They took a financial risk by doing this.

In a related business conflict based on colors, an American manufacturer could not sell its white appliances in Hong Kong. However, after they discovered that the Chinese associated white with death and would not have these funeral symbols in their homes, the company shipped only almond-colored products, which sold very well. Of course, this manufacturer had greater motivation than the first company because the color decision directly affected sales.

Although Richard's company chose yellow as a symbol of approved products, that color more often has negative connotations, as in the association of yellow with cowardice—"He has a yellow streak in him." This relationship has cross-cultural counterparts. The French streak a traitor's doors with yellow paint; Judas is often pictured in yellow; the Nazis made Jews wear yellow stars; Spanish executioners wear yellow.

- It would be best if American companies did not use yellow tags on approved merchandise exported to Chinese customers.

Foodways

Cracked Eggs

(See also: Uzbeks, p. 248.)

Aware of salmonella hazards from eating cracked raw eggs, Carolyn becomes apprehensive as her hostess in Uzbekistan removes one from the refrigerator, cracks it open, adds some lemon juice and honey, and mixes it together. Because her hostess is always urging her to try new local foods, Carolyn searches for a way to excuse herself from eating the potentially sickening concoction without offending the other woman. Only when the hostess applies the mixture as a face mask does Carolyn feel relieved.

- When traveling outside the United States, it becomes difficult to ignore inculcated warnings about food dangers and hygiene risks in places that do not emphasize such concerns.
- Rather than take on the mantle of the "Ugly American," some U.S. tourists ruefully go along with acts they would not consider doing at home.

Travelers have learned that they offend hosts when they refuse their food. (See also: Refusing Food, p. 72.) Sometimes this results in conflict when trying to interact positively with locals. Carolyn was relieved of making choices, but other Americans describe similar feelings of discomfort, such as the couple staying in a Romanian village home. The hostess prepared her best meal for her guests, yet seemed unperturbed by the ants crawling over the homemade pastries. The guests followed her lead and merely brushed them aside as they took some of the delicacies from the platter.

Refusing Food

(See also: Azerbaijanis, p. 239.)

Galib Mammad tells about two American relief team workers visiting a refugee camp in Azerbaijan—a male physician and female companion. A villager has just finished baking bread on a makeshift hearth. She offers some to the doctor, but he does not want to deprive the needy family of food, so he declines her offer. She is offended.

The doctor was unaware of how highly valued hospitality is among the Azerbaijanis. Despite his concern for the physical well-being of the woman, he had injured her pride. His companion knew more about Azerbaijani customs. She accepted the bread, tore off a very small piece, and returned the rest to the woman, restoring the woman's dignity.

- By rejecting the bread, the doctor rejected the woman and her culture.
- By accepting the bread, the doctor's companion built a bridge between the two cultures.
- Azerbaijanis believe that if you share food, you expose your heart and soul to the other person and are forever linked in friendship.
- In many cultures, rejecting another person's food is frequently interpreted as an insult. To avoid this, Americans in post–September 11 Afghanistan learned to accept cups of tea whenever they interacted with the local people.

Changing Food Habits

The school nutritionist at the Missouri conference voices her concern about newly arrived Bosnian students who discard the meat from their hamburgers and eat only the bread and the pickles.

Later the school staff learns that these Muslim children fear that the meat may contain pork and wish to take no chances in eating taboo food. To be on the safe side, they don't eat the meat.

In addition, despite coming from a yogurt-eating culture, the students rejected the yogurt at school. They had been accustomed to yogurt mixed with water and savored as a drink. They were unfamiliar with the sweet thick fruit-flavored form, which eventually they learned to enjoy.

Likewise, the Vietnamese children at this school ate only baked fish and rice when they first arrived. Now, along with the Bosnian children, they relish pizza, nachos, and hamburgers.

- It is difficult to overcome entrenched food habits and accept unfamiliar food. However, over time, and with frequent exposure, food habits can be changed.

Hospitals, too, must deal with cultural differences in food preferences. California hospitals, like hospitals elsewhere, are mandated by law to ensure that patients receive adequate nutrition despite conflicting cultural habits. For Asian patients at Mission Hospital in Mission Viejo, California, they serve rice—for every meal, if necessary. (See also: What Makes a Meal?, p. 76.) They provide kosher food for observant Jewish patients, vegetarian food for vegans and Hindus, and special Mexican dishes such as enchiladas for Mexican patients. When the kitchen cannot provide all the customizing required, with permission from doctors, some families may bring in home-cooked ethnic foods.

Offering Food

(See also: Refusing a Gift, p. 98; Believing What They Say, p. 197.)

Greg, a non-Tongan, accepts an invitation from his Salt Lake City, Utah, high school classmate, Epafasi, to join him and other Tongan schoolmates after school at Epafasi's home. While the guys are sitting in the living room, Epafasi's mom returns from work.

As soon as she spots Greg, she loudly scolds her son in Tongan. Although the language is unfamiliar, Greg senses the mom is talking about him.

She then places a large bowl of food in front of Greg; she serves no one else. Because it is such a large quantity, Greg offers to share it with the others, but they refuse. Although he feels awkward, Greg begins eating for fear of insulting his hosts. Again, he asks the others to join him, but they decline.

After stuffing himself, he announces that he cannot eat anymore. Then he again asks if the others would like some. The boys dig in.

In Tonga, when a chief visited a home, the hosts served him enormous portions of food and no one else could eat until he finished. Then they ate the leftovers. Later, that custom was extended to the missionaries, and today it applies to non-Tongan guests as well. It is a custom that has carried over to Tongan families in the United States. Additionally, Tongans will not accept food until it is offered at least three times.

For Javanese, too, food must be offered three times before guests can accept it. Filipinos and Koreans, as well, frequently wait until after the third invitation before accepting.

How can such situations be avoided? One way is to automatically serve the food and drink. This relieves guests of the pressure of propriety. Another way is to offer and if necessary repeat the offer more than three times to circumvent guests' social discomfort from breaking their own rules of courtesy.

- If guests decline the first offer of food, try offering it at least two more times.
- If you are hosting guests who may observe this custom, you can automatically serve the food to relieve the guests of the pressure of propriety. Or offer the refreshments more than three times to circumvent their social discomfort from breaking their own rules of courtesy.
- In some places, guests of honor, like Greg and the missionaries before him, are supposed to eat first. This practice extends to Thai temples, where temple members must wait to eat until after the monks have eaten.

Milk Intolerance

Charles reminisces about his childhood, when he enjoyed a popular children's local television show, *Engineer Bill*. Each day Engineer Bill asked his young viewers to bring a glass of milk in front of the TV and participate in a game called Red Light, Green Light. On the green signal, the children were supposed to take a big drink of milk and not stop until Engineer Bill called, "Red light." As much as Charles enjoyed playing the game, drinking the milk caused stomach cramps.

While the intention of the Red Light, Green Light game was good nutrition, the producers were unaware that not everybody needs milk, including Charles, who was a newly arrived Chinese. Globally, 90 percent of Asians, Africans, and Native Americans are lactose-intolerant due to a missing lactase enzyme that breaks down lactose, a complex sugar found in milk. Lactase is present in infants, allowing them to digest their mothers' milk, but after weaning, the enzyme disappears in the majority of the world's population. For them, milk and milk products produce cramps and diarrhea. Nowadays, special milks and tablets are available to aid those who lack the lactase enzyme. These items allow them to enjoy milk products without discomfort.

- If members of ethnic groups refuse to eat milk products, it may be due to physical limitations. It may also be due to food taboos. (See also: Food Taboos, p. 77.)

Potluck

Carol asks her English as Second Language students if they like potluck dinners. The response is negative. A Puerto Rican student stands up, bends her left arm upward, and makes a fist in front of her own face. Then, with her right fist, she raps her bent left elbow. Some laugh heartily; others don't get it, especially Carol.

Carol's students jovially explain, "It means cheap, stingy." This delights the class. With the exception of family members bringing food to family meals, potluck is a nonexistent concept in their own countries: Latin America, Yemen, Haiti, Dominican Republic, and China. Hosts prepare all the food with extra available in case neighbors stop in, where they are welcomed.

Likewise is their dismay about "Dutch treat." In many countries, a person who suggests meeting in a restaurant for a meal is expected to host everyone.

- Potluck and Dutch treat are unfamiliar concepts to many from cultures outside the United States.
- Elsewhere hosts are expected to take complete responsibility for providing food and drink for their guests.

What Makes a Meal?

(See also: Nepalese, p. 224.)

While visiting Nepal, Doug accepts an invitation to dine at the home of some Nepalese. Sangita, the hostess, tells him that her husband, Lopsang, will do the cooking.

She ushers Doug into a lower-level room of their two-story home and invites him to sit on a bench among several that surround a large coffee table. Soon, Sangita and her son, Rinji, begin bringing down food: buffalo, chicken, lentil pancakes. After about one and one-half hours of eating and talking, Doug thanks Sangita and rises to leave.

In disbelief, Sangita asks, "Where are you going? We haven't had dinner yet." Doug is astounded until Sangita explains, "These were just snacks. From now on you should know that if you haven't had the rice, you haven't eaten yet!"

The three ascend the stairs to the upper level of the house where the husband greets them before a dinner table set with rice, vegetables, buffalo jelly, and *dal* (lentil stew). From that evening forward, Sangita makes jokes about rice whenever she sees Doug.

- This is a widespread sentiment in Asia, where a meal includes two categories: rice and items served with rice.
- In Indonesia snacks do not constitute a repast, and the Indonesian term for snacks is *lauk-pauk*, meaning all things that go with the rice. In other places where rice is the staple, the other foods are basically condiments.

- Most cultures have their particular staple food without which a meal is incomplete. For some it may be bread, rice, or rice and beans.
- Sangita's ongoing use of humor about the incident helped to defuse Doug's embarrassment.

Food Taboos

Lakshmi has just arrived from India to study at an American university. Unaware of the Hindu prohibition against beef, a classmate invites her to dinner at the best steakhouse in town. When Lakshmi explains the Hindu beef taboo to him, he apologizes and encourages her to order lobster, another specialty of the house. He then orders a sixty-second steak for himself, one barely seared that oozes blood all over the plate. Although Lakshmi has seen cooked meat before, she has never witnessed bloody meat served at the table. She instantly loses her appetite.

Food taboos are powerful. When persons from any religious group break a food taboo, they are subject to condemnation by members of their group. Even if someone accidentally eats a taboo food, the repercussions are potent. There have been situations where people unknowingly ate a taboo food and later, when they discovered their mistake, became physically ill.

In addition to daily taboos, many religions have special dietary laws that outlaw the eating of foods on certain holy days. Until 1966, for example, the Roman Catholic church prohibited eating meat on Fridays. That's no longer true, but dietary prohibitions still exist on Ash Wednesday and Good Friday, when no meat is allowed. One nonobservant Catholic recalls how he offended his Catholic friend's family as he munched on beef jerky while visiting their home on Ash Wednesday. Similarly, observant Jews eat no leavened breads and use no leavening agents during the eight days of the festival of Passover. Special foods made without leavening are designated "kosher for Passover."

In addition, many observant Jews follow the taboo of mixing dairy products with meat. According to Orthodox rules, there must be a six-hour space between eating meat and dairy products. Those who comply with these laws keep two separate sets of pots and dishes, one for dairy products and the other for meat.

Mainstream America may think certain food taboos strange, but there's hardly a person who does not have strong notions about what should or should not be eaten. Some Asians are surprised by the American taboo of not eating dog, because in a number of Eastern countries, dog is considered a delicacy. In recognition of this strong American taboo, during the 1988 Olympics, Korean restaurants in Seoul removed dog entries from their menus.

In a turnabout, when Missouri-born June first visited India, she went to the home of business associates. Vegetarians themselves, her hosts prepared a special chicken dish for her. Noting that she finished so quickly, her host asked, "Would you care for more flesh?" June had never considered calling chicken *flesh* before, and that terminology gave her pause about her own customs.

- Seeing our own customs from the eyes of outsiders can be startling. Sometimes it can lead to the broadening of perspectives.

Most Americans have definite opinions about culturally taboo foods for children and bolster these opinions with moralistic epithets such as "good for you" or "bad for you." Coffee and tea among most Americans are considered "bad" for children, as is alcohol, which is legally prohibited. These are not universal beliefs. A French immigrant recalls how the nuns at his first American grade school reacted with horror when they discovered wine in his thermos.

Here are the most common food and drink taboos. As with most rules, however, members of all ethnic groups vary in how strictly they adhere to the restrictions.

- Muslims and Jews don't eat pork.
- Hindus don't eat beef.
- Jews don't eat seafood without fins or scales.
- Seventh-Day Adventists don't eat meat.
- Some Puerto Ricans will not eat pineapple in combination with other foods.

- Navajos, especially the older generation, don't eat fish. Younger Navajos are less strict.
- Hindus, Mormons, some Protestant sects, and Muslims do not drink alcoholic beverages.

After the Matthias family first hired a newly arrived Macedonian housekeeper, they couldn't find their children's shoes. They finally discovered them stashed in an empty wine rack under the stairs. Because the housekeeper was Muslim, she was unaware of the true function of the rack and assumed that its structure was meant for storing shoes.

Utensils

American-born Alfred and Khaled, who is Arabic, work together in a video shop. Both men are in their early twenties. A camaraderie develops between them, and Khaled invites Alfred to meet his father's friends at a dinner. When the food is served, no utensils are placed on the table, and the guests begin eating with their fingers. Alfred asks Khaled if he can ask for a fork or a spoon, but Khaled says that would insult the father.

Alfred must eat with his fingers, but he feels awkward.

People from Arabic countries, parts of Africa, India, Sri Lanka, and certain parts of the Philippines often eat with their fingers from a common platter. They expect their guests to follow suit. It would be insulting to refuse. However, guests need to be observant about the ways in which hosts carry out the maneuver, for there are a number of variations in style. Indians from northern India, for example, do not put their fingers into the food beyond the second joint of the fingers, whereas people from southern India insert their entire hand into the food.

Regardless of where people come from or what their particular eating style may be, those who eat with their hands only use the right hand for touching food or drink. They consider the left hand unclean because it is used for cleaning oneself after using the toilet. Even when these hygienic customs no longer exist, many people still regard use of the left hand as taboo.

Chinese, Japanese, Koreans, and Vietnamese people generally use chopsticks. However, there are slight variations in the length, shape, and materials used. Chinese chopsticks are longer, have squared sides, and are made of bamboo, plastic, or ivory. Vietnamese use Chinese-style chopsticks. In contrast, Japanese chopsticks tend to be shorter and pointed at the end that goes into the mouth. Wooden ones are frequently lacquered. Korean chopsticks are often made of metal, such as stainless steel. They are thin, flat, and the same length as the Japanese.

Whereas Japanese people drink soup by lifting the bowl to the mouth with both hands, Koreans and Chinese use soup spoons. Koreans use spoons to eat rice, but the Chinese and Japanese do not.

Note that people from Thailand, Indonesia, and most parts of the Philippines generally do not use chopsticks unless they are of Chinese descent. Their tables will be set with forks and spoons. Cambodians, Lao, and Hmong generally do not use forks and rely solely on the spoon. However, Lao and Hmong people will also use their fingers when eating sticky rice.

People from Asian countries rarely set knives on the table. This goes back to the time when knives were primarily considered weapons. As a sign of trust, weapons were set aside when people ate together.

- When eating with fingers, only use the right hand to touch the food.
- When you're finished eating with chopsticks, place them in a parallel position across the top of the dish or bowl or on a chopstick rest, but never on the table, never crossed, and never upright.
- If you are a guest, it may be considered rude to rub wooden chopsticks together to remove any splinters.

Making Eating Noises

Two girls, Janice, a Vietnamese Chinese, and Yoki, from Japan, meet in a California high school and become friends. On Yoki's birthday, she invites Janice to her home to celebrate. Yoki's family acts pleased to meet Janice. As the family eats their meal, they make loud slurping sounds. When Janice does not make these sounds, Yoki's family becomes displeased.

In Japan, as in Hong Kong, slurping is not rude; it is a sign of approval and appreciation for the cooking. Slurping pays tribute to the chef. Therefore, when Janice does not slurp, Yoki's family believes Janice does not like their food. They are insulted. However, Janice's Chinese eating traditions do not include noisemaking while eating. In Janice's family, slurping is considered ill-mannered.

In most parts of Asia making sounds while eating is acceptable and encouraged. In Hong Kong and in other countries, lip-smacking tells the cook his food is delicious. Belching is another complimentary sign, as in some parts of the Philippines and in Saudi Arabia.

Of course, there are exceptions. People from Thailand, for example, do not make noises while eating. In addition, there are many customs related to whether it is impolite or polite to eat with your mouth open. The Japanese believe that it is rude to show the inside of the mouth. That is why they also cover it when they laugh.

In Janice's situation, she did not understand the meaning of the slurping sounds. However, if guests know that the sounds are complimentary, then why not try to do it, too? In a way it is fun, especially if, as a child, one has been taught *not* to make noises. Nevertheless, if guests feel self-conscious about making these sounds, then it's best to admit that their customs prevent them from doing it. If hosts understand the reasons for not participating, they will be more sympathetic.

- Many Asians and Saudi Arabians make eating noises to show their appreciation of the food. Interpret this as a compliment and not bad manners.

Cleaning Your Plate

Scott, born and raised in Los Angeles, and Marina, who spent her childhood in Cambodia, plan to marry. One evening, Scott joins Marina and her family for dinner, which they enjoy while sitting in a circle on the floor, Cambodian style. Each place setting has a small bowl of liquid. Scott observes the elderly Cambodian guest sitting next to him pick up the small bowl and drink from it. Scott does the same, emptying the bowl completely. As soon as he does, Marina's mother asks, "Good?"

"Good," says Scott, and Marina's mother refills it. Once more, Scott drinks the entire contents and again Marina's mother refills it. This happens one more time, but now Scott's face has turned red and he has a dripping nose. He keeps leaving the table to get a cold drink. The more he drinks from the small bowl, the more Marina's mother gives him. He doesn't know what to do.

When Cambodians empty the bowl or glass or clean their plates, that means they want more. If Scott had wanted to discourage the constant refills, he should have left less than half in the bowl. Marina might have told him this, but she was so busy helping her mother that she was unaware of her boyfriend's plight.

The act of cleaning one's plate and emptying the glass has different meanings, depending on the culture. Jordanians leave a small amount as a sign of politeness. Filipinos keep a little on the plate to show that the hosts have provided well. Conversely, as with Marina's family, cleaning the plate sometimes signals that the guest still wants more and the hosts have not provided sufficiently.

With Koreans, the glass will not be refilled if there is still some liquid in it, and Egyptians leave some food on the plate as a symbol of abundance and a compliment to the host. For Thais, leaving food means you are finished or it was delicious. For Indonesians, leaving food on the plate means the diner is impolite. For the Japanese, cleaning one's plate means the guest appreciates the food. Finishing the rice in the bowl signals that the diner has finished the meal.

Americans frequently caution their children to not waste food and to clean their plates, often citing some place in the world where people are starving. Parents elsewhere employ similar techniques for warning children not to waste food. A Chinese American recalls her childhood when her mother admonished that for every grain of rice left on the plate the youngster would have one pock mark on her face.

- When you're at a new acquaintance's house and you're not sure whether or not to clean your plate, observe how other guests ask for more food and how they signal when they have had enough. When in doubt, ask. If there is a language barrier, experiment.

Boxes of Food

Kay, a well-known folklorist, is invited to attend a Samoan wedding. She thinks she knows what to expect—whole roasted pigs presented to the newlyweds, paper money pinned to the dancing bride, and traditional island music and garb. Nevertheless, she is totally unprepared for the food.

At each place setting sits a large open cardboard box holding a slab of corned beef, cooked plantains, large portions of roast pork, pork ribs, fried chicken, a can of soda pop, containers of potato salad, and fruit salad. Kay knows that as a sign of friendship she must eat the food, but she cannot consume the entire contents of the box.

Kay didn't know that instead of having to eat all of the food, she was expected only to sample it. She discovered that guests merely tasted the food, then afterward carried the boxes to their cars to be taken home to share with family members.

Samoans, like other Pacific Islanders, place high value on the welfare of their extended families and the exchange of material goods. Thus, sharing festival food is a custom that can be found as far south as the Cook Islands and as far west as the Republic of Palau, where on festive occasions hosts distribute baskets of woven banana leaves filled with whole crab, tapioca, taro, and breadfruit.

- At Samoan weddings, if food is served in boxes, it should be taken home to be shared with the family.

Food and Politics

Executive members of a major corporation decide to tap into and expand their Chinese customer base. They select Ms. Garey to plan a luncheon to introduce the company's services to this community.

Ms. Garey is adept at such tasks. She selects a lovely Chinese restaurant in a prosperous Chinese business community and invites two hundred Chinese guests. On the appointed day, everything is in readiness, except the guests. Out of the two hundred invited, only six appear.

Unwittingly, Ms. Garey had selected a restaurant owned and operated by Chinese from Taiwan. The guests, however, were from Mainland China, and they did not wish to patronize a Taiwanese establishment. Bitterness about political differences between Mainland Chinese and Taiwanese remained strong, even in their new country. The few Mainland Chinese who showed up did so only out of embarrassment for the host company.

Ms. Garey found out about her error from the restaurant owner, who recognized the problem. Subsequently, she contracted with a restaurant owned by Mainland Chinese, who agreed to cater the luncheon. She reinvited the errant guests, who happily appeared and subsequently became customers.

It is easy to make mistakes about political divisions, especially when they take place outside this country, yet these partisan splits have implications for businesses here at home. Ramifications can also be found in medical settings when translators and patients come from opposing political sides. If the patient is from South Vietnam and the interpreter is from the North, the patient may be unwilling to reveal the true nature of the physical ailment in front of an old-time enemy.

- Politics in other countries may adversely affect personal relations and business practices here.

Fast-Food Bags

(See also: The *Qur'an*, p. 153.)

Anticipation of interest in the Summer 1994 World Cup soccer championship games inspires businesses to create promotional tie-ins. One fast-food chain produces a take-out food bag showing flags of the twenty-four competing nations. However, government representatives from one of these countries object when they discover their country's flag on the bag. Their ambassador contacts corporate headquarters and demands that the flag be removed.

The offended country was Saudi Arabia, whose green flag with a sword contains words in Arabic taken from their sacred book, the *Qur'an* (Koran). The inscription reads, "There is no God but God. Mohammed is the messenger of God."

To the Saudis, the idea that the food bags containing these holy words inevitably would be crumpled and thrown into the trash was sacrilegious. To jettison sacred words in such a casual way would insult not only the Saudis, but Muslims everywhere. According to Saudi officials, the only acceptable way to dispose of anything containing quotations from the *Qur'an* is to recycle or shred them. Holy words must never be thrown away.

Liz Claiborne Inc., licensed by Donna Karan International, made a comparable error when they incorporated verses from the *Qur'an* into some jeans design. What especially offended was that the verses were printed on the back pockets. After complaints from the Muslim community, they recalled eight thousand jeans. (See also: Boutique Boo-boos, p. 55; Camouflage, p. 52.)

- Casual treatment of words to one person may be blasphemy to another.
- When cultural gaffes happen, quick action to repair the damage may save the relationship.

Food as Medicine

(See also: Heart Transplants and Licorice, p. 103; Alternative Healers, p. 107.)

Nurse Bassett is in charge in the hospital emergency room, and phones are ringing off the hook. A teenager is now on the line panicked about her father. He has just cut himself with an electric garden edger and is bleeding profusely.

Bassett questions the girl about how the injury is being treated. Bassett is astounded when she hears that the grandmother has put honey on the wound. Bassett urges the girl to have someone drive the father to the hospital at once. He needs *real* medical care.

When the family arrives, Bassett expects that the father will need stitches, but she is amazed when she sees his hand. The bleeding has stopped, and the wound has already begun to close— no stitches are necessary.

The family was from Iran, where they believe that honey has the power to heal a wound. There is often a truth to be found in home remedies, and shortly after Bassett questioned the validity of putting honey on the wound, she read a column in *Natural Health* magazine recommending the same treatment. The article extolled the value of honey as an antibacterial ointment and recommended unprocessed honey (unheated and unfiltered) for killing a wide range of germs. The article cited a scientific study in which honey had been applied to the various wounds of forty patients. Researchers found that it promoted healing in 88 percent of the cases.

Honey has long had a good reputation as a curative. Many people from Central America and the Caribbean mix it with lemon as a tea for soothing upper respiratory problems. Some Russian immigrants add it to warm milk, butter, and baking soda for sore throats.

A wide range of cultures use other foods as curatives. Russian immigrants have been known to parboil cabbage leaves and place them on foreheads to draw out fevers. Some Central Americans chew on cloves with lemon to ease toothaches. Puerto Ricans often put tomato sauce on burns.

Many people believe garlic and ginger are cure-alls, although no one has accurately analyzed their healing properties. Garlic is heralded for its antibacterial qualities, while ginger tea is thought to aid digestion and colds.

And who doubts the efficacy of chicken soup to soothe a cold? Jewish mothers and grandmothers have long been associated with chicken soup, affectionately known as "Jewish penicillin" or "bubbamycin." Many Southeast Asians place equal stock in the power of this sustenance. Scientifically, the value of chicken soup has been corroborated by Dr. Marvin Sackner of Mount Sinai Medical Center in Miami, who claims that drinking the golden liquid works better than other hot liquids for relieving nasal congestion by increasing nasal mucus velocity.

- If you work in a health care profession, encourage patients to tell you what home treatments they have been using.
- It may be difficult to dissuade patients from using folk remedies because they are closely bound to cultural customs that are important for patients to maintain.
- If patients are reluctant to give up home remedies, encourage them to use their remedies, as long as they are not harmful, along with prescribed treatment.
- If home remedies are harmful, don't overreact and put patients on the defensive. Instead, try to reeducate them.
- Some folk remedies may be effective.

Hot/Cold

(See also: Alternative Healers, p. 107.)

Mrs. Wong, recovering from a spinal fusion, tells her morning nurse, Lois, how hungry she is. Later when Lois comes to check on her, she sees that the patient hasn't touched her orange juice, cold cereal, and milk. "I thought you were hungry," says Lois.

"I am, but the food is cold," the patient answers.

"Of course it is," says Lois.

"I can't eat cold food," says Mrs. Wong.

Lois is baffled.

Mrs. Wong couldn't eat the cold food because she believed that following surgery or childbirth, one must take warm fluids. This is based on a system of labeling food, drink, medicines, herbs, illnesses, and medical procedures as either hot or cold. This system originated with the ancient Greeks, and through the spread of Islam, it moved through Central Asia. It is based on the premise of balancing the four humors (body fluids). According to this system, illness is the result of humoral imbalance.

In the Asian interpretation of the system, as the result of a "hot" procedure, like surgery or childbirth, the body loses heat. Therefore, the heat must be replaced. This accounts for Asian resistance to drinking cold water or taking showers after surgery or childbirth.

An extreme reaction to fear of losing heat comes from those who practice "mother roasting," a form of replacing heat lost during childbirth. In Cambodia, mother roasting consists of placing the mother on a slatted bed that has a heat source underneath it. Every few minutes, an attendant turns the mother to a different side of her body, much like turning a turkey or a cut of beef in the oven to ensure even browning. This procedure continues for thirty days. In this country, the request by Asian patients to pile on many blankets following childbirth or surgery is a modern adaptation of replacing and retaining the heat.

The classification of foods, medicines, and medical procedures as either hot or cold is not limited to Asians. Middle Eastern and Latino peoples do the same. However, what may be considered hot to one group may be considered cold by another. Principles vary also. With one group of people, after a hot procedure, like childbirth, they may want to balance it with something cold rather than replace the heat.

Whether a food is labeled hot or cold has nothing to do with actual temperature. For example, Iranians classify grapes as hot and cantaloupe as cold; mint as hot, spinach as cold. The Lao classify ice as hot. Obviously, there is no easily observed principle in this classification scheme. Health practitioners find this confusing. However, if the nurse or doctor notices that a patient routinely refuses meals, it would be useful to ask the patient just what combination of foods would be helpful.

To provide the best nourishment for infants, people who hold beliefs in the hot/cold system follow strict rules during pregnancy and after birth. During the first trimester of pregnancy, Vietnamese women eat hot foods, such as meat, ginger, and black pepper. In the second trimester, they eat cold foods, such as squash, melons, fruit, and foods high in fat, protein, sugar, and carbohydrates. In the last trimester, they limit hot foods to prevent indigestion and to avoid rashes and sores on the newborn's skin.

Latinas believe they are in a hot state during pregnancy, so they avoid cold foods to maintain the heat. After childbirth, they avoid eating hot foods such as pork, chile, and tomatoes.

New Cambodian, Chinese, and Vietnamese mothers believe they need hot foods after childbirth due to loss of blood, energy, and heat. They can change their breast milk to hot by eating meat, salty fish, chile, and herb-steeped wine. (See also: Breast Milk, p. 31.)

- When patients refer to hot or cold, they may not be referring to actual temperature.
- Hot/cold systems vary with people's different backgrounds; for example, a Middle Easterner and a Latino may give opposite classifications to the same food or procedure.
- Always ask the patient what is specifically hot or cold to them.

Gifts

(See also: Odd or Even?, p. 135; Red Envelopes, p. 136; Political Differences, p. 163.)

Yellow Flowers

(See also: Yellow Tags, p. 68; White Flowers, p. 92; Funeral Flowers, p. 93; Odd or Even?, p. 135.)

In Armenian culture, when you give someone yellow flowers, it means "I miss you." That is why Anahid, an Armenian girl, brings yellow flowers to the mother of her Iranian friend, Leila Golestani, who is away on her honeymoon. Anahid misses Leila and phones Leila's mother. She discovers how lonely Mrs. Golestani is for her daughter. Anahid goes to visit Mrs. Golestani.

Mrs. Golestani is pleased to see Anahid and hugs her; but as soon as Anahid gives her the yellow flowers, her face turns red. She ushers Anahid into the living room but immediately excuses herself to prepare some tea. After waiting an inordinate length of time, Anahid walks into the kitchen to see if she can help. She sees that Mrs. Golestani has been crying.

Alarmed, Anahid asks, "What's wrong? Has something happened to Leila?" Before Mrs. Golestani can answer, Anahid notices that her yellow flowers have been thrown on the floor in the corner of the room.

"I didn't know you hated us so much," Mrs. Golestani says accusingly.

In Iranian culture, yellow flowers represent the enemy, and giving someone yellow flowers means that you hate them. It can even mean that you wish the person dead. Anahid had to plead

91

with Mrs. Golestani to reveal this information, but the explanation shocked her. In defense, Anahid explained that Armenians give an opposite meaning to the gift of yellow flowers—I miss you. Ultimately she convinced Mrs. Golestani of her sincerity, and their relationship was restored.

Peruvians have this same belief about yellow flowers, and they, too, would never give them to anyone. Among Mexicans as well, yellow flowers have a negative connotation, related to funerals. They are always used for Day of the Dead celebrations.

- The colors of flowers have different meanings for different cultures. Yellow in particular has negative connotations for many people, such as Iranians, Peruvians, and Mexicans. It would be safer not to give yellow flowers as a gift.

In 2003, I attended the funeral of an elderly Iranian man and was surprised to note several flower arrangements that contained yellow flowers. I assumed that they came from American business associates and was astonished when I discovered that they had been sent by other Iranians.

- The longer immigrant families have been in this country, the more likely it is that rules will relax.

White Flowers

(See also: Wedding Guests Wearing White, p. 66; Yellow Flowers, p. 91; Funeral Flowers, p. 93; Odd or Even?, p. 135.)

Another color error in choosing appropriate flowers happened to Marilyn, who, when working as a substitute high school teacher, met another substitute, Joe Chen.

Marilyn and Joe Chen become friends and go out together for meals and movies. One day, Joe invites Marilyn over to meet his family and have dinner at the Chens' family home. She is delighted and stops at the florist to pick up a bouquet of white gladioli.

When she enters their home carrying the flowers, the family gasps.

For Chinese people, white is the color of mourning. In addition, gladioli are frequently used in funeral sprays. When Marilyn brought these taboo objects into the home, she was symbolically bringing death to the family.

Throughout the meal, the family was very cold to her. At first, she wasn't sure what was wrong but noticed that after giving them the flowers, they never put them in water, nor did they bring them out to display.

Several months later, Marilyn met Joe's sister and found out why the flowers had not been displayed. Joe's mother had become very anxious having these death tokens in the house, yet Joe never mentioned this to Marilyn. In retrospect, Marilyn realized that Joe probably had been interested in pursuing a romantic relationship with her, but her white flowers killed that possibility.

Many people are unaware that they have flower taboos. When I ordered a bouquet of flowers for my daughter's college graduation and the florist asked if I wanted to include gladioli, I surprised myself with a vehement "No!" As a person who was born in the States, I had been to too many funerals where gladioli were the mainstay of the floral displays, so gladioli have unconsciously become a taboo flower for me.

- Chinese and most other Asian people respond negatively to white flowers because white has death connotations. It would be safer not to give white flowers as a gift.

Funeral Flowers

(See also: Yellow Flowers, p. 91; White Flowers, p. 92; Odd or Even?, p. 135.)

Angela works in a Chinese-owned bakery. She, as well as most of the other workers, is Latina, and they all work together very well. One day the owner's brother dies, and the workers decide to buy some flowers out of respect for their boss. Because they don't have the address of the home of the deceased, they have the flowers delivered to the bakery. From there, they assume the manager will be able to deliver them to the right place.

When the manager sees the flowers, she becomes upset and quickly hides them in the walk-in refrigerator.

After hiding the flowers from the Chinese workers and boss, the Chinese manager found the address of the mortuary, and within a few minutes, a delivery truck arrived to pick up the flowers and take them to the funeral home.

She explained that objects of death should not be placed among the living. Having flowers brought to the bakery or any place of business was equivalent to bringing death and bad luck to the business and to those who worked there. However, she also complimented the workers on their good intentions, thus easing everyone's agitated state.

The next day all the workers received a little red envelope with a dime in it from the boss to bring the workers good luck and to show his appreciation.

- Never send funeral flowers to an Asian place of business.

Bribery

Professor Morris is a stickler for high standards, and he gives low grades when he sees fit. One day, a Korean student comes to his office about the F she received on her paper. She brings him some fruit, which he graciously accepts. On a subsequent visit about another non-passing paper, she brings more fruit. Although the teacher is uncomfortable about this, he thanks her and says he will share it with the office staff.

On a final visit, she presents him with solid gold cuff links, which he refuses. She informs the professor that if she does not pass the class, her husband will beat her.

This situation has been repeated often between American teachers and foreign or immigrant students. It is difficult for a teacher not to feel upset and torn when students reveal that if they fail a class, physical consequences will occur—beating by husbands or parents. Still, most teachers do not yield to this pressure, and students eventually learn that this kind of coercion will not work. No matter how disturbed Professor Morris was, he did not change the student's grade, nor would he accept the cuff links.

The threat of physical harm is more difficult to deal with than the mere acceptance or rejection of a gift that may be perceived as a bribe. Elsewhere, bribes are an accepted part of doing business. In other countries, bribes are known as *baksheesh* (Middle East), *mordida* (Mexico), *dash* (Africa), and *kumshaw* (Southeast Asia). On the other hand, while Americans openly abhor the use of bribes, businesspeople create similar obligations between parties, for example, by buying clients expensive meals or providing box seats at ball games.

Teachers have to be sensitive when receiving gifts. Accepting a student's present always raises the specter of bribery. Sometimes students will use the excuse that it is "Teacher's Day" in their native countries, or they may say that it is their custom to present teachers with gifts in appreciation of their dedication. Both reasons may be true, but teachers should be leery of the failing student who suddenly presents the instructor with a costly gift, such as jewelry. It is incumbent upon the teacher to explain the inappropriateness of such behavior.

On the other hand, if a student presents a gift or if a class chips in to buy something for the teacher at an accepted gift-giving occasion, such as the end of the semester or Christmas, this is acceptable and there should be no strings attached.

- Some students may attempt to affect grades through gifts or by revealing that physical harm may come to them if they do not pass or get high marks. This may be the truth.
- Teachers must convince students that expensive gifts cannot be accepted and may be negatively interpreted.

Gift Taboos

(See also: Yellow Flowers, p. 91; White Flowers, p. 92.)

Jeff has a Chinese girlfriend named April who invites him to her twentieth birthday celebration. At the end of the party, April opens her gifts, saving Jeff's present for last. When April unwraps Jeff's gift—an umbrella—she becomes infuriated.

In Chinese, the sound of the word *umbrella* is the same as the word for *separation*. April interpreted this present to mean that Jeff didn't want to see her anymore. For Chinese, gifts of knives and scissors also symbolize the severance of a relationship.

In the past, Americans had a similar reaction to a gift of a sharp object, such as a knife or scissors; the recipient had to give the donor a penny to symbolize the transaction as a sale and not a gift, which could sever the relationship. Nowadays, gift-givers frequently include a penny when giving a sharp object.

Another Chinese gift taboo is the giving of a clock. The grandparents of a Chinese girl who received a clock as a birthday gift demanded that she end her relationship with the person who gave the present. In Chinese, the sound of the word "clock" is a homophone for a word that means "attending the dead." To counteract the negativity of such a gift, the recipient of a clock can give a coin in return, symbolically buying it instead.

The following are some guidelines for giving gifts to the Chinese and Japanese.

- Avoid giving umbrellas, knives, scissors, and clocks as gifts.
- Cash gifts to the Chinese should be in even numbers and given with both hands. (See also: Numbers, p. 132.)
- Don't expect the Chinese to open gifts in front of the donor.
- Don't open gifts in front of the Japanese.
- Avoid wrapping gifts for the Japanese in either black or white paper.
- Don't give the Japanese gifts that number four. Avoid giving wedding gifts, such as teacups, in even numbers because they can be divided. (See also: Odd or Even?, p. 135.)

White Envelopes

(See also: White Bonnets, p. 65; Wedding Guests Wearing White, p. 66; White Flowers, p. 92.)

On a Saturday morning, Sally calls Dao, her Vietnamese manicurist, to see if she can make an appointment for that same day. Dao apologizes, saying she is booked solid. "How about tomorrow?" she asks.

Sally says that is impossible because she needs the manicure to look good for her father's funeral taking place the next day. Dao hesitates, then tells Sally to come at noon and she will work her in.

When Sally's nails are done, Dao surprises Sally by handing her a white envelope. "What's this?" Sally asks as she begins to open it and look inside.

Dao scolds, "No! Don't open it now!"

Startled, Sally obeys, places the envelope in her purse, thanks Dao, and leaves the shop. As soon as she gets home, she looks inside the envelope and finds twenty dollars.

Dao's gift to Sally was a sign of her regard for her as a customer and out of respect for Sally's father. The white envelope represents the color of death and mourning in most Asian traditions. The envelope is an important symbol in Vietnamese and Chinese tradition.

At Chinese wakes, the family of the deceased will often pass out white envelopes with nickels in them to take away the bitterness or to buy something sweet. Often one piece of candy is enclosed in the envelope, or there will be a bowl of candy for people to help themselves.

At the funeral, the family will pass out red envelopes with dimes in them to represent life. (See also: Red Envelopes, p. 136.) The dime has another significance: just before the casket is closed, a dime is put on the lips of the deceased to pay for passage to the other side. Sometimes Chinese families will elect to hand out both white and red envelopes at the funeral service.

Sally was obliged to accept the envelope in spite of knowing what a financial sacrifice it was for Dao to give her twenty dollars. Dao would have been offended if Sally had returned it. Sally felt guilty to accept the money from this hard-working, low-paid young woman but made it up to the manicurist by giving her a generous Christmas gift.

- If a Chinese or Vietnamese person gives you a white envelope on an occasion of death, accept it graciously, but do not open it in the presence of the donor.

Refusing a Gift

(See also: Offering Food, p. 73; Evil Eye, p. 138; Believing What They Say, p. 197.)

Julie, an art student, and Farid, her Iranian boyfriend, have been seeing each other for several months. Farid has just invited Julie for dinner at the home of his brother, Reza, and sister-in-law, Maryam. Julie is delighted.

When they arrive, Julie "ooohs" and "aahs" over their Iranian folk art collection. She is particularly drawn to a miniature on the bookshelf and admires its beauty and fineness of handwork details.

Julie is so enthusiastic that Maryam insists on giving it to her. Surprised and a bit embarrassed, Julie refuses, but Maryam persists in her offer. Not wanting to hurt Maryam's feelings, Julie graciously accepts the gift.

Julie is happy. Maryam is not.

Many Middle Easterners feel obligated to offer as a gift an item that is admired. It is, in part, due to graciousness, but there is another reason. If a person were to admire an object belonging to you and you did not offer that object to the person, he or she might covet it. Out of envy, that person might cast an evil eye toward you. Believers in the evil eye think that accidents, sickness, and death can be caused by the voluntary or involuntary glance of a person or animal. Arousing the envy of others makes one vulnerable.

Maryam did not want to inspire envy. Therefore, she offered the gift to Julie. What should Julie have done? She should have persisted in rejecting the gift, convincing Maryam that even though she admired it and appreciated the offer, she could not possibly accept. It probably would have taken several rounds of "No, thank you" to reset the balance.

Maryam's response is not limited to Iranians. This tradition is found all over the Middle East and in India as well.

- After admiring someone else's possession, the person may be culturally obligated to offer the object to you, but you are not obligated to accept it, and indeed, you should not. Most of the time, you should persist in your refusal.

Birthday Cake

(See also: Evil Eye, p. 138.)

Roxanne wants to surprise her Iranian boyfriend, Peyman, by ordering a small birthday cake to be served at an Iranian restaurant where they are going to celebrate with another couple.

When the waiter brings out the cake, Peyman is not pleased.

Roxanne discovered that Peyman worried because the cake was not large enough to share with diners at adjacent tables. He was afraid they might become jealous. This might make him a target for the evil eye. The only way to have avoided such a situation would have been to order a cake big enough to share with other restaurant patrons.

- Many Middle Eastern people are cautious about making themselves the cause of someone else's envy. This places them in a vulnerable position.

Health Practices

(See also: Coining, p. 34; Breast Milk, p. 31; Dress for Respect, p. 62; Food as Medicine, p. 85; Hot/Cold, p. 87; Hospital Roommates, p. 146.)

AIDS

(See also: AIDS Education, p. 143.)

At a party, Danny shares a can of soda with Julie, who points to another man and observes, "He's really cute." Danny answers, "Not as cute as the guy I've been dating." In horror, Julie drops the can of soda to the floor.

Danny mistakenly thought that Julie knew about his recently revealed homosexuality. Likewise, Julie jumped to the conclusion that because Danny was gay, he also had AIDS or was HIV-positive. Accusingly, she asked, "Why did you let me drink out of the same soda can as you?"

Julie had made false assumptions:

- Not all homosexuals have AIDS or are HIV-positive.
- Drinking from the same can of soda cannot spread the virus.
- According to the National Centers for Disease Control (www .CDC.gov), AIDS is a disease that occurs when HIV destroys the body's immune system.

HIV is spread in the following ways:

- Having unprotected sex, sex without a condom, with a partner who has HIV. The virus can be in an infected person's blood, semen, or vaginal secretions that can enter the body through tiny cuts or skin sores, or in the lining of the vagina, penis, rectum, or mouth.

- By sharing a needle and syringe to inject drugs or sharing drug equipment used to prepare drugs for injection with someone who has HIV.
- By receiving a blood transfusion or blood-clotting factor prior to 1985.
- To babies born to HIV-positive women and infected during pregnancy, during birth, or while breast-feeding.
- You *cannot* get HIV by working with or being around someone who has HIV; from sweat, spit, tears, clothes, drinking fountains, phones, toilet seats, or through everyday things like sharing a meal; from insect bites or stings; from donating blood; or from a closed-mouth kiss (but there is a very small chance of getting it from open-mouthed or "French" kissing with an infected person because of possible blood contact).

Misunderstanding the Doctor's Orders

In California, Dr. Linda Chassiakos tells about the worried non-English-speaking family she encounters in the ER. They are convinced that their baby's ear infection has gotten worse since taking antibiotics. An examination confirms that the parents are correct in their assessment of the child's worsening condition.

The doctor questions the parents about the medicine, and they admit that it is difficult to give the child the liquid medicine from the dropper: the pink liquid leaks from the ear. Dr. Chassiakos now understands the problem.

Instead of giving the medicine orally, the parents inserted the dropper into the ear canal. Since the antibiotic could not get past the eardrum to treat the infected middle ear, the infection had become more severe.

These parents assumed that they should put the medicine directly into the ear; the original doctor was unaware of this assumption. This time, Dr. Chassiakos carefully explained to the parents the correct way to give the medicine and why it had not previously worked. The concerned parents followed her precise instructions, and the child quickly recovered.

- Health practitioners must make certain that patients fully understand instructions. Never take their comprehension for granted.
- Interpreters are crucial when language barriers exist.

An enraged patient arrived at a New York City hospital clinic. Because she already had twelve children, the woman had previously asked for a contraceptive and had received a spermicidal jelly. She now complained that she had followed the instructions and used it before having sex, but it tasted "lousy." She tried it on crackers with peanut butter and grape jelly, but it still tasted "lousy." And now she was pregnant again!

- Even without language differences, misunderstandings about correct methods of treatment occur.

Heart Transplants and Licorice

When the doctor recommends a heart transplant for his Latino patient, the patient is concerned. He asks, "Whose soul will live inside me?"

This is not an uncommon worry in the Latino community. Many believe that the soul resides in the heart. They fear that after a heart transplant, they will take on the character and behavior of the donor. In *Healing Latinos: Realidad y Fantasía*, Ismael Nuño, M.D., describes this reaction and explains that the concept is rooted in Aztec beliefs.

Beyond the Latino community, an abundance of anecdotal material suggests the possibility that aspects of the donor's personality may be transferred to the donee. Some organ recipients claim having foreign memories, eerie new personal preferences, and unexplained emerging talents. The phenomenon, called cellular memory, was the subject of a 2003 Discovery Channel television show, *Transplanting Memories*. It told of an eight-year-old girl who received the heart of a murdered ten-year-old and subsequently began having nightmares in which she relived the crime. Her dreams helped police solve the murder. Another recipient was a shy, reserved woman who, post-op, became more assertive and had vivid dreams of the donor she had never met. A third example was a man who, strangely, picked up his donor's musical tastes.

The show referred to biochemist Dr. Candace Pert of Georgetown University, who offers that the mind is not just in the brain, but also exists throughout the body. She asserts that every cell in our body has its own mind. When transferring tissues from one body to another, the cells from the first body will carry memories into the second body. She claims that the mind and body communicate with each other through chemicals known as peptides. According to Pert, the peptides are found in the brain as well as in the stomach, muscles, and all major organs. She says that memory can be accessed anywhere in the peptide/receptor network. For instance, a memory associated with food may be linked to the pancreas or liver, and such associations can be transplanted from one person to another.

Jeff Punch, M.D., a transplant surgeon at the University of Michigan, disputes the concept. "A transplant is a profound experience and the human mind is very suggestible. Medically speaking, there is no evidence that these reports are anything more than fantasy," he challenges. Punch is not alone in his skepticism, dismissing the strange phenomena as postsurgery stress or reactions to anti-organ-rejection drugs. Yet a growing number of experts are beginning to express the possibility that cellular memories can be transplanted with organs.

Sometimes folk beliefs are valid, but it may take a long time until they are proven. As one example, the ancient Greeks, Egyptians, Chinese, and Hindus recognized the natural medicinal qualities of licorice. Tutankhamen was buried with licorice root. Today, the root is a botanical ingredient in modern Chinese medicines used to manage cancers. And now Professor Mohamed Rafi of Rutgers University's Cook College in New Jersey has discovered a new molecule, BHP, in common dietary supplements made from licorice root. For the first time, he and his colleagues have demonstrated that BHP arrests the growth of breast and prostate cancer cells.

- While it is easy to dismiss folk medicine beliefs that contradict scientific knowledge, these beliefs may contain clues to cures and the truth.

Patients may have beliefs that cause problems in the health care environment: Southeast Asians may resist when doctors wish to draw blood, fearing that the blood will not be replenished; patients from Eastern Europe and Russia become anxious about X-rays because of the Chernobyl explosion and the spread of radiation and subsequent illness.

- Some ethnic health beliefs may impede effective treatment.

Hospital Accommodations

Martha works as a hospital nurse and is attending a child who has just died. The family requests that Martha open the window to release the child's soul, but the hospital windows do not open.

Taking the situation in stride, the family, while chanting, escorts the soul out the hospital room, into the elevator and out again on the first floor to be released through the front door.

Martha's willingness to accommodate patients' ethnic beliefs is not unique. More and more hospitals are making these kinds of concessions, aware that by doing so, their patients and families will thrive. Here are some examples:

- At hospitals with large Chinese populations, chopsticks are served with meals; cesarean sections may be scheduled according to astrologers' recommendations; the number four is not used for room numbers (see also: Numbers, p. 132); mah-Jongg is available for recreation and occupational therapy.
- A hospital in Sunset Park, New York, has Muslim prayer rooms and tropical fish for Chinese patients who believe that fish are healing symbols; a Patient's Bill of Rights is posted on the wall in Arabic, Chinese, Russian, Spanish, and English.
- Maimonides Hospital in Brooklyn serves glatt kosher food to their Orthodox Jewish patients and provides rooms for husbands studying the Torah while waiting for their wives to deliver. To avoid

violating the Sabbath taboo of pressing buttons or levers from sundown on Friday to sundown on Saturday, other accommodations are made here and at other hospitals serving large numbers of Orthodox Jewish patients, such as Cedars Sinai in Los Angeles. The staff opens sealed packages and adjusts electronic beds; one elevator automatically stops at every floor to avoid the need to push buttons. They also recommend that a family member stay in the room to personally advise the desk if a patient needs help, averting the need to press the call button.

Ignoring the Baby

(See also: Evil Eye, p. 138; Giving Praise, p. 185.)

A Vietnamese woman has just delivered a beautiful healthy baby boy, but the new mother's reaction puzzles Ms. Crane, her delivery nurse attendant. The new mother ignores the baby when the nurse presents him to her.

On the hospital records, Nurse Crane describes the mother's response: "Bonding—0."

Nurse Crane did not know that many Asian people believe a baby is in grave danger when first born. To recognize the child's presence by fussing over it would bring too much attention that might place the baby in jeopardy, a concept related to the evil eye.

The Vietnamese mother was not unconcerned about her baby. On the contrary, she cared so much for her child that she made a pretense of ignoring him to safeguard him from what she perceived as perilous influences. When Nurse Crane later discovered her misunderstanding of the situation at a hospital-sponsored cross-cultural awareness workshop, she felt regretful.

In the 1992 Academy Award–nominated film *Indochine*, the same attitude toward babies was revealed in Catherine Deneuve's character's comments about a newly born Vietnamese baby: "The evil spirits are listening. If we say we like him, they will harm him."

People from many cultures are reluctant to draw attention to a baby for fear of attracting misfortune. After complimenting a child's physical attributes, many Jews of Eastern European heritage try to protect the baby by saying *Kain ayinhore* ("Not one evil eye").

- A seeming lack of demonstrated appreciation for a child may have different meanings for people from different cultures. It may be a form of protection rather than indifference.

Alternative Healers

(See also: Food as Medicine, p. 85; Hot/Cold, p. 87.)

The hospital conference room is packed with nurses, doctors, and administrative staff gathered to hear a diversity trainer offer advice about the most effective way to provide health care to multiethnic patients.

One attendee suggests that upon admission, patients should be asked what kinds of alternative healers they consult and what kinds of nonstandard treatments they use.

Although the staff responds favorably to this suggestion, the diversity trainer assures them that it will not work.

- Patients hesitate to reveal information about traditional healers lest they put the healers in jeopardy, either related to immigration or to legal issues, for example, practicing medicine without a license. This particularly applies when the patient is first entering a health care system and dealing with an unfamiliar staff person. Likewise, patients are reluctant to reveal their sources of herbs and other supplies. Additionally, they worry that their methods will be frowned upon by Western medical practitioners. (See also: Food as Medicine, p. 85.)
- Generally, members of ethnic groups first seek help from a practitioner within their tradition. When that fails, they may turn to standard Westernized medicine. Sometimes they simultaneously consult with both, which can negate the effectiveness of the medications or cause complications.
- Information about a patient's use of non-Western healers and treatments will only be revealed after rapport has been established

between the professional and the patient, and only after patients feel confident that they will not be denigrated for their behavior or that healers and suppliers will not be reported to authorities.

- Mexican patients may consult with a *partera* (midwife), *curandero* (folk healer), *hierbera* (herbalist), or *bruja* (witch). Cambodians may use a *kru Khmer* (a channeler) to contact *shamans* (gifted spirits from the past). Hmong use shamans, folk healers who enter the spirit world by chanting themselves into a trance, to diagnose and perform treatments asking good spirits to help fight the evil ones. Cubans, Puerto Ricans, and Brazilians who believe in Santería may consult with a *santero* (priest) who may invoke an *Orisha* (saintlike deity) to assist in the cure. Haitians may consult with voodoo priests and priestesses seeking prevention and treatment of illnesses. Puerto Ricans may also consult with a *santiguadora* (folk healer) or spiritualists called *señorías, espiritistas*, or *curanderos*. Cajuns may seek help from a *traiteur*. Pennsylvanian Germans may use Powwow doctors or *brauchers*.
- *Botánicas* supply healing substances and objects to Caribbeans and Latinos. They sell amulets, candles, teas, books, bath salts, crystals, shells, and statues of saints.

Sacrificing a Rooster

When a Hmong child falls down in the girls' bathroom at school, her parents believe that an evil spirit has entered her body and caused an illness. Belief in evil spirits as a cause of illness is a common Hmong concept. To restore the child's health they must appease the evil spirit by having a shaman sacrifice a rooster in the school bathroom, where she fell down.

Doctors, however, diagnose the girl as having kidney failure. They recommend dialysis and a subsequent kidney transplant, but the parents are adamantly against it. Equally resolute is the school's refusal to have an animal sacrifice on school property. Meanwhile the girl's condition worsens.

To save the child's life, a Hmong intermediary negotiates with the school to allow the ritual sacrifice in exchange for the parents' permission, initially for dialysis and later for a kidney transplant. The sacrifice takes place after school hours. Subsequent medical treatment is successful.

- Sometimes school administrators must make painful decisions. (See also: Ashes, p. 124.) In this situation, no one was hurt, except the rooster, who was eventually cooked and eaten. Only the maintenance man complained—about having to clean up splattered blood in the bathroom. (See also: The Voodoo Squad, p. 127.)
- Although medical authorities may be reluctant to support unusual beliefs of their patients, if it's in the patient's best interest, it may be beneficial to incorporate the patient's own health constructs into the Western mode of medicine. (See also: Alternative Healers, p. 107.)

Physical Examinations

(See also: Chastity, p. 147.)

Dr. Bradley greets his new patient, a woman in her late thirties, who has stopped menstruating. Assuming that she is experiencing premature menopause, he orders tests to check her hormone levels and starts to perform a pelvic examination to make sure there are no internal abnormalities. The patient adamantly refuses to be physically examined.

The patient was Rom, or Gypsy. The Rom have very strict rules about chastity. In their culture, an unmarried woman cannot spread her legs before a man, even for medical purposes. If this patient had done so, she would have been considered ineligible for marriage. This stymied Dr. Bradley, who was limited only to the results of the bloodwork and patient history to make his diagnosis and prescribe treatment.

- Culturally specific perceptions of women's modesty may impede medical treatment in profound ways.

Gypsies have strict rules about chastity. In 1997, the city of Spokane, Washington, settled out of court with a Gypsy tribe for

$1.43 million, in part because the local police had illegally performed a strip search of some of their unmarried girls. Consequently, the girls were considered defiled and unclean and could not marry other Gypsies. The Gypsy family was ostracized and unwelcome at other Gypsy weddings and funerals and could no longer visit hospitalized relatives.

Gypsy modesty and chastity also affect their disdain for hospital gowns that too easily expose the genitalia. Other concerns relate to their system of pollution and purity: they believe that food arrives on impure dishes. They are terrified of being alone, accounting for the large numbers, thirty or forty, who hang around the hospital for a minor problem. Visitors may number one hundred or more when a patient is in critical condition.

Birth Attendants

Accustomed to having expectant parents take childbirth preparation classes, nurses are surprised when Mrs. Rodriguez declines to have her husband assist with breathing and massage during her labor. She wants her mother instead.

Mexican traditional men do not assist during childbirth. Likewise, it is taboo for Orthodox Jewish husbands to assist because the wife is considered unclean, due to the presence of blood. (See also: Menstruation, p. 164.) Some Arabic husbands will not assist, and for some Chinese families, the mother-in-law may be the preferred labor companion.

• During the birth process, some cultures exclude men.

Prayer Position

The nurse cannot understand why her newly admitted patient, Mr. Asfar, is so agitated about his assigned room. He keeps insisting that the bed should be against the opposite wall, but that is impossible: the oxygen and all the telemetry for measuring respiration and heartbeat have been permanently installed on this side of the room. There is no way to move the bed because the wires are not long enough to reach to the other side.

Mr. Asfar insists that the room is unsatisfactory in its present layout. In exasperation, the nurses switch him to another room that meets with his approval.

Mr. Asfar was a Muslim, and he needed to be able to face the east, toward Mecca, to say his prayers five times daily. The staff at this hospital was annoyed by having to change Mr. Asfar's room. However, most hospitals are sensitive to this highly emotional response and cooperate with patients who have such beliefs.

- The direction a hospital bed faces can affect the emotional state of a patient: those who believe in the principles of *feng shui* prefer to have their beds face south. (See also: *Feng Shui*, p. 129.) Muslims must face the east.

Birth Control

Cheryl, a gynecology nurse practitioner, has just opened a new private practice. Her fifth Latina patient, Alicia, is in for a general checkup. Cheryl provides information about various birth control methods, indicating their advantages and disadvantages and ease of use. However, she notices that when she describes the diaphragm, Alicia, like previous Latina patients, giggles, shakes her head, and ultimately says "No!"

Because the diaphragm is inexpensive, easy to use, and has a high safety rate, Cheryl is baffled by the negative response.

Cheryl eventually discovered that there is a Latino cultural stigma about touching one's own genitals, so much so that during menstruation, most Latinas prefer not to use tampons. On the other hand, for birth control, they will agree to the use of the IUD because that is inserted by the health specialist. However, with IUDs, Latinas want assurance that their husbands will not be aware of their presence because so many spouses oppose any form of birth control.

Even if there were no religious restrictions, birth control presents problems for Latinas. Many Latino men refuse to use condoms or to have vasectomies. In addition, they frequently won't allow their wives to have tubal ligations. Cheryl found that most of her patients preferred birth control pills, but hid them from their husbands.

Cheryl later learned that many Southeast Asians do not practice birth control either, especially the Hmong. In addition, they do not condone open discussion of birth control methods; this is considered personal and strictly a family matter.

Cambodian women have similar disregard for the diaphragm and for the same reasons as the Latinas. Their society pressures against any form of birth control.

- Cultural background impacts choice of birth control method. Most Latinas and many Southeast Asians oppose use of the diaphragm.
- Although a woman may individually desire to practice birth control, social pressure from her ethnic group may be so disapproving that she will not follow through.

No Heroic Measures?

Medical staff at a major hospital attempt many procedures, including life-support machines, on a sixty-eight-year-old woman who has suffered a severe heart attack and whose lungs, kidneys, and liver have failed. When the patient does not respond to treatment and loses consciousness, specialists consult with the patient's husband and sons. Since the patient has no chance for recovery, they advise phasing out life support. The family refuses.

Weeks later the doctor calls to inform them that the woman is now dying. He asks what the family wants him to do. The son is adamant: "You do what you're supposed to be doing. You keep her alive."

Against better judgment the hospital follows the family's instructions and administers drugs to the patient's failing heart. According to reporter Benedict Carey, one of the doctors who was desperate to spare the dying patient CPR chest-pounding pleaded with the family, "Someone please tell me not to do this. I don't want to do this." Still they declined.

Finally, the son asked the doctor to make the decision, later admitting, "We could not make that decision ourselves."

The family was from Iran, and had this situation occurred there, someone else would have made the decision for them, a doctor they trusted or a close family friend. To place the decision in the family's hands was unbearable, something totally unfamiliar to them. Once the doctor was given the authority to make the decision, the family was relieved and the woman died peacefully.

Variations on this scene have been replayed frequently among families, especially first-generation immigrants, who believe that patients should be kept alive at any cost, and to whom advance directives may be an abomination.

An immigrant patient may also not want to know the truth about his condition, either. A family member may request that a health practitioner withhold the truth from the patient, so informed consent is not possible.

- In some cultures, a trusted physician is expected to make life-and-death decisions rather than the immediate family.
- For some immigrants, informed consent is undesirable, yet they may sign the release form fearing that treatment might be withheld if they refuse.
- If patients refuse to sign, it may signal that they don't understand the language.

Holidays

(See also: Permanent Wave, p. 125; Red Envelopes, p. 136.)

Ramadan

Roberta's new neighbors happily accept her invitation to take them out to lunch. However, the night before the event, an embarrassed Roberta realizes that it is Ramadan and her neighbors are Muslims, who traditionally fast until dinnertime during this thirty-day holiday.

She phones to apologize, but the husband says, "Don't worry about it. We're sitting here drinking wine anyway." The next day they meet for lunch, as scheduled.

- Not every Muslim observes Ramadan with the same rigor. That the neighbors were drinking wine the night before indicated that they did not observe the official taboo on alcohol.
- Like Jews who do not fast during Yom Kippur, or Christians who only attend church on Easter, a wide range of behavior exists for people who consider themselves members of religious groups.
- Customs are not static. Changes occur whether or not they are sanctioned by religious laws.
- During Ramadan, which usually falls sometime during November/December, the devout fast from dawn to dusk for a month and abstain from sex, tobacco, and other pleasures. In the evening, they frequently break their fast by eating dates and taking a sip of water.

Thanksgiving

It's Thanksgiving, but in this neighborhood, no turkeys are being carved, no cranberry sauce and stuffing served. Instead, close to eighty bridal couples jam the local establishments in rented formal attire for marathon wedding ceremonies witnessed by busloads of relatives (sometimes up to five hundred per couple) arriving from all over the country and jamming the streets.

The neighborhood is New York's Chinatown on East Broadway, where Thanksgiving is traditionally slow because desires for Chinese food plummet. This offers restaurant employees, mostly from China's Fujian province, a day off and a rare calendar opportunity to get married. For these restaurant workers, Thanksgiving has become a new annual wedding day custom.

- Immigrants create new takes on traditions of their adopted countries. In New York's Chinatown, the need for marriage vows has been adapted to American calendar observations and eating habits.

Similarly, in their Lao homeland, the Hmong observe the New Year in November, but that is not compatible with either U.S. school or work schedules. Consequently, they now celebrate it one month later, during the rest of the U.S. winter holidays.

Halloween

Maureen takes a new position as a school speech therapist. Halloween is approaching, so she asks the students about their costumes for trick or treat. To her amazement, none plan to participate.

Maureen's new school was an Orthodox Jewish day school, and while she knew that singing Christmas carols was unacceptable, the lack of Halloween observance surprised her. At this school and in the Jewish Orthodox community, they only observe religious holidays, and not secular holidays such as Halloween or Thanksgiving.

- Although the Orthodox ignore Halloween, they do have an annual masquerade holiday, Purim, near the beginning of March. Often they wear costumes related to the story of Esther in the Old Testament. Sometimes boys who ordinarily wear black suits and hats masquerade as American teenagers in jeans.
- Halloween is not accepted in all U.S. schools.
- Some fundamentalist Christians do not approve of this holiday as well, associating it with pagan/satanic traditions.

Jumping over Fires

Dolores Smithson is an active member of the Neighborhood Watch in a beautiful suburban community. One day she panics when she looks out in the street and sees the teenage sons of her new neighbors jumping over seven piles of burning brush. Laughter and high spirits prevail for the boys, but not for Mrs. Smithson. She dials 911.

Mrs. Smithson's neighbors were newly arrived Iranians, and their sons were jumping over the fires as part of a purification ritual before the start of Iranian (or Persian) New Year. When the authorities arrived, the fire department put out the fires, and the police took the boys into custody. However, a lenient judge dismissed the case with a warning to the boys' family about never doing this again. The family also had to pay a fine.

Like Mrs. Smithson's neighbors, many Iranians transplanted to America discover that because of strict fire codes, they cannot build fires in urban areas, even for religious purposes. Consequently, Iranians in Southern California often go to beaches where fires are allowed and jump over them in safe settings. Those who risk jumping in urban areas often select public parking areas for their sites.

Persian New Year, or *Nouruz*, takes place on the vernal equinox, which falls on April 20 or 21. One of the features of this thirteen-day celebration is a ritual meal ornamented by seven items that begin, in Iranian Farsi, with the letter S, including garlic and a wheat pudding; a bowl of goldfish is also on the table. On the last day, it is considered bad luck to stay indoors, so commonly they participate in special picnic events.

Other ethnic group members have been disappointed when their home-country customs were not met with enthusiasm here. The Vargas family, for example, wanted to celebrate *Las Posadas* as they had in Mexico. For nine days before Christmas, Mexicans musically and dramatically reenact the story of Mary and Joseph searching for lodging.

Celebrating in their backyard, the Vargas family offered shelter to Mary and Joseph and food to the many pilgrims. As part of the festivities, they hung a piñata, but when one of the guests broke it open, a hard candy flew out and smashed against a neighbor's window. The irate neighbor stormed over and chewed out the Vargas family. Although they tried to explain their *Posadas* tradition to him, he only reluctantly accepted their apology. Sorrowfully, the Vargas family realized that not all traditions can simply be transplanted.

- New immigrants should check local laws before engaging in home-country rituals.
- When entertaining large groups during ethnic celebrations, alert neighbors beforehand. Explain the occasion and, if possible, include them in the festivities.

New Year's Offerings

(See also: Permanent Wave, p. 125; First Foot, p. 119; Sweeping Away the Luck, p. 120.)

One midnight, while driving home from a party, Jan and Herb England spot something puzzling. They notice a twelve-year-old boy stealthily looking around as he walks toward the corner, carrying something unrecognizable.

When the boy reaches the corner, he places the object on the ground and runs away. Moments later, when the Englands reach the corner, they discover that the boy has left a plate that contains a king-sized shrimp, a piece of meat, some uncooked rice, and salt, with a dollar bill lying on top.

Jan and Herb can't figure it out.

Jan and Herb didn't know that this day was *Tet*, the Vietnamese Lunar New Year. The youngster was helping his mom with her Lunar New Year's traditions by bringing an offering to this busy intersection. Placing an offering at the heavily trafficked corner was the woman's way of petitioning the gods to prevent any accidents from taking place there in the new year.

- Making offerings to ensure an auspicious new year is a common Asian practice.

First Foot

(See also: Permanent Wave, p. 125; New Year's Offerings, p. 118; Sweeping Away the Luck, p. 120.)

Ellen, a divorced mother, notices the Dieps, her Vietnamese neighbors, preparing for *Tet*.

Demonstrating her respect and fondness for them, Ellen knocks on their door on New Year's morning with a bouquet of flowers. However, when the Vietnamese grandmother opens the door, she storms off bitterly proclaiming, "It would have been better to have kept the door closed!"

For the Vietnamese, the first person who crosses the threshold on New Year's Day foreshadows what will happen for the year. Unfortunately, Ellen didn't know that the Dieps had arranged for a successful businessman with many children to be their first guest. That would have brought them good luck in financial and family matters. Unwittingly, Ellen got there first. Because she was divorced, she symbolized a broken family and lack of success.

The "first foot" tradition is not limited to Asian cultures. It is an ancient and well-known custom in the British Isles. Families there often try to rig the tradition by prearranging for the right person to be the first one to step through the front door, ensuring good luck and prosperity for the new year. One British family in New York would all walk out the front door after the stroke of midnight on December 31. The oldest man in the group would then enter the house first, followed by the rest of the family. Unlucky first foots are a woman, a flat-footed or cross-eyed person, or one whose eyebrows meet across the nose. They usually dislike a red-haired first foot, especially in Wales.

For most people around the world, the first day of the new year is significant. If bad things happen, it is interpreted as a negative omen for the entire year. Sadly, on Chinese New Year, one newly arrived Chinese family received an advertisement in the mail from a funeral home. They felt doomed, certain that during the coming year someone in their family would die.

• Many people believe that what occurs on New Year's Day foretells what lies ahead for the entire year.

Sweeping Away the Luck

(See also: Permanent Wave, p. 125; New Year's Offerings, p. 118; First Foot, p. 119.)

Amy's grandmother is an elderly Chinese woman from Vietnam. She holds on to the old traditions. On New Year's Eve, all the relatives come to Amy's house for dinner. Afterward, the children play games, and the married adults give the children red envelopes with money inside. When the party is over, Amy helps her grandmother clean the dishes and the tables.

The next day Amy wants to do something nice for her grandmother, so she sweeps the food and dust from the floor. Grandmother becomes so angry about this that she ignores Amy for the whole day.

What Amy didn't know was that while she was sweeping up the food and dust, Grandmother believed Amy was also sweeping away all the wealth and good luck. That's why Grandmother was furious. Similarly, many Chinese people believe that one should not shower on New Year's Day for fear of washing away all the good luck.

Amy's misunderstanding with her grandmother is typical of problems caused by generational differences. As the youngest members of the family become more Americanized, they become less familiar with the traditions of their elders.

- Many Chinese avoid sweeping on New Year's Day, for this may get rid of good luck for the new year.
- Cultural conflicts may occur between family members of different generations.

Luck and Supernatural Forces

(See also: Green Hats, p. 63; Red Ink as Death Sign, p. 64; Funeral Flowers, p. 93; Gift Taboos, p. 95.)

Gris-Gris

(See also: The Voodoo Squad, p. 127.)

Karen has dental implants with metal posts that often set off airport metal detectors. Consequently, she carries her dental X-rays with her as proof.

This morning, she has an appointment at the headquarters of a high-security international corporation. As she enters through the building metal detectors, she hands her X-rays to the uniformed security guard, who casts one glance, fearfully drops them to the ground, and exclaims, "It's bad *gris-gris* [gree-gree] to look at bones!"

He calls for his supervisor, who passes her through.

While at first Karen is amused, upon reflection she is concerned about security. The guard's instincts had taken over despite his high-tech training. His behavior seemed to repudiate the scientific environment.

Gris-gris is a form of voodoo (*voudun*) and magic practiced in New Orleans. It defends against hostility and danger. Forms of *gris-gris* protection can be found in objects such as amulets, bound packets, sealed bottles, and gourds. Sometimes it refers to a small bag containing charms, herbs, stones, and other items to draw energy, luck, love, or prosperity to the wearer. *Gris-gris* origins are traced from West Africa, to Brazil and the Caribbean, to Louisiana.

Approximately half of the over seven million people of Haiti practice *voudun*. Emigrés numbering in the tens of thousands have brought these beliefs and practices to Miami, New York, and the Boston area, where many Haitians, Brazilians, and Cubans reside. In New Orleans there are additional thousands of followers.

- Ancient beliefs guide human behavior more than science and technology, especially when triggered by stressful circumstances.

Ashes

A sixteen-year-old girl brings a heart-shaped box to her Arizona high school English class. The box contains the cremated remains of the girl's mother, who died two years before. While showing the ashes to a girlfriend, the teenager inadvertently spills some of the ashes on the floor. The next day, a hundred students are absent from the school.

The students whose families boycotted the school were Native Americans from the Hopi and Navajo nations, which represent about half of the school's eight hundred students. According to their beliefs, they could not enter a room where the remains of the dead had been spilled. They believed that if the classroom were not spiritually cleansed, the spirit of the deceased would remain in the area, posing a threat to them. Administrators of the school had a dilemma about the separation of church and state. They weighed their options and subsequently a traditional Navajo medicine man and a Hopi spiritual leader conducted a cleansing ceremony that returned the spirit of the student's mother to its resting place and allowed the students to come back to school. In order to keep a low profile, the ceremony was conducted after school hours.

Generally, Native Americans do not cremate their dead, preferring the burial tradition. In preparing for burials, Navajos wash the deceased, and afterward many will not touch the body lest they leave their handprints or fingerprints on it. Older Navajos won't go near the grave after a person is buried, but many in the younger generation will visit veterans' cemeteries and other grave sites on memorial holidays.

- Sometimes school administrators are placed in a bind. In this situation, they opted to bend the rules in order to bring students back to campus to continue their education, their primary mandate. (See also: Sacrificing a Rooster, p. 108.)

Permanent Wave

(See also: New Year's Offerings, p. 118; First Foot, p. 119; Sweeping Away the Luck, p. 120.)

Preparing for a Hawaiian vacation, Winnie calls her hairdresser, Kim, and requests an appointment for a permanent on February 16. Horrified, Kim refuses to give her one on that date.

Kim is Vietnamese and February 16 was the first day of the Vietnamese New Year, called *Tet*. (The date varies according to the lunar calendar.) Many Vietnamese believe that washing one's hair or showering on that day washes away good luck for the ensuing year. Even though Winnie was not Vietnamese, Kim did not want to jeopardize Winnie's future. Ironically, Winnie, who is a fourth-generation Chinese American, long ago discarded many of her family's old Asian customs. Now, out of respect for Kim's beliefs, she was observing an age-old taboo that she personally did not embrace. Winnie rescheduled for the next day.

- Actions taking place on New Year's Day foretell what will happen throughout the year.
- On Tet, Vietnamese don't throw away rubbish; children shouldn't cry; parents shouldn't scold their children; no one should shower or sweep.
- On Chinese New Year, reckoned by the same calendar as the Vietnamese, Chinese also don't sweep; don't open red envelopes in the presence of others; don't wear black; don't use bad language or words pertaining to death; don't eat from chipped or broken

dishes; don't give an odd amount of money; do not use knives or scissors.

Hot Rocks

At Uluru-Kata Tjuta National Park in the Australian Outback, stolen rocks, as heavy as 75 pounds, are regularly being mailed back to park headquarters. Within fifteen months between 2003 and 2004, three hundred packages arrive, mostly from Australia, but also from the United States, Britain, Italy, Japan, and the Netherlands.

At Maui's Haleakala National Park, site of the dormant Haleakala Crater, and at Hawaii's Volcano National Park, home of Kilauea, the world's most active volcano, packages of stolen rocks have been arriving almost daily since the mid-1980s.

Visitors who send back rocks they have stolen are attempting to divest themselves of misfortune. In Australia, the stolen rocks come from two sites: Ayers Rock, a holy site for the Anangu tribe of the Australian Aborigines, who call it Uluru; and Mt. Olga, known to the Anangu as Kata Tjuta, considered more sacred than Uluru.

Australian park officials have labeled the returned rocks "sorry rocks" because letters of apology often accompany them. Many relate that bad luck has befallen them as a result of the theft. One visitor to the outback in 1992 claimed that getting the mud on his shoes and keeping the sacred red soil as a souvenir led to a string of misfortunes: his kidneys failed; he suffered chronic depression, had two strokes, and received kidney and pancreas transplants; and his wife had an affair, divorced him, and won custody of their daughter. For these reasons, he mailed back the soil.

In Hawaii, rock thieves attribute misfortunes to offending the revenge-seeking goddess Pele, who governs volcanic activities on all the islands. Since the rocks are contained within United States national parks, they are protected resources, so removing them is also illegal. Many rock returners apologize and claim innocence, stating that at the time they took them they were unaware that they were breaking the law. By returning the rocks, they hope to ease their consciences and revoke their bad luck: illness, car accidents, spouses leaving.

Because the items taken are from sacred places, those who steal them may believe that possessing a piece of these sacred sites will empower them. Anthropologists call this "contagious magic." But when the magic doesn't work in their favor, people sometimes reconsider their actions.

- When misfortune strikes, humans tend to look for explanations. Some people may blame it on external forces or scapegoats. Others may look internally to see if they have erred in some way. Returning stolen goods relieves a bad conscience and may provide relief.

The Voodoo Squad

2003: Grayish powder covers courtroom seats and evidence boxes. The prosecuting attorney complains about his awesome dry-cleaning bills to remove the powder from his suits. The judge orders extra security measures in her Florida courtroom—that the room be vacuumed and locked during each recess.

At the Richard Gerstein Justice Building in Miami, Florida, Santería supporters of the defendant believed that by disseminating a special powder they could bring good luck and sway the jury, judges, or prosecutors in favor of the accused. They made the powder by writing the names of the judge and prosecutors on paper, burning it, mixing the ashes with ground-up twigs, then strewing the powder around the courtroom. However, for this defendant, accused of money laundering, it didn't work.

Santería practitioners in South Florida number approximately 100,000. Since animal sacrifice is one of their practices, dead chickens, doves, and goats can often be found outside the courthouse, as well as puzzling candle formations. Consequently, the building's cleanup crew has been dubbed "The Voodoo Squad." But "Voodoo Squad" is a misnomer. These are Santería practices, which are not the same as voodoo or *voudun*. (See also: Glass-Bead Necklaces, p. 57; *Gris-Gris*, p. 123.)

- Voodoo is practiced by those from Haiti. Santería followers are more commonly from Cuba and Puerto Rico.
- It is not illegal for Santería practitioners to sacrifice small animals for religious purposes. (See also: Glass-Bead Necklaces, p. 57.)
- In Florida, Caribbean exiles practice religions that combine elements of old African religions with those of Christianity, such as Santería, voodoo, and Palo Mayombe.
- To deal with some of the religious practices more efficiently, police personnel attend classes taught by anthropologists and leaders from these Caribbean religions so that officers will not automatically assume that artifacts and altars are evidence of criminal activity or that practitioners in a trance are engaged in devil worship.

Eclipse

(See also: Classroom Behavior, p. 37.)

Recognizing the educational opportunity offered by the solar eclipse occurring during school hours, principal Sharon Daniels sends a memo to her elementary school faculty. She encourages them to view the eclipse either on classroom TV monitors or by using viewing devices that the children have constructed.

Most of the students are excited about observing this astronomical phenomenon and eagerly view the dimming of the sun. However, a small group of students refuse to watch the eclipse by any means. They are terrified.

The children were Hmong, people who emigrated here from isolated mountain villages in Laos after the Vietnam War. The Hmong believe that spirits control nature. Consequently, any force powerful enough to cause the sun to disappear could potentially carry them away as well. The students try to protect themselves by not looking.

The Hmong are not unique in attributing the eclipse to supernatural powers. In Taiwan, when a solar eclipse occurs, they say that the sky dog is eating the sun. Consequently, many Taiwanese go outdoors and beat gongs to chase the sky dog away. In addition, numerous people believe an eclipse can harm pregnant women: in the Philippines, Afghanistan, and Iran, women are sometimes warned to stay indoors and to not touch their bodies for fear of marking the babies with shadows (dark spots) on their faces or bodies.

- Safety experts warn against looking directly at the sun during an eclipse to avoid damage to the retina of the eye. Some groups accomplish the same goal by attributing the eclipse to dangerous supernatural forces. Since the safety goal is satisfied, it is best not to encourage people from these groups to look at an eclipse through artificial means.

Feng Shui

(See also: Prayer Position, p. 110.)

Jane is a successful real estate broker. She has shown her Chinese clients several houses, and even though they seem enthusiastic about them, they ultimately reject them as future homes. They blame it on the location of the front stairs. Although they claim that they like the property, clearly they do not because they never return. Jane is puzzled about their reticence to explain what they don't like about the houses.

Jane didn't know that her clients observed the rules of *feng shui* (pronounced *fung shway*, meaning the wind and the water), an ancient Chinese philosophy related to the *I Ching* and the principles of *yin* and *yang*. The goal of *feng shui* is to find the most harmonious and auspicious place to live and work. One seeks a smooth flow of positive energies. Thus, before buying a house, many Chinese clients will consult with a *feng shui* expert to see if the energy of the house will be beneficial or harmful to them. *Feng shui* dictates how a room or a house should be built, with each angle corresponding to a sphere of life—health, love, money.

Feng shui has rules about the placement of buildings: a hospital, for example, should not be located opposite or next to a temple or church. *Feng shui* affects the design of a building. The front doorway should face the east; for the door to face west brings bad luck—that is where the sun sets, where the day ends, not begins, so it symbolizes death. The front door should not be aligned with the back door; that would cause luck and money to enter and immediately exit. Likewise, the front stairs must not lead to the street because this causes money to leave the house. Being at the center of a cul-de-sac is not desirable either, for it allows the evil spirits to proceed directly to the front door.

The foot of the bed should not face the door but should be placed sideways in relation to the door. This is connected to the Chinese practice of carrying out the dead feet first. Ideally, the bed should face south, and the kitchen should be on the east side of the house.

If negative structural features of a house cannot be changed, they can at least be ameliorated by taking certain steps; for example, a tree outside the front door might block prosperity from entering, but this can be counteracted by placing a special invocation for wealth on the tree.

To improve the interior of a house, practitioners may refer to a *ba-gua*—an eight-sided mirror. Its design correlates body parts, colors, and life situations with layouts of rooms. The *ba-gua* provides guidance about making physical adjustments to improve one's condition. Sarah Rossbach, an authority on *feng shui*, cites an example: to enhance financial opportunities, one might place a plant or fish tank in a particular spot in a room related to the position of money on the *ba-gua*.

Jane's Chinese clients were reluctant to reveal their beliefs in *feng shui*, but that needn't occur any longer. *Feng shui* followers are becoming more outspoken about their beliefs. A restaurant column in the *Los Angeles Times* mentions that the chef-owner of an elegant Chinese restaurant was having a new piece of property evaluated by a *feng shui* master before purchasing it for a second location.

Belief in the system has crossed cultural boundaries as well. Major corporations such as Rupert Murdoch's News Corporation, Coca-Cola, Procter and Gamble, Hewlett-Packard, and Ford Motor have enhanced their environments based on *feng shui* principles.

At a Motorola office in Phoenix, Arizona, two waterfalls were placed at the entrance of the computer-chip company, which, according to *feng shui* philosophy, would bring money to the firm and create *chi*, the life force.

- Real estate brokers and housing developers with Chinese clients will be more successful if they familiarize themselves with the principles of *feng shui*.

Walt Disney Company used *feng shui* masters not only to assist in the building plans for their Hong Kong Disneyland facility, but also to select the opening day of their theme park, September 12, 2005, considered a "fabulous" date according to *feng shui* principles. Don Robinson, Hong Kong Disneyland's group managing director, said, "A lot of our work has gone through *feng shui* masters." Disney's use of ancient Chinese beliefs to guide its $3.5 billion investment is indeed a testimony to the power of tradition.

Moving and the Almanac

Rick and Mai-Wan have worked hard putting their new home in order. They are about to receive their first guests, Rick's parents.

Mai-Wan proudly shows her in-laws through the meticulously prepared house. However, the older couple is surprised when they look into the master bedroom. Although the furniture is in place, Rick and Mai-Wan have been sleeping on the floor.

Taiwanese-born Mai-Wan had consulted with a Chinese almanac about the most propitious time for the couple to settle into their new home. The book had recommended a date more than three weeks after she and Rick would actually move in. However, Mai-Wan believed that if they did not sleep in the bed until the recommended date, technically they would not have settled in until then and thus might ensure good luck while living there.

In addition to consulting the almanac, many Chinese immigrants confer with astrologers to determine, for example, the best dates for weddings, funerals, and surgery.

Chinese almanacs are not the only books to give advice about moving. The *Old Farmer's Almanac* regularly recommends the best times for moves; for example, in 1994, they advised that the new moon was the best time. The *UCLA Archive of American Popular Beliefs and Superstitions* contains myriad examples of days considered either good or bad to change residences. Friday seems by far the most risky, as expressed in this proverb: "Friday flits have not long sits."

- Many people believe that the day on which one moves can affect the resident's future in a new location.

Numbers

(See also: Gift Taboos, p. 95; Birthday Dates, p. 160.)

It is a very busy morning in the city's planning department. A long line impatiently waits for the clerk, Robert Seltzer, to answer questions. The next couple in line introduces themselves as Mr. and Mrs. Lin. Their real estate agent has recommended that they speak to Seltzer about an important matter regarding the house they have just purchased.

The couple wants to change their address from 314 to either 316 or 318. They are adamant in their desire to make this change, but Seltzer does not understand.

"Why the big deal of this slight change in numbers?"

Mr. and Mrs. Lin were Chinese, and in both Mandarin and Cantonese dialects, the word for the number *four* sounds like the word for *death*. It has a meaning of death for Japanese and Koreans as well. For the Lins to have death in their address would bode poorly for their future in this new home.

Whereas Seltzer had never had to deal with this kind of request before, planning departments in cities with large immigrant Chinese populations have become familiar with this issue. In fact, some municipalities charge as much as $1,000 to handle the processing of such address changes.

A change of address necessitates changes in the records of numerous agencies, such as the county assessor, tax collector, registrar of voters, school district, post office, utility offices, and waste haulers. All these bureaucratic adjustments justify charging large fees by those cities that do so.

Numbers have positive and negative values for the Chinese. Sometimes the sound of the number word is the same as that of a negative concept, like death. Sometimes the number has negative connotations; for example, seven is related to the notion that ghosts return seven days after death.

Positive meanings are associated with other numbers: one for guaranteed; two for easy; three for life; six for happiness; eight for prosperity; nine for long life. Furthermore, combinations of certain numbers have significance—by placing a five, which by itself is neutral, in front of an eight, the good effect of the eight is cancelled.

Auspicious numbers are important not only for private residences but for businesses as well. China, Hong Kong, and Taiwan hotels often eliminate the fourth floor. Some Asian airports eliminate Gate Four as well. The elegant Hong Kong–owned Peninsula Hotel in Beverly Hills, California, has 9882 as its address numerals. Whether or not they made special arrangements to obtain the good-luck numerals meaning "long life," "prosperity," and "easy" cannot be verified, but one can be certain that heavy consideration was given to the symbolism of these important numbers.

Having lucky phone numbers is portentous, too. In some heavily populated Chinese immigrant neighborhoods, entrepreneurs buy up propitious numbers from the phone company and then resell them to new residents as they move in. Intercultural business consultant Angi Ma Wong suggests that one of the reasons why so many Chinese companies located in the San Gabriel Valley in California was because the area code there is 818, which means "prosperity guaranteed prosperity." Unfortunately for those residents, in 1996 the area code was changed to 626. Those numbers total fourteen, and the presence of the number four distressed the residents. Despite protests to the phone company and the Public Utilities Commission, the area code 626 has remained.

Akin to this, a Japanese-owned hotel in San Diego, California, has paid no attention to American beliefs about numbers. Accordingly, they have a thirteenth floor—missing from most American hotels—and even a room number 1313, which, according to the desk clerk, most Americans will adamantly refuse. However, hotel guests seem to be less open about aversions to being placed on the thirteenth floor. They will usually just ask, "Do you have something on a different floor?" Savvy to this taboo, Santa Monica, California, calls their 13th street "Euclid."

- Just as many Americans believe that thirteen is unlucky, the Chinese have strong beliefs about the good luck or bad luck associated with particular numbers. Four is the most negative number, since its sound is the same as the word for *death*.
- The Japanese have a death association with the number four as well; thus Mormon missionaries are instructed never to knock four times on the door of potential Japanese converts.
- The number 666 has ominous connotations for some Christians who associate it with the mark of the devil. In 2002, Kentucky Mountain Bible College finally changed their 666 telephone prefix. A relieved administrator said that the 666 phone number was like having a scarlet letter attached to them. And in 2003, Route 666 in the Southwest changed its number and identity as the Devil's Highway. Politicians in Colorado, Utah, and New Mexico, led by Governor Bill Richardson of New Mexico, successfully argued that the New Testament's association of 666 with Satan was impairing the economic vitality of towns along the route.
- Additionally, when President and Mrs. Ronald Reagan first moved to Bel Air, California, after leaving office, their address was 666 St. Cloud. To avoid Satanic implications, the Reagans changed the house number to 668.
- Among the Navajos, four is not only their sacred number, but when they are in a court of law, they will not answer a question until it has been asked four times. A question asked only once comes across to them as less important than other issues. It also doesn't give the person time to think through the potential answer. Couple this behavior with their habit of not looking someone in the eyes when speaking. Both of these customs are likely to send erroneous messages to non–Native Americans.

Numbers in Photos

The high school graduation ceremony has just ended. Excitement and jubilation fill the air. Cameras click and flash as parents and students proudly record the moment.

Mickey, an Anglo, María, a Latina, and Pau, a Chinese, have become close friends over their school years and want to mark this moment of friendship and achievement. They gather together to take a picture, but as soon as María steps in between Mickey and Pau, Pau's parents both shout, "No!"

Many traditional Chinese people believe that having an uneven number of people in a photograph brings bad luck. To have three people is of greater consequence—the person in the middle will die.

The impassioned reaction of Pau's parents bewildered both Mickey and María, but after Pau explained their belief, María apologized and stepped out of the picture. Pau's parents felt relieved and happy. Although this belief seemed strange to them, María and Mickey both accepted it out of respect for their friend. As a result, they took turns stepping in and out of the shot until they each had pictures with one another.

- Many cultures associate bad luck and death with specific numbers or number sequences.

Odd or Even?

Vigen Sakian works for a construction company as a carpenter. He becomes friendly with Chris Howell, a fellow worker, and Vigen invites Chris and his wife to his home for dinner.

As a hospitality gift, the Howells bring a dozen roses to Vigen's wife, Sima. As soon as Sima accepts the flowers, she removes one of the roses and puts it in a separate vase. This mystifies the Howells.

Armenians from the former Soviet Union believe that giving an even number of flowers brings bad luck. That is why Sima removed the single rose from the bouquet. Even numbers are linked with death and funeral rituals, which require even numbers of candles and flowers. Consequently, on happy occasions, Armenians will give an uneven number of flowers.

- On happy occasions, give an uneven number of flowers to Armenians. (See also: Gift Taboos, p. 95.)

Black Magic

When Lidia, a housekeeper from Nicaragua, fails to show up for work one day, her employer, Mrs. Borden, becomes worried. Mrs. Borden phones her at home, but Lidia's number has been disconnected. After two weeks, Lidia calls to tearfully announce that she must leave her job and move away.

Lidia was convinced that black magic had been used against her family. Someone was even trying to break up her marriage. After conferring with a spiritual advisor, Lidia was advised to move away, have her new residence and automobile ritually cleansed, and start afresh. In spite of her skepticism, Mrs. Borden did not challenge her beliefs.

This is not so rare a story among Central American immigrants. Social workers report difficulties in dealing with clients who have been victims of wrongdoing yet are fearful of testifying against perpetrators. They reveal fear of spells and powerful supernatural retribution.

There is a positive side to this as well. Some patients with chronic pain and other psychosomatic afflictions exhibit benefits from alternative supernatural powers; for example, believers in the spirit of the *Niño Fidencio*, a famed Mexican healer, report relief from pain and recovery from ailments after praying to him. (See also: Alternative Healers, p. 107.)

• Although many people find it difficult to fathom others' spiritual beliefs, it is best to leave alone what is not understood.

Red Envelopes

(See also: Colors, p. 63; New Year's Offerings, p. 118; First Foot, p. 119; Sweeping Away the Luck, p. 120.)

Karina, a young woman, has just arrived in New York from Mexico. She is going to study English and visit her mom, who works in a sewing factory in Chinatown.

One day, Karina's mother telephones from work, asking Karina to bring her lunch. The dutiful daughter hops a bus bound for the factory. As soon as she arrives, her mom's Chinese boss walks up and hands her a small red envelope. When she looks inside and discovers twenty dollars, she becomes indignant and thrusts it back at him.

The boss stares at her in stunned disbelief.

Being a newcomer, Karina didn't know it was Chinese New Year. According to Chinese custom, during this holiday, older people give red envelopes with money inside to unmarried children for good luck.

The boss intended to wish Karina good fortune. Her refusal was an affront he could not comprehend: Why would anyone reject money and good luck?

From Karina's point of view, the boss was an older man she had never met before. When he handed her the money-filled envelope, she thought he was making an offer for sexual favors. Consequently, she was offended and angrily returned it.

Later, when Karina learned of the boss's true intentions, she accepted the gift. Since then, she happily receives the red envelope each Chinese New Year.

Chinese people call these red envelopes *lai see*. Often they are decorated with gold characters expressing good wishes, like greeting cards. At other times of the year, red envelopes filled with money indicate congratulations, gratitude, or compensation and are given on such occasions as wedding celebrations and the birth of a child or to a doctor before surgery.

- To the Chinese, red envelopes filled with money express two positive things: the red signifies good luck, while the money signifies prosperity.

Baby Furniture Delivery

Mrs. Del Signore comes to stay with her daughter during the last few weeks of the younger woman's pregnancy. Anxious to have everything ready before the child is born, they go to a local baby furniture store to order a crib and chest of drawers. After Mrs. Del Signore pays for the merchandise, she tries to arrange for immediate delivery, but the store owners refuse to deliver it until after the child is born.

The owners of the store were Orthodox Jews who believed that the birth of a child can be fraught with problems and danger. Since they do not want to tempt fate, they wait until after the child is born before bringing any baby supplies into the home. This also explains why Orthodox Jews do not give baby showers before the birth.

From the store owners' point of view, they were performing an act of kindness by refusing to deliver the furniture before the child was born. They were trying to prevent anything negative from happening to Mrs. Del Signore's grandchild. Even though she was Italian, not Jewish, Mrs. Del Signore accepted the owners' customs. Following their instructions, she notified the store as soon as the baby arrived. As promised, they delivered the furniture before the new mother returned from the hospital with her healthy infant daughter.

- Some peoples believe that pregnancy is a time of potential peril for the unborn. Consequently, this rite of passage is surrounded by many beliefs and customs designed to protect the expected child. (See also: Evil Eye, p. 138.)

Evil Eye

(See also: Refusing a Gift, p. 98; Birthday Cake, p. 99; Ignoring the Baby, p. 106; Baby Furniture Delivery, p. 137; Complimenting a Baby, p. 183.)

American-born Janet marries Samy, an Iranian graduate student. Their first child has just been born, and Janet's mother goes to the couple's apartment to ready it for Janet and the baby's homecoming from the hospital.

Just prior to picking up his wife and infant, the new father places some dried leaves in a flour sifter, sets the leaves on fire, and carries this smoking, crackling material in and out of each room and each exterior door.

Janet's mother curiously watches her son-in-law's actions, reluctant to ask anything about this procedure.

Janet's mother later learned that Samy was protecting his new baby from the evil eye. The evil eye can cause death, illness, and accidents. Babies are favorite targets, but by burning *espand* (rue), a shrub with bitter-tasting leaves and berries, Samy believed he was forcing the evil spirit out of the house. The crackling sounds of the popping seeds are like the sound of eyes—evil eyes—popping.

Frequently, the evil eye comes from the glance of an envious stranger, and people all around the world have devised methods of protecting new babies from this sinister force. Afghans write a verse on paper covered with a clean cloth and hang it as a necklace around the newborn. Puerto Ricans place around the baby's wrist a charm of a black clenched fist with protruding thumb (*mano fica*) topped by a red bead. Orthodox Jews hang prayers in the baby's room to protect the newborn. Armenian parents pin a blue bead to the baby's clothing. Jews with Eastern European backgrounds tie a red ribbon to the crib or handle of the baby carriage. Mexican parents hang a deer's eye (*ojo de venado*)—a brown pit topped with red yarn—on a red string around the baby's neck.

- People everywhere have devised methods for symbolically protecting the newborn child from evil spirits.

Rocks

(See also: Shoveling Dirt on the Coffin, p. 164.)

Louise loves to go camping and rock collecting. She hopes to become a geologist when she grows up. One day she brings part of her rock collection to the elementary school to share with her fifth-grade class.

Mrs. Kaufman, her teacher, admires the beautiful rocks and compliments Louise on her hobby. Then she carefully examines all the rocks, selects one, and asks if she might keep it.

Although Louise is surprised, she agrees to give the rock to her. When Mrs. Kaufman says she wants to place the rock on her father's grave, Louise becomes confused.

Placing a stone on top of a grave is an old Jewish custom. Today it is used as a way to let the deceased know that someone has visited the grave. Although the origins of this custom are not certain, the most logical explanation is that in ancient times, when a body was interred, stones were placed over the gravesite as a marker and also to keep animals away. Later, when visitors came to the grave site, they would bring stones to keep rebuilding the monument. Nowadays, a small stone or pebble is left at the grave as a symbolic remembrance of the past and as a token of the visit.

Louise was not Jewish, and she had no idea that her teacher was Jewish; neither was she aware of Jewish customs. However, once she learned how her rock was to be used, Louise realized that in a way, she was being honored by Mrs. Kaufman's using the rock to pay tribute and send a message to her beloved father.

- Jewish people may leave a stone at a gravesite as a memento of their visit.

Male/Female Relations and Gender Issues

Gender Expectations

(See also: Japanese, p. 218.)

A Japanese publishing company purchases rights for a Japanese edition of Sharon Bertsch McGrayne's book *Nobel Prize Women in Science.* When the finished product arrives from Japan, McGrayne excitedly opens the package. However, she cannot decipher the Japanese characters of the title and is puzzled by what she sees. The cover features a kitten, steaming bowl of food, teapots, and a cartoon mother holding a spoon. A child tugs at Mom's apron while she thinks about molecules shown floating above her head. Teapots decorate the inside pages; the endpapers are pink.

McGrayne assumes that they have mistakenly sent her someone else's book and is stunned to discover it is her book, now retitled *Mothers Who've Won Nobel Prizes.*

Although the gender gap is beginning to close, traditionally, Japanese women have not had access to important career positions. The publishers stressed domesticity, perhaps as a way to allay men's anxieties about women's achievements, to reinforce that they are homemakers first. Japanese housewives might buy the book because the cover relates to them. The artwork suggests that in spite of domestic responsibilities, women may now think about becoming scientists, too. By using a domestic context to honor women scientists, neither Japanese men nor women would feel threatened.

- The gender gap in many places outside the United States persists. Women are supposed to be wives and mothers first. In many occupations, they cannot attain the highest roles.

Lesbian Bridesmaid

Celeste invites her close lesbian friend Jillian to be a bridesmaid at her wedding to Michael. When the reception is just about over, Jillian leaves the room to change her clothes. While she is gone, Celeste tosses the bouquet to the bridesmaids. An irritated Jillian asks Celeste why she didn't wait for her to participate in the ritual.

Celeste explains, "I didn't think you wanted to catch the bouquet because you're never going to get married."

Jillian was angry. She thought Celeste had been very shortsighted. After all, there are many different kinds of pairings. Jillian had a life partner, and she would have liked to catch the bouquet just like any of the straight unmarried women there. Jillian's desires to commemorate a union were just as strong as those of any of the others.

- Don't omit homosexuals from rituals assumed to pertain only to heterosexuals. Homosexual desires are often the same as everyone else's. Witness the gay marriages in Boston and San Francisco. They would like to acknowledge committed relationships, and some may choose to raise children or choose not to raise children, as well.
- Don't omit homosexual offspring and their partners from family traditions. Include them in family portraits, Christmas letters, and family vacations. Leaving them out is hurtful.

At one lesbian wedding, the newlyweds tossed four bouquets: one each for the straight men, the straight women, the gay men, and the lesbians.

AIDS Education

(See also: Classroom Behavior, p. 37; AIDS, p. 101.)

The adult education principal hires an AIDS education representative to address a class, demystify the disease, and explain modes of protection. The speaker brings a bagful of props, including condoms and bananas.

Tension fills the classroom as he begins his discourse. Students squirm as he talks about the correct way to use and remove a condom and how to dispose of it. Eventually he unwraps and opens a condom and brings out a rubber replica of an erect penis. Students drop their heads onto their desks or flip papers in front of their eyes to screen the speaker from their vision.

The class consisted of middle-aged women, Yemeni Muslims wearing head coverings, and Latinas. Although the principal had requested a female presenter, a male was sent. The women students were clearly offended.

His presentation would have been unsettling for many women. From the point of view of these women, however, it was especially disrespectful and embarrassing to have a male present explicit sexual details to them. Although the information was important, this educational experience was counterproductive. Students were so emotionally distressed that they could not absorb the facts.

- When imparting sexual information, it will be more effective to separate the sexes and have male educators talking to males and female educators talking to females.

Spousal Abuse

(See also: Inequality, p. 148.)

After receiving calls from an alarmed neighbor about screaming and loud noises, police officers Barg and Marshall pull up to the Oh residence. Once inside, they encounter a pathetic scene.

Lamps and bric-a-brac lie broken on the floor; Mrs. Oh in a torn housecoat has a bleeding lip and one eye so bruised it is nearly swollen shut. Mr. Oh has scratches on his arm and looks disheveled; their four children are pale, silent, and terror-struck.

Mr. Oh assures the officers that there is no problem. His wife merely fell while standing on a stool to put away some dishes.

The officers don't believe the husband, so they question the wife, who in broken English corroborates her husband's story. Barg then asks the oldest daughter if anyone has done something to hurt her mother. She hesitantly supports her parents' story.

Barg and Marshall depart, certain that all parties have been lying.

This is a typical scenario in homes where domestic violence occurs. When the police come, often called by a neighbor, family members lie and say they were hurt in a different way. Wives deny their abuse by husbands and refuse to report them. This is especially common in Asian cultures. According to the Asian Pacific American Legal Center in Los Angeles, 60 to 70 percent of cases of domestic violence in Asian families are not reported at all.

Representatives from different Asian Pacific social service agencies agree: Spousal abuse is a problem in part because in many of their home countries it is socially acceptable for men to batter their wives as a method of training them. Spousal abuse is allowable where people believe that men are superior to women. Even if their lives are in jeopardy, wives fear letting authorities know. The women suffer in silence because they don't want to bring shame to their families.

In the Asian family, the man is the head of the household. He dominates. Thus, no one is supposed to take action against his authority. And because spousal abuse has been a traditionally accepted form of husband/wife interaction, many women have likely seen their mothers abused and view spousal abuse as a norm.

Furthermore, part of the Asian wife's established duty is to please her husband. That is what it means to be a good wife. If there is a problem, she must change herself. She is also reluctant to bare the truth. To share family secrets runs counter to her cultural code.

Asian Pacific wives are not the only immigrant victims who fear getting involved with the legal system to stop abuse. Latin

American and Armenian women, too, are fearful. While they might at first call the police, they often back down when it comes to filing formal complaints. Their problems are compounded by language barriers, no access to funds, and lack of extended family support.

- Social service agencies catering to specific ethnic groups should offer more education regarding the illegalities of spousal abuse in this country.
- Women and their children need to be informed about availability of counseling and shelter services.
- Women need to be taught how to obtain restraining orders against abusive spouses or boyfriends.
- Police need to be sensitized when trying to assess whether abuse has taken place.
- Children of an abused parent are not reliable informants. They are placed in a culturally conflicting position of power when the police question them. The children feel it is disloyal to accuse the abuser.
- Authorities need to seek evidence of spousal abuse from other sources, such as medical records.

Romantic Implications

(See also: Greetings, p. 15; Hospital Roommates, p. 146; Chastity, p. 147.)

While working at her desk, Mrs. Roy, an elementary school principal, receives word about a fracas in the schoolyard. She dashes out to discover Yasmin punching out Jack. Mrs. Roy pulls them apart. She asks Jack what happened. Jack answers, "All I said was, 'You like Billy.'"

Saying "You like Billy" to Yasmin was the equivalent of Jack accusing her of being a prostitute. Yasmin was Muslim, and the implication of her having any kind of relationship with a boy was unacceptable, so much so that she felt the need to physically attack him in order to uphold her reputation of being chaste.

Muslims have very strict rules about interactions between the sexes, for children as well as adults. Mrs. Roy had many Muslim children in her school, some directly from Arabic countries, as well as some African American converts. Their restrictions affect several activities; for example, since Muslims allow no body contact between members of the opposite sex, Mrs. Roy had to eliminate folk-dance activities to avoid the conflict caused by boys and girls holding each other's hands.

Asian newcomers, too, often experience conflict over such school activities as folk dancing. In their home countries, many schools are sexually segregated, and boys and girls are not allowed to play together. As a sign of respect, no body contact with a member of the opposite sex is allowed.

- Muslim children are not allowed to touch members of the opposite sex. No relationship between males and females may even be implied.
- Asian children often experience cultural conflict when they are asked to hold hands with members of the opposite sex.

Hospital Roommates

(See also: Romantic Implications, p. 145.)

In a Boston hospital, Ahmed's mother tends to her ten-year-old son recovering from an appendectomy beset with complications. She ministers to his every need and sleeps next to his bed each night.

The hospital brings another seriously ill boy into the room. He is Patrick, victim of a hit-and-run accident, suffering from multiple injuries. Patrick's worried father is a widower, and now he, too, sits by his child's side both day and night.

Ahmed's mother becomes frantic.

Ahmed was Muslim and because of a taboo against relationships between members of the opposite sex, Ahmed's mother could no longer be in the same room as Patrick's father.

It took a while before the hospital staff understood what the problem was. Fortunately, when they did, they moved Ahmed into a private room.

- Even in medical crises and with the curtains drawn between the beds, Muslim taboos regarding interaction between nonrelated members of the opposite sex must be maintained.

Chastity

(See also: Green Hats, p. 63; Physical Examinations, p. 109; Romantic Implications, p. 145.)

Iranian-born Mahmoud marries Donna, an American. One day while shopping at the mall, they run into Phil, Donna's high school classmate. She introduces Phil to her husband. Phil is friendly and very happy to meet Mahmoud. "I knew your wife before you two were married," he says enthusiastically.

Mahmoud responds politely. Donna and Phil reminisce for a few moments and then part. Later, when the married couple is alone in the car, Mahmoud explodes in rage.

Mahmoud interpreted Phil's statement—"I knew your wife before you were married"—to mean that Phil had had sexual relations with Donna. No Iranian Muslim husband wants to hear that phrase. A woman is supposed to be a virgin and without any prior relationships with men, no matter how casual or nonsexual. The only acceptable relationship between a nonrelated woman and a man is in marriage. Therefore, any inference of a prior relationship between a woman and a man who is not her husband is taboo.

After a verbal battle, Donna thought she had convinced her husband that she and Phil had only been good friends, like a brother and sister. Although she wanted to continue her friendship with this old school friend by merely talking over the telephone once in a while, Mahmoud would not allow it. It became a nonnegotiable and painful issue in their marriage.

- When a man converses with a Muslim husband, he should not refer to having previously met the wife.

Inequality

(See also: Gender Expectations, p. 141; Spousal Abuse, p. 143; Menstruation, p. 164.)

Mae has been teaching nursery school for years and has made the following discovery—the Japanese mothers in her school always have something sweet in their sons' sandwiches. Even if it is a fried-egg sandwich, there is jelly rolled in it. The same parents pack different lunches for their daughters—without the sweets.

Mae thinks this is unfair.

Japanese parents begin early on to demonstrate differences in expectations for boys and girls. Boys are treated differently—better—than girls, and that is accepted.

Mrs. Wakematsu, mother of twins Peggy and Henry, exemplified the differences in treatment. Mrs. Wakematsu sweetened only her son's sandwich. She trimmed off Henry's bread crusts, but not Peggy's. She addressed her twins differently, too. She spoke to Peggy as if she were older than Henry, babying him more.

Unlike Henry, Peggy was expected to be her mother's helper. If Henry left his sweater at school, Peggy had to go back and get it. Peggy had to carry her own *and* her brother's lunch box. When Mrs. Wakematsu came to pick up the children, Henry would often crash into her, grabbing her leg, whereas Peggy approached her mother more tentatively. Peggy never received the same affection and was never indulged like her brother.

The Wakematsu family may be an extreme example. Nonetheless, it demonstrates how parents teach children about gender roles. Naturally, as newcomers become more Americanized, expectations for women will change.

- Ethnic groups do not all perceive gender roles in the same way. Some encourage equality of the sexes, and some do not.
- Unequal treatment of sexes begins early in life. Parents instill differences in subtle ways, including what they pack in their children's lunch boxes.

Child Custody

Michelle, a beautiful American waitress, becomes quite taken with Haitham, a handsome and charming Iraqi customer ten years her senior. They fall in love and, over objections from Michelle's mother, they move in together, have a son, and marry.

The marriage doesn't work out, so Michelle files for divorce. She and her child move in with Michelle's mother, and Haitham is allowed visitation rights. One weekend when he is supposed to be camping with his son, Haitham abducts the child and flies him to Iraq.

This scenario is not rare. It has been frequently played out in marriages where the father is from the Middle East, where, according to tradition, the child automatically belongs to the father. In the United States, it has been quite different. In the past, child custody was usually given to the mother without question, although nowadays joint custody is becoming more common.

Haitham, like most Middle Eastern men, believed he had the right to take his child back to his homeland. This has a lot to do with Islamic law and the patriarchal families in the Middle East. In those societies, men are dominant over their wives and children, who are often considered possessions of the men. Therefore, they assume they are the ones to make decisions and to be in charge of the children.

The story of Haitham, his escape to Iraq, and his subsequent capture created headlines in 1994. Michelle was eventually reunited with her child in England.

- In divorce proceedings, Middle Eastern men usually assume they are the most appropriate parent to have custody over the children.
- In most Middle Eastern marriages, the father's opinion will more likely prevail, since he is considered superior to his wife.

Home Alone Together

(See also: Chaperone, p. 33; Chastity, p. 147.)

Jim, a mainstream American, has been steadily seeing Silvia, who moved here from Ecuador six years ago. They intend to be married.

One Friday afternoon, Jim goes over to visit Silvia, who is home alone cleaning the house. She invites him to watch television while she finishes her tasks. Within fifteen minutes, Silvia's father arrives, sees Jim, and loses his temper.

In many Latin American cultures, girls are supposed to preserve their virginity until they get married. Any situation that might prevent this from occurring is unacceptable.

Silvia's father came from such a place. An unmarried female's reputation could be easily ruined if community members learned that she had been alone in the company of a man. In these communities, people pay a lot of attention to what others think and say about them. A slur against a single woman's reputation could ruin her chances for a good marriage.

Silvia's father yelled at her, shouting that she should not have let Jim into the house. Crying, Silvia insisted that they had done nothing wrong. They weren't even sitting together or kissing. Meanwhile, Jim quietly left the house.

Later, Jim called and apologized for leaving without saying good-bye. He hadn't known what to do or say to Silvia's father; he was afraid of him. He also didn't understand this cultural difference because in his family they didn't see anything wrong when his sister had male guests without adult supervision.

Silvia later enlisted her mother's assistance. Her mother talked to Silvia's father and tried to get him to understand that Silvia and Jim had done nothing wrong and that he shouldn't be so worried about what others might say or think. As the father began adjusting to this culture, he tried to change his way of thinking, but it was difficult for him.

- A traditional unmarried Latina should not be alone in the company of a man.

Miscellany

Traffic Violations

Visiting San Diego, California, for the first time, Mel cannot believe his eyes. A driver runs a red light, and when a police officer pulls him over, instead of the driver remaining in his seat with his hands on the wheel, he gets out of his car and unself-consciously hands the officer money.

What astounds Mel even more is that the officer does not seem threatened by the driver advancing toward him. Nor does he take offense at being offered money. Instead, he talks the driver into putting the money back into his pocket and returning to the vehicle.

San Diego, California, is home to over ten thousand refugees from the East African countries of Eritrea, Ethiopia, Somalia, and Sudan. Because some of their customs can be easily misinterpreted, the San Diego Police Department Community Relations Division has created a training video to alert their officers to significant cultural differences that can lead to problems.

The East African training video explains that in those countries, drivers get out of their vehicles when pulled over. The violator pays the fine directly to the officer, something easily misinterpreted here as a bribe. If the offender doesn't have enough money in East Africa, the officer takes the driver's license and holds it at the station, where the driver may redeem it after paying the fine. The training video offers other insights regarding East Africans.

- Those from rural areas know how old they are, but accurate birth records are not kept, so immigration authorities have assigned them the same birth date of January 1, which can seem suspicious to those without background knowledge.

- They are reluctant to call the police or to be a witness. (See also: Fear of Authority, p. 39.)
- Since many are Muslims, males and females should never be placed in the same patrol car.
- Same-sex touching (arms and chin) is commonplace, especially to get attention.
- When dealing with family issues, the tape recommends that officers speak with an adult male.
- Phone reminders of appointments are recommended because time does not have the same priority as it does for Americans.

Points of View

In *The Anguish of Snails*, folklorist Barre Toelken asks white teachers on a Navajo reservation how often they visit their students' homes. The teachers report that they have tried, but when they drive up to the hogans, the Navajos run inside and slam their doors. The teachers assume they aren't wanted and, not wishing to intrude, they leave.

The Navajo also complain. They can't understand why white people drive up to their hogans as if they want to visit, but as soon as the Navajo go inside and take their places to prepare for the visit, the white people drive away. They think the whites are acting superior and in too much of a hurry for a normal visit. They wonder if the whites are trying to make fun of them.

Toelken, a white man who has been adopted into the Navajo Nation, decodes the misunderstanding. The whites assumed that the Navajo were avoiding contact, while the Navajo saw the sudden departure of the whites as impatience, which many equate with ill will.

- Like so many examples of cultural miscommunication, no one was wrong and no one was right. Each side responded according to its own cultural traditions. Each group interpreted behavior of the other group based on completely different sets of cultural norms.
- It is easy to misjudge the behavior of those whose cultural backgrounds are different.

- To effectively interact with persons different from ourselves, it behooves us to acquire cultural information about them so as not to misinterpret and act in bad faith according to their point of view.
- The reverse is also true.

The *Qur'an* (Koran)

(See also: Iraqis, p. 250.)

During the 2003 occupation of Iraq, an Iraqi woman balks when an American soldier uses his sniff dog to check her purse. When the officer on duty opens the purse and empties the contents on the ground, including the *Qur'an*, the woman and bystanders become enraged.

The *Qur'an* is the holy book of the Muslim world. To throw it on the ground is a great offense because the ground is dirty and pollutes the holy words. Compounding the offense, the soldiers were unaware that Iraqis, like most Muslims, consider dogs unclean. They only use them for guarding or hunting and never as household pets. And they would certainly never let an unclean dog near their Holy Book.

Akin to this, U.S. Muslim customers complained to a chain bookstore about the placement of the *Qur'an* in one of their stores. Unaware of the sacredness of the book, staff members had placed the book on the lowest shelf. After learning that this was offensive, sales associates moved it to a higher shelf.

- The *Qur'an* is the sacred text for all Muslims and requires physical as well as psychological respect. (See also: Fast-Food Bags, p. 84.) Being placed on a shelf close to the ground and being sniffed by dogs are offensive acts.

Generosity

Arlee and Don become sponsors of Reyna, a Native American child living on the Santo Domingo reservation. Reyna is close in age to their own daughter, Alice, a child who has been brought up in affluence.

One day Arlee, Don, and Alice bring Reyna a box of crayons as a gift. Reyna immediately hands the brand-new box to Alice and says, "Take what you want." This puzzles Alice's parents.

At a swimming pool party, Reyna is the last to arrive, as the other children are finishing up their hot dogs. As soon as she receives her food, she hands the plate to Alice and asks, "Is there anything on my plate you'd like?"

When Don later sees Reyna's mom, he comments upon her daughter's generosity. The mother explains Native American ethos: If I take care of you today, you will take care of me in the future. Similarly, at the Navajo party commemorating the baby's first laugh, the baby is taught generosity at a very early age by an adult helping the child to release some salt from its fist onto each guest's plate. From infancy, the baby learns to share.

- Native Americans, like many other ethnic groups, believe that the welfare of the community is more important than the welfare of the individual. They eagerly share because they know that others will share with them.

This plays out in other ways. Witness the dedicated new science and math teacher on the Hopi reservation arranging competition for individual academic achievement prizes. Once he realizes that the students cannot perform in this manner because it counters tribal values of putting community first, he changes his tactics and successfully creates group competitions instead.

- The concept of individual striving for excellence conflicts with those whose cultures place community values higher. (See also: Absenteeism, p. 49; Urgency, p. 177.)

Temples

During the winter holidays, Bill Cooper, an insurance agent, purchases a gift for his boss, Mr. Collins. Cooper has often heard

Collins talk about his temple, so he buys a Hanukkah card to go with the gift and has fellow employees sign it. Collins thanks his staff for the thoughtful present and card, but adds, "You might want to know that I'm not Jewish."

When Collins referred to his temple, he meant the Mormon temple, the place where the holiest of Mormon rituals take place. Mormons also attend local churches of Jesus Christ of Latter-Day Saints, where they go for regular Sunday meetings.

- Several other religions call their houses of worship temples: Hindus, Buddhists, and Jews, who also use the term *synagogue*. *Wat* is the Thai name for their temples. Sikhs call theirs *gurdwara*.

Japanese Business Cards

An early scene in the film *The Japanese Story* shows actress Toni Collette portraying an Australian geologist who greets a Japanese businessman and first-time visitor to Australia. He hands her his business card with two hands, which she casually accepts with one hand and stuffs into her back pocket. She has insulted him.

In the next scene, two Australian businessmen enter. The Japanese visitor hands each of them his business card with two hands, then bows. They accept his card with two hands, bow, then seemingly study it before placing it into an upper front pocket. This pleases the visitor.

Called *meishi*, Japanese business card exchange is highly structured.

- They hand business cards with two hands and expect recipients to accept them with both hands and a slight bow. Recipients study the card, shake hands, then bow a few more times. They carefully place the card in a card case or an upper front pocket.
- The Japanese never write on business cards. To place the card in a back pocket is also an affront.
- If Americans wish to do business with Japanese, they should print their business cards in English on one side and Japanese

on the reverse side. When they hand it to the Japanese with both hands, the Japanese side should be up and face the recipient, ready for him or her to read.

Temporary Nuns

When Leilei returns from a visit to Myanmar, her native country, her American friends are shocked to see her with a shaved head. They fear that she is undergoing chemotherapy and are relieved to find out that she is not, yet they are confused when she tells them that she has become a nun.

In Western countries, being a nun is a lifetime commitment. Not so in Asian countries, where, in pursuit of spiritual renewal, people join monasteries on a temporary basis for as few as three days. Leilei spent three days living as a nun; she shaved her head and donned peach-colored robes. Daily, she rose at 4:00 A.M. for prayers, ate breakfast at 5:00 A.M., and meditated until lunch at 11:00 A.M. After noon, she ate no more food and meditated until 10:00 P.M.

In many Asian countries, men and women can join separate monasteries on a temporary basis. Sometimes children join during school vacations and are called Summer Monks. This custom has been brought to this country where there are concentrated Asian populations, such as the Cambodians in San Diego and the Thais in North Hollywood, California.

- Participation in religious life is more varied than we might assume. In some cultures, it is not necessary to make lifelong commitments.

Business Practices

(See also: Dress for Respect, p. 62.)

Ms. Youngson, head of a corporate sales division, sends her representatives out to solicit new Chinese and Korean merchants in the city. Her crew is bright, outgoing, and effective. However, this time, each one returns unsuccessful and dejected.

She asks them to review their procedures. They describe introducing themselves, sitting down, and getting down to business in order not to take up too much of their client's time.

Youngson can't see anything wrong with their methods but realizes that something must be amiss. She must find out how to overcome the barriers that prevent success. She enrolls her reps in sensitivity sales-training workshops for courting Asian customers, sponsored by a local university, and discovers many errors in the employees' procedures.

Youngson's reps were put into mock selling situations and then critiqued for their sales protocol by different Asian consultants. The first thing they learned was not to place objects on or lean on the desk of a prospective client because the desk is considered the boss's territory.

The worst error was getting down to business too soon. When conducting commercial transactions with Koreans, Chinese, and other Asians, friendship must be established first. The first encounter should be considered a courtesy call, which can be enhanced by presenting a small token such as a calendar or a pen. Only during a follow-up call should business matters be initiated.

Another mistake was sitting down before being invited to do so. Finally, the sales reps learned that it is advisable to do more listening than speaking, just the reverse of American sales habits.

In business transactions with Middle Easterners and Latinos, the same rules apply: establish friendly relationships before getting down to business.

- Avoid the Yankee getting-down-to-business attitude in initial business encounters with Koreans, Chinese, and other Asians.
- Sit down only when invited to do so.
- Establish a cordial, friendly relationship, which can be improved by giving small gifts.
- Do not be either too casual or overly friendly.
- Listen more; speak less.

Sealing a Deal

(See also: Bargaining, p. 195.)

In colorful details, Jean, a member of one of the Plains Native American tribes, describes her daughter's wedding to a folklorist conducting research for her next book. As agreed, the folklorist writes up the interview and mails it back to Jean to check for accuracy.

For convenience, the folklorist encloses a self-addressed stamped envelope to facilitate return of the information. But instead of returning corrected copy, Jean sends a note canceling her agreement for the interview and requesting that her information not be released.

After consulting with the medicine man who performed her daughter's wedding, Jean discovered that she had broken some spiritual laws and consequently was not permitted to reveal anything about the sacred ceremony. This was because, according to the medicine man, no proper tobacco exchange to seal the agreement had occurred between the folklorist and Jean, and specific wedding details had to be kept secret for one year. Finally, it was the bride and groom's right—not the bride's mother's—to share wedding ceremony information with outsiders.

- Depending on custom or civil or tribal law, sealing a deal can take a variety of forms: shaking hands, signing on the dotted line, a verbal agreement, or sharing tobacco.

Welcoming Home Ceremonies

(See also: Greetings, p. 15.)

March 19, 2004: High-pitched ululations and ritualistic drumbeats emanate from the Billings (Montana) Logan International Airport. By special arrangement, one hundred fifty Native Americans and an anxious mother, Kathleen Beartusk, wait on the concourse for a serviceman's return. Her son deplanes and approaches, but she must wait before she can greet him.

Cheyenne Pfc. Uriah Two Two received a Warrior's Welcome on his return from occupied Iraq. Elders crowned him with a feathered war bonnet and laid a star blanket over his shoulders. Through these acts he was ritually cleansed from the pollution of war and death, and his mother could now embrace him. Gaiety and native dancing ensued as tribal members crowded to hug the returning hero. One of the elders proclaimed, "When a serviceman comes home, everyone dances."

In Montana, where numerous Native American tribes live, such as the Crow, Sioux, and Shoshone, their young men who join the Armed Forces receive ceremonial welcomes upon return.

Salt Lake City International Airport: Excitement mounts as the passengers deplane. Suddenly the room is filled with fifty dark-suited young men and a few dozen fresh-faced young women, all wearing name tags. Awaiting them are over one hundred elated family members holding colorful balloons and banners: "WELCOME HOME ELDER JOHNSON." "WELCOME HOME ELDER SMITH." "WELCOME HOME SISTER WILLIAMS."

This scene is commonplace when young Latter-Day Saints (Mormon) men and women ages nineteen to twenty-one return from their two-year missionary posts all over the world. When they arrive, the clean-shaven young men are still wearing their official garb: dark suits, white shirts, and ties. The young women wear modest dresses or blouses and skirts, but no pants or shorts.

The young men and women have been away for two years, and they have only spoken to the family by phone on Mother's Day and Christmas. Parents revel in the euphoria of reuniting with their children. They kiss, embrace, and proffer treats that their children might have been deprived of while stationed far away: cheeseburgers and peanut butter.

- Regardless of religion or ethnicity, separation from children is one of the most difficult experiences parents endure. Expressions of reuniting may take many forms, but parents' joy is universal.
- Airports are excellent places to observe cultural differences in body language, clothing customs, and relationships between the sexes.

Birthday Dates

The Cao family, from Vietnam, has just moved into the neighborhood, and their son Van becomes friendly with Randy Wallace, who lives next door. Randy is going to be six years old, and the Wallace family invites Van to Randy's party. During the celebration, Mrs. Wallace asks Van when his birthday will be. Van becomes flustered.

Traditional Vietnamese do not celebrate individual birthdays. Everybody celebrates his or her birthday on *Tet*, New Year's Day. This is the time when everyone becomes one year older. A Vietnamese newborn is one year old until the last day of the last (nineteenth) month of the lunar year. The child becomes two years old on the first day of the first month of the following year, even if he or she was born the day before—on the last day of the previous year.

Certain birthdays—40, 50, 60, 70—have special significance for the Vietnamese and require celebrations. Of course, as Vietnamese children become more Americanized, they usually participate in birthday parties of their neighbors or classmates and eventually want to have them for themselves. In that way, the Vietnamese unbirthday custom is undergoing some transition.

Traditional Chinese men celebrate birthdays at the beginning of each decade of life—21, 31, 51, 61, 71, 81. Emphasizing the odd number of the decade relates to the active male principle (yang). Traditional Chinese women also celebrate special birthdays—20, 30, 50, 60, 70, 80—the even numbers representing the passive female principle (yin). Note that both the fortieth and forty-first birthdays are ignored because of the death connotations related to the sound of the four. While these birthday customs have somewhat faded among Chinese Americans, they have been invigorated by the new influx of Chinese immigrants. (See also: Permanent Wave, p. 125; Numbers, p. 132.)

Others reckon birthdays differently. Before the Hmong arrived here, they counted a person's age from the time of conception. They were considered one year old at birth and added another year at

New Year's. This caused some misunderstandings here when filling out forms requesting birth dates. Now, like other groups, they are adopting American customs.

- Not all cultures figure age from the actual day of birth.
- Iranian immigrants have two different birth dates: one according to the Islamic calendar, a strict lunar calendar; the other adjusted to our own Gregorian calendar.

Friendship

(See also: Signs of Affection, p. 18; Dropping In, p. 179; Too Friendly, p. 186.)

Sheila, who is outgoing and has many friends, is a regular customer at a neighborhood coffee shop. There she befriends Souad, one of the waitresses. Souad is Palestinian and lives alone. Her family plans to join her in the United States. Sheila and Souad are both in their early twenties, and they start going to movies or parties together on weekends.

One day Souad has an accident at work, cutting her foot badly. She phones Sheila, who drives her to the emergency room, waits for her, pays the bill, and drops her back at home. Sheila is shocked when, the next day, Souad calls and complains, "How come you didn't bring me any food today?"

Most Americans treat friendships more casually than people from Middle Eastern, Asian, and Latino cultures. Those people are often surprised when Americans say, "Let's get together," yet never do. While on the surface Americans may seem friendlier, in fact, they are more reserved than foreigners about close friendships. This confuses those who take friendship more seriously and for whom friendship involves a greater obligation.

Sheila believed she had done quite a service for her friend and didn't dream of taking on the responsibility of feeding Souad, too. On the other hand, Souad considered Sheila as family and expected more from her, including having her provide meals.

- The rules of friendship are as varied as the people who engage in it.
- People from Middle Eastern, Asian, and Latino cultures might attach greater significance to friendship than Americans do and have higher expectations regarding obligation.

Hospitality

In San Francisco, the Andersons send out invitations for the forthcoming wedding of their daughter Leslye to Guatemalan-born Ricardo Sandoval. Since the Sandoval family lives in Los Angeles, the Andersons enclose with the invitations a map and the following information: "For your convenience, we have included the rates and phone numbers of hotels and motels located close to the reception hall. You should make your reservations as soon as possible."

The Sandovals become outraged when they receive their invitations. They refuse to go to the wedding.

The Andersons included the map and hotel information as a convenience for the out-of-towners. They believed they were being considerate, but to the Sandoval family, hospitality meant more. From their point of view, the family of the bride should have welcomed the groom's family into their home, no matter how crowded they might have been.

To the Sandovals, sharing worldly possessions would have expressed family closeness; hotel recommendations represented coldness and distance, translating into rejection. After all, the Sandovals believed they had demonstrated their closeness by taking time off from work to drive five hundred miles to the ceremony.

Once they discovered the reason for the misunderstanding, the Andersons felt embarrassed but did not alter their plans. In deference to the bride and groom, the Sandovals attended the wedding and stayed in a motel, but they remained miffed, and relations with the other side of the family stayed strained. No happy solution existed for these two families.

- Wedding party family members from other ethnic groups may be offended when not invited to stay over in new relatives' homes.

Political Differences

(See also: Food and Politics, p. 83.)

Monsy and Margaret are close friends. Monsy is Mexican American and Margaret is Anglo. Over the years, Monsy has repeatedly mentioned her grandfather, a general who was assassinated during the Mexican Revolution.

One day while at an art fair, Margaret sees a beautifully framed sepia photograph of heroes of the Mexican Revolution, including Alvaro Obregón, Emiliano Zapata, and Pancho Villa. Excitedly, she buys it as a present for her friend. On Monsy's birthday she feels triumphant as she gives this "perfect gift." As soon as Monsy unwraps it, her face falls, and she hands it back to Margaret.

"These were my grandfather's executioners!"

Margaret had naively assumed that Monsy's grandfather had been with the revolutionary forces. It had never occurred to her that he was a part of the established Mexican regime.

Correspondingly, Vietnamese seniors at California State University, Fullerton threatened to boycott their 2004 graduation. The school had planned to display eighty flags representing the national backgrounds of their students. Unwittingly, officials selected the flag of the Socialist Republic of Vietnam despite their graduates being from South Vietnam. Because students protested that the communist flag did not represent them and was immoral, the university administration scrapped the entire flag display to avoid controversy.

- Political divisions cause deep emotional rifts that don't necessarily ease with time.
- Ask, don't guess, from which political side a person comes.

Shoveling Dirt on the Coffin

(See also: Rocks, p. 139.)

Beverly, a Protestant, is a member of the language department at a small university. The faculty are very close to one another. Beverly is particularly fond of one of her colleagues, Nick, who is Jewish. She feels terrible when she learns that he is HIV-positive. Beverly remains attentive to him throughout his painful and unsuccessful battle with AIDS and is in constant contact with his family.

Beverly sadly attends Nick's funeral. At the end of the ceremony, after the casket is lowered into the ground, the rabbi invites the mourners and friends to stand in line and shovel dirt onto the coffin.

Although she has been supportive of Nick throughout his struggle, Beverly cannot bring herself to participate in this farewell rite for her friend. She feels guilty, and she is sure she has offended Nick's family.

Jewish people often have family and friends shovel dirt onto the lowered casket. This is a sign of respect and love for the deceased. The rule is that the shovel should not be passed from person to person, as this will transfer the death to others. Instead, people line up to toss three shovelsful of dirt onto the coffin and then stick the shovel into the ground. Then the next person picks up the shovel and repeats the act. Psychologically, this becomes an act of closure, completing the life cycle.

It is not obligatory for either family members or friends to participate in this ritual. No social or religious offense is created by someone not wishing to participate. Therefore, Beverly had not done anything to offend either Nick's memory or his family.

- At a Jewish funeral, shoveling dirt onto the coffin is not obligatory for either family or friends.

Menstruation

(See also: Inequality, p. 148.)

Libby attends college in New York and becomes close friends with her Indian dormmate, Jayasri. When Jayasri invites Libby to her home for *Ganapati*, an important Bombay Hindu celebration, she accepts with great anticipation. In honor of the occasion, Libby dons a sari, and Jayasri's family and friends compliment her on how good she looks.

Later, Libby mentions to her friend that she doesn't feel well. Jayasri asks if she has the flu, and Libby confides, "No, I have my period."

Jayasri nods, walks away, and sends over a few non-English-speaking Indian women, who quickly usher Libby upstairs to a sequestered space where, for the rest of the event, she is allowed only to look down on the festivities.

Afterward, Libby asked Jayasri if she had done something to offend her because she couldn't understand why she had been escorted away from the activities. Jayasri assured her that there had been no offense and explained that because she had her period, she was considered religiously unclean and could not be with the other participants. Menstruating women cannot go to the temple either. Libby was mortified when she realized that by her isolation, everyone at the party knew she had her period. She was also embarrassed that she put Jayasri in an awkward position.

Orthodox Jews similarly maintain that when women have their menstrual periods, they are unclean. When a woman is menstruating, she must sleep in a separate bed from her husband; she cannot touch the same household utensils or dishes as her husband; and she is forbidden to cook for the family.

Furthermore, everything the woman lies on or sits on or anyone who touches her bed will also be considered unclean. Because of menstrual prohibitions, in temple, women must sit separately from the men at all times. These rules are taken from the laws of *Niddah* (isolation, condition of uncleanness).

- Some societies separate the sexes according to biological functions, with menstruation believed to be a socially threatening condition.
- If a woman in menses is invited to attend an event given by people who maintain menstrual separateness, she has two choices: stay home or don't tell.

Prejudice

Post–September 11

A young cab driver/student feels uneasy as he shears his long hair and shaves his beard, yet he is unprepared for his family's reaction. When his mother sees him, she bursts into tears. His father screams, "What did you do? Why did you do it?" Relatives urge that the father throw his son out of the house.

The offense the son committed was cutting his hair and trimming his beard, acts that show disrespect for his Sikh religion. (See also: *Kirpan*, p. 60.) He had traded in the required religious appearance for one that might protect him from violence. Just the night before he had been attacked by youths after dropping off a fare in Brooklyn. They smashed windows of his cab and taunted, "There's Osama's relative. Let's do the job now." Terrified, he replaced his turban with a floppy hat. (See also: Hats Off—Not! p. 51.)

The assault on this young man was not unique for Sikhs post–September 11. They were victimized by a string of hate crimes: the murder of an Arizona gas station owner, beatings, verbal attacks, a threatened throat-slashing, the burning down of a Sikh temple in Queens. Prejudiced, nonthinking citizens automatically linked beards and turbans to Al Qaeda.

- Sikhs are not a branch of either Islam or Hinduism. Sikhism is the fifth-largest religion in the world.
- Most Sikhs in the United States come from the Punjab region of India.
- The first Asian American member of Congress was a Sikh, Dalip Singh Saund, from 1956 to 1962, representing Riverside and Imperial counties in California.

- Although *Singh* is the most common Sikh last name, other Indians bear that name but do not follow the Sikh faith.

On November 18, 2001, teenagers in Oswego County, New York, set fire to a Sikh temple because they misheard its name, Gobind Sadan. They heard it as "Go Bin Laden," which provided the rationale for their crime. Dismayed, Mark Lichtenstein, president of the local school district, set out to cure his own and the community's ignorance. He traveled to India to apologize at the Gobind Sadan temple and to learn more about their religion. Lichtenstein has since been enlightening the community through PowerPoint presentations about India and the Gobind Sadan branch of Sikhism. Subsequently, other community members have become involved in a cultural exchange, including the distribution of clothes and books at the temple in India.

Five nights after September 11, in a Queens, New York, Egyptian-owned coffeehouse, four youths broke into the business at 3:00 A.M. They smashed windows, drinking glasses, and mirrors. The owner, still in the shop with other customers, called the police. As reported in *Crossing the BLVD* by Warren Lehrer and Judith Sloan, instead of pressing charges or asking for financial damages, the owner had the boys released. An hour later the boys returned, apologized, and offered to fix whatever they had broken and to pay for expenses. They helped with the cleanup and offered to buy drinks for everyone. Then they sat and talked with the owner and his friends until eight in the morning, clearing up cultural misconceptions and diffusing anger.

- Education may ameliorate and prevent hate crimes. One person's initiative can make the difference.

In post–September 11 Brooklyn, in an incident where local Pakistanis came under suspicion, the Pakistanis reprinted their business cards. Before, 786 appeared on the cards, meaning "In the name of Allah," signifying that they were Muslims. They removed the numbers. In addition, the cards had previously recommended, "Ask for Abdul." This was changed to "Ask for Eddie."

During the Iran hostage crisis of 1979, Iranian Americans also changed their names to avoid the prejudice. Mahmoud became Moe; Amir became Tony; Jafar became Jim.

- To avoid becoming targets of discrimination, people will make name changes and other alterations of self for protection and camouflage.

Race Manners

In spring 2001, Mayor Carty Finkbeiner of Toledo, Ohio, appoints an African American committee to find an appropriate way to honor Dr. Martin Luther King Jr. The committee decides that Collingwood Boulevard should be renamed for the African American hero. However, Collingwood Boulevard contains the largest collection of Victorian homes east of the Mississippi, and the residents are predominantly white. The community becomes sharply divided between African Americans supporting the change and most whites against it.

Public hearings and community debate ensue. Rather than change the street name, the committee creates the Martin Luther King Train Station, which also has space set aside for a future civil rights museum. From this resolution, a workshop is born called "Building Relationships Toward Racial Harmony" (BRRH), an organization of cross-racial conversation. Since May 2001, the fifty-member BRRH has met monthly, working on race issues in Toledo.

- Racial tensions/conflicts need not end in violence or bitter stalemates. Enlightened community members, with support of local government, can find innovative alternatives for diffusing conflict.

Here is one method the BRRH found to ease racial tensions in Toledo. They read Bruce Jacobs's *Race Manners*, a book that tackles black/white issues in the United States. Then they brought the author to town for three speaking engagements during the 2002 Martin Luther King Jr. weekend. The results were so inspiring that BRRH partnered with sixteen other agencies to expand the *Race Manners* reading project. They trained facilitators, and over a period of five weeks, three hundred people read and discussed the book. Finally, they invited Jacobs to return to Toledo, where he spoke to an enthusiastic audience of 450. The newly elected mayor attended and issued a proclamation. As Jacobs describes, "There was a real charge in the air." The community felt positive and hopeful that dialogue would continue and positive changes would be made.

- This method could serve as a model for other communities dealing with racial dissension.

Green Card

Shortly after moving to Los Angeles from New Mexico, Jaime Salinas goes to the DMV to apply for a California driver's license.

The clerk tells Jaime that he must show some sort of photo ID, such as a birth certificate or a passport. When Jaime explains that he has neither with him, the clerk asks, "Well, then, did you bring your green card or your work permit?"

Taken aback, Jaime responds, "No. I'm a United States citizen."

The clerk incorrectly assumed by Jaime's appearance and name that he was not an American citizen. However, Latino surnames indicate only ancestry, not nationality. Because stories about aliens, legal and illegal, have become a staple of the news, the impact has made many forget that originally much of the Southwest belonged to Mexico. Many Latino families were citizens of the territory long before the Anglos took possession.

Eighth-grader Sahnaz Mirshafi was summoned from her Orange County school math class. The office attendant told the black-eyed brunette, "Sahnaz, we want you to take a test to see how well you speak English." Sahnaz protested. She and her mother were both Americans, and English was their first language. Nonetheless, Sahnaz was required to take an English as a Second Language placement test because school administrators assumed she lacked English-speaking skills.

- Appearance and names can lead to false conclusions. Don't assume that people with Latino names are aliens.

- Don't assume that people who look like immigrants don't speak English.

Mosque Phobia

While renting a seaside apartment in Spain, Rachel, an American, feels uneasy living one building away from an Islamic center. Being Jewish in the post–September 11 environment, she has become so fearful of the mosque that she avoids walking by it. She regularly circumvents its entrance by ascending a flight of stairs, then walking above the building and down another flight of stairs.

One late evening, Rachel walks along the heavily trafficked street and, while looking up at some scaffolding, falls down. Immobilized, her legs protrude into the onslaught of cars. Observing her plight, a man rushes out of the mosque and urgently asks, "Are you okay? Are you okay?" as he moves her legs out of the path of the traffic and helps her up. Rachel believes he has saved her life.

Rachel no longer shuns the mosque. She now walks by it with ease.

The man's act of kindness demonstrated to Rachel that she shouldn't automatically be afraid of people because of their differences.

- Unfamiliar places of worship can seem daunting, but through positive interaction, prejudice toward them can be overcome.

Bridge Builders of Anchorage

On a cold January night at midnight, a car with several teenagers cruises the Anchorage, Alaska, downtown streets. Each time they spot Native Americans, they beckon them to the car, call them vile names, shoot them with paintballs, and then videotape each escapade. Eventually the boys are arrested, and their videotape airs on television. The community becomes enraged.

Stepping up quickly to involve themselves in the fracas was Bridge Builders of Anchorage, an organization whose goal is for Anchorage to become the first city without prejudice. They not only exposed the common bias against Alaskan natives but encouraged the authorities to pursue solutions to cold-case homicides of female Native Americans. Largely as a result of their efforts, in 2002 Anchorage was recognized as an All-American city, being one of ten winners out of 150 competing cities.

Anchorage has a population of over 260,000, and one hundred different languages are spoken in the schools. Fourteen different ethnicities comprise the makeup of the Bridge Builders' board, including Japanese, Filipino, Thai, Tongan, and Vietnamese. Former mayor Rick Mystrom created the organization, and members of different ethnicities pair off to share meals together, in each other's homes or at picnics.

President Malcolm R. Roberts says, "Over a meal, if you create the right environment, you can talk about anything." He called the process "magic," describing the bonding that takes place when entering another person's home to share a meal. Trust is established. Barriers come down. You enter their lives as well as their homes. With pride, he mentioned being invited to a Gambian naming ceremony and a Chabad Lubavitcher Sabbath dinner.

- The sharing of meals is one method for creating bonds among people of unlike backgrounds.
- Having antiprejudice organizations in place before an incident occurs makes a difference. Committed leaders are already identified, so actions can be quickly taken and community solidarity demonstrated.

Math Skills

(See also: Giving Praise, p. 185.)

Mr. Craig announces the results of the last math test. Registering mock disbelief, he turns to Tiffany Kwan and says, "How come you only got a B this time? I thought all Asians got straight A's in math."

The rest of the class hoots and howls.
Tiffany feels humiliated.

Mr. Craig believed he was complimenting Tiffany on her usually outstanding math skills. Unwittingly, however, he revealed prejudice by linking her ethnicity with a particular characteristic. For Tiffany, to be singled out in such a manner was painful. On the one hand, she realized that Mr. Craig was sort of paying her a compliment, but she also recognized a derogatory attitude.

Mr. Craig thought his teasing manner softened the cruelty of the joke. The rest of the class enjoyed it, unfortunately, at Tiffany's expense.

Until now, Tiffany had consistently received high grades in math and the other students resented her for this. Sometimes they accused her of being a born math genius. Other times they complained that she skewed the grading curve and ruined it for the rest of them.

The non-Asian students would not accept that Tiffany sometimes studied four or five hours before each test. She wanted to, and her family pressured her as well. Her parents had successfully instilled the value of taking schoolwork seriously.

Other teachers have made similar mistakes and embarrassed students by ostensibly complimenting while at the same time degrading them. By connecting a particular ethnic group with a quality or ability to do something well is to single them out and make them feel self-conscious.

- Even if it seems complimentary, avoid linking any one ethnic group with a particular characteristic.

False Assumptions

Aida was born and grew up on the Mexican side of the Texas/ Mexican border. Now living in the United States, she has just published a critically acclaimed novel and is being honored at a "Meet the Authors" luncheon.

A reporter comes to Aida's lovely two-story home for an inter-view and is visibly shocked by what she finds. "Paintings? I don't have paintings," the reporter observes. She asks for a tour of the house and enthusiastically comments on the carpets, furni-ture, piano, and artifacts. "You've done all right," the reporter says admiringly.

Aida is offended.

By her comments and reactions, the reporter revealed that she hadn't expected such a high standard of living from the author. When she said, "You've done all right," Aida interpreted it to mean, "You've done all right—for a Mexican."

The reporter had no notion of Aida's background. She proba-bly assumed that Aida had pulled herself up out of poverty. No doubt she would have been astonished to discover that Aida's mother was the principal of an exclusive school in Mexico City and that the family had long been a part of the social elite in Mexican government and the arts.

This was not Aida's first experience at being assumed to be a member of a poverty-stricken minority. Once when she visited a self-proclaimed psychic, the seer declared, "You have overcome great hardship. You might have chosen the wrong path of crime and degradation. Your people are proud of you." Both the reporter and the psychic had come to the same conclusion based on a cul-tural stereotype.

Another writer, Puerto Rican–born Judith Ortiz Cofer, described prejudices she encountered. She grew up in the tropics, where bright colors were the norm and exposing the skin was a way to keep cool. This affected her choice of clothing here. "I may dress in scarlet, but don't mistake me for a hot tamale," she complained.

She chose primary colors over pastels and wore bold jewelry, tight skirts, and frilly clothing. Her teachers attacked her and other Puerto Rican girls for wearing too much jewelry and too many accessories. This fed a misconception that the females who dressed this way were vulgar and loose.

Adding to that misconception are the different ways that Amer-icans of Northern European descent and people from the Carib-bean islands move their bodies. Northern Europeans tend to have rigid torsos, whereas the torsos of most of those from the Caribbean are flexible and seem to move as if they were made up of separable parts, which leads to the "wiggling hip" movement often misinterpreted as a sexual invitation.

- Being a minority and being deprived are not synonymous. There is a wide range of socioeconomic classes among all ethnic groups.
- Brightly colored tight clothing and showy jewelry are not necessarily sexual signals.
- Cultural upbringing has shaped how people move their bodies. People with roots in Northern Europe tend to hold their torsos rigidly. Those from the Caribbean move their bodies more fluidly.

Time

Urgency

Documenting the lives of the Rom (Gypsies) living in Queens, New York, musician/writer Yale Strom visits a *bulibasha*, a respected elder. While Strom is there, the elder receives a phone call. He hangs up announcing, "A friend of mine has passed away. Let's go!"

When Strom asks, "Where?" the *bulibasha* answers, "Not very far."

Four and one half hours later, they arrive in Washington, D.C., to pay their respects to the deceased, lying in state in his home surrounded by Rom family and community. Strom and the *bulibasha* stay overnight.

Rom values dictate that family and community needs cannot be put on hold. One drops what one is doing to aid those in need. The *bulibasha* never asked Strom if he had other commitments that might conflict. Nor was there any concern about packing a bag. It was a spontaneous act of community rallying. An urgency prevailed.

Native Americans have similar attitudes. When Curtis, a non–Native American, sets up an intercultural event to honor a distinguished Native American leader, Curtis is dismayed when the honoree is a no-show. A tribal emergency had arisen, so he stayed home to solve it. Regardless of the pay or recognition the leader was to have received, tribal loyalty came first.

- Ethnicities with a strong sense of community will discard personal commitments if community members are in need. (See also: Absenteeism, p. 49; Generosity, p.153.)

- The Rom in Queens number a few thousand. They have only been there about a dozen years and are originally from Transylvania, Romania.
- Approximately one million Rom from all over the world live in the United States. Originally from India, they migrated through the Middle East and Europe over the past eight hundred years. Most arrived here at the end of the nineteenth century.

Being on Time

Professor Enell enjoys teaching and invites his students to his home to celebrate the end of the semester with him and his wife. He asks them to come for dessert and coffee at three o'clock in the afternoon.

At two thirty, the doorbell rings, and Mrs. Enell—not yet ready to receive her guests—opens the door to find her husband's Korean students standing there. Flustered, Mrs. Enell ushers them in.

Not everyone interprets time in the same way. Most Americans expect that guests will arrive at the appointed time or perhaps a few minutes later; they are generally not prepared for guests who arrive ahead of time, especially thirty minutes. However, both Japanese and Korean guests tend to arrive early. This is their interpretation of being "on time."

Carol tells about a Nigerian man who invited her to an eight o'clock dinner here in the United States. He reminded her to be prompt because the dinner was on "American time, not Nigerian time." Previously, she had learned what Nigerian time meant—she had attended a one o'clock Nigerian Catholic wedding that did not begin until three o'clock.

Judy, too, made a discovery about ethnic time differences when she showed up at five thirty for a six o'clock Indian wedding, and no one else was there. The ceremony finally began at eight forty-five. Afterward, she asked if there had been a misprint on the invitation. "Oh, no," she was told. "We never pay attention to the time."

American regional interpretations of time differ as well. Margie arrived thirty minutes late for a brunch, and when her Vermont hostess scolded her, she retorted, "In Tennessee, twelve o'clock means twelve thirty. At home, if I were to arrive at twelve for a noon brunch they would ask, 'What are you doing here?' In the South, people don't expect you until thirty to forty minutes after the set time."

- Cultural background affects ideas of what is on time, what is early, and what is late. To avoid unpleasant surprises, explain your expectations about time and ask those from different regions and cultures about theirs.

Dropping In

(See also: Friendship, p. 161.)

The community college brings students together from a wide variety of backgrounds. This is how Madge, a native-born American, meets Alina, a newly arrived young woman from Armenia. They become friendly with one another, and to Alina, Madge becomes her best friend. Eventually, Madge suggests that it might be nice if Alina visited her at home. Alina is delighted, but they set no date or time.

One morning during semester break, Madge hears a knock on the door. When she opens it, she is astonished to see Alina standing there.

In Alina's culture, you can visit somebody's house anytime, especially when you have a close relationship. It is not necessary to call ahead to notify your friends or family. However, Alina quickly learned that visiting customs are different here. Even though Madge invited her in, Alina noticed that her friend kept looking at the clock. Finally, Alina asked if Madge had other plans. When Madge said that she had a doctor's appointment, Alina felt very ashamed. She realized that she should have called first and apologized many times. Madge was understanding and convinced Alina that she wasn't angry.

This scenario has been played out many times by immigrants who come from cultures where dropping in without notice is the norm. It usually takes only one unfortunate experience before they learn the custom of calling first that is prevalent in much of the United States.

- It's best to tell friends from a different country that while you welcome their visit, you expect a call in advance.

Taboo Times

(See also: Food Taboos, p. 77.)

The urban newspaper's advertising department thinks they have planned their campaign carefully. They distribute two sample boxes of cereal with the Sunday edition and enclose both the paper and the cereal in a plastic bag for their home-delivery customers.

On Monday, the phones ring off the hook with intense reactions from incensed subscribers.

The planners had forgotten to check the calendar. If they had, they would have discovered that the Sunday of their cereal distribution was also the first day of Passover, a holiday that is marked on most American calendars. At this time, observant Jews must keep their homes free of all *hametz* (bread and grain products) for the weeklong festival. Jewish customers had just finished days of conscientiously removing these taboo foods from their homes. To have the newspaper toss some back on their doorsteps was a frustration of the highest order. The subscribers could not bring the paper indoors because it touched the cereal box. Consequently, they were deprived of reading the newspaper on this day.

School administrators have made similar scheduling misjudgments by setting the opening day of the fall semester at the same time as *Rosh Hashanah*, the first day of the Jewish New Year, when observant Jews are obligated to attend temple services.

- Businesspeople should check the calendar for religious holidays of their clientele when planning special events such as advertising campaigns.

- School administrators should check the dates of religious holidays of their school population when planning such events as the opening of the school semester.

In 2001, the New York State Board of Regents scheduled their two-day, six-hour English Regents exam, required for high school graduation, on the first and second day of the Chinese Lunar New Year. Chinese students complained, comparing the Regents' cultural gaffe equal to scheduling the exam for Yom Kippur, the Jews' holiest day of the year. Other Chinese Americans said that the Lunar New Year was of deeper significance than Passover or Christian Easter because it is more ancient.

Verbal Expressions

Complimenting a Baby

(See also: Ignoring the Baby, p. 106; Evil Eye, p. 138.)

Melanie is excited to be invited to a party honoring the birth of her neighbor's baby, but imagine her surprise when she hears relatives say about this beautiful baby, "Oh, what a flat nose spread out all over its face." "Oh, what big ears."
Melanie is shocked.

Melanie's neighbors were Hawaiian, and like many other ethnic groups, they were reluctant to compliment the baby. Whether or not this belief is grounded in the evil eye is hard to ascertain; nonetheless, some people may not appreciate receiving compliments about their new child, lest the baby be put in jeopardy.

If you compliment a Jewish baby, members of the older generation may say *"Kein eyn ahora"* (not one evil eye) or "Poo, poo, poo," to indicate spitting to keep away the evil eye.

- Avoid complimenting Hawaiian, Hmong, Indian, and Mexican babies.

Beating around the Bush

American scholars attending an academic meeting in Romania are well prepared with their learned treatises but unprepared for cultural differences.

When Jeanne asks, "What time will the bus come?" Romanian hostess Silvia answers, "The bus will come." When Lisa queries,

"Tell me what tour arrangements you have made for tomorrow," Marius replies, "Yes, but first I must organize the drinking of more plum brandy."

Americans expect precise answers to questions. This is called direct communication. However, Romanians often avoid direct responses. Silvia knew the bus would be late, and the truth would have caused complaints from the Americans. Sylvia's dodge kept them hopeful. Two hours later, when the bus finally appeared, the conventioneers were so relieved they forgot their impatience. Likewise, Marius knew that the details of the next day's tour were not yet fixed. He shifted the topic to a Romanian hospitality custom, the serving of *tuica*, a strong plum brandy. After a few rounds of this libation, Lisa's anxiety about travel arrangements disappeared.

By the end of the conference, many Americans cheerfully accepted the Romanian indirect style of communication.

- Indirect communication is not unique to Romania. Other countries that utilize this mode include Spain and Italy.
- Outside the United States communication may be less direct. Depending on ethnicity, within the United States, indirectness may also prevail.

"Hello!"

Jala Garibova and Betty Blair relate the travails of Ahmad, an Azerbaijani student newly enrolled in an American university.

On his first day of class Ahmad arrives early. As other students enter the class, they take their seats but ignore their classmates, even those sitting in adjacent seats. Ahmad is dismayed by their behavior.

Azerbaijanis say hello and good-bye to all the people in a room, including students in classrooms. Ahmad was grateful that he waited to observe their behavior beforehand. He thus avoided making a fool of himself by greeting all students as they entered and left.

Similarly, an Azerbaijani girl working in the United States considered her boss rude because he never said hello to her in the morning. At first she thought it was because she was a foreigner or because she was in a low position. Over time, she realized that she had culturally misinterpreted his behavior.

- Saying hello and good-bye in Azerbaijan is required. Even policemen will first say hello to errant drivers before writing up their traffic violations.
- It is easy to take offense when you don't understand the cultural behavior of other people.
- In unfamiliar situations, observe behavior before taking action. When in doubt, ask questions regarding protocol.

Giving Praise

(See also: Math Skills, p. 172; Compliments about Appearance, p. 193; Indonesians, p. 228.)

John takes a job making videos throughout Asia. In Indonesia, he hires a local young man to help him organize an event to be videotaped in a large stadium. Arrangements are complex, and the young man excels in handling all details.

Grateful, and in front of the hundreds in attendance, John acknowledges his assistant's skill. The next day, the young man quits.

The compliment may have backfired because the young man was embarrassed, perhaps even demeaned by being publicly singled out. He might even have been insulted because from his point of view, he was just doing his duty.

While Americans place high value on being singled out for achievement, many Asians feel awkward and embarrassed. In addition, praise is often considered a subtle way of suggesting that prior to the moment of praise, the person's performance had been inadequate.

Part of this incongruity in interpreting praise is because of American emphasis on competition and being number one. (See also: Cheating, p. 44.) Most Americans believe that praise moves them ahead. However, praise for people from other cultures may mean being singled out and thus a target for negative reaction from peers. (See also: Birthday Cake, p. 99; Ignoring the Baby, p. 106.)

Gail, a hospital administrator, tells how she wanted to promote Angelica, a Filipina nurse, because of outstanding performance. However, Gail didn't realize that by putting Angelica in charge of other Filipinas who had formerly been her peers, the administrator was altering the social relationships between them. Angelica preferred to stay in the same position and keep social relationships even and maintained. To Gail's amazement, Angelica refused the promotion.

- After receiving praise, many Asians feel uncomfortable and embarrassed. They may even consider praise a form of subtle criticism.
- Public criticism should be avoided when dealing with Asians, as this may lead to loss of face.
- Some Asian employees may be reluctant about promotions if they threaten social relationships, which may be deemed more important than upward mobility.

Too Friendly

Monica and her Ethiopian husband, Teshome, attend a concert, and at intermission Monica begins chatting with the woman sitting next to her. Before long, Monica has told her that she is a teacher, the name of her school, and the kinds of CDs she collects.

Going home, Teshome criticizes her habit of talking to strangers. He cautions that Monica has given away too much of herself. "People may use the information against you." He believes it is undignified to reveal oneself to a stranger.

Americans are often perceived as being too friendly when they speak freely to people they don't know. They give misleading messages with this behavior.

- In many cultures, being open and quick to talk to strangers is not respected. Reserve is more the protocol.
- People may misinterpret friendliness as intended friendship.

Accent

An English as a Second Language (ESL) class comprising adults from at least ten different countries warily greeted their new teacher. She was the third instructor in only four weeks.

The teacher asked, "What American idioms confuse you?" An attractive Middle Eastern woman in her twenties responded. "'Feel her up' is an idiom?"

The teacher, a twenty-year classroom veteran, was reluctant to begin the opening class talking about sexual matters. Stalling, she asked, "Feel her up?"

"Yes," the student insisted. "Feel her up."

Once more, the teacher delayed. She didn't know whether to speak about sexual harassment or the American breast fetish. Biding for time, she once more affirmed, "Yes, 'feel her up' is an idiom."

Frustrated by the teacher's hesitation, the young woman spoke more emphatically. "Feel her up!

"You know, you go to the gas-a station and you say, 'Feel her up!'"

The instructor was so relieved. Rescued by her own hesitation, she had been spared a terrible embarrassment. That small difference in the pronunciation of a word might have plunged her into a cross-cultural morass. Had she attempted to explain American sex habits, the students would have been astonished and offended. Most of them came from cultures where sexual information would not be disseminated to males and females at the same time—especially by a woman. Some might even come from places where sexual information is withheld or limited to basic procreation issues. Certainly, sexual arousal techniques would not be discussed in a coeducational language class.

- Be cautious when trying to understand what someone with an accent is trying to say. It's easy to misconstrue and blunder.

When Ginger, an Apache-speaking Anglo anthropologist, attends an Apache girls' puberty ceremony, she asks one of her friends for a cup of coffee. At least, that's what she thought she said. However, Apache is a tonal language, and she inadvertently altered one of the sounds. Instead of asking for a cylindrical-shaped object filled with liquid coffee, she inadvertently asked for a male dancer's filled cylindrically shaped object, a euphemism for penis.

The mistake brought great amusement to all and became the source of a running gag. In this situation, her mistake did not alienate her. Instead, the shared laughter pulled her closer to the Apache community.

- Through humor, cross-cultural blunders can sometimes be turned into positives.

Forms of Address

(See also: Respect for Teachers, p. 46.)

A delightful encounter takes place in an ethnic food shop when Sandy, a bubbly American in her twenties, meets Mr. and Mrs. Rao, a lovely older couple from India. They have such a good time together that the Raos invite Sandy to their home for supper. Soon after her arrival, Sandy goes into the kitchen to chat with her hostess as Mrs. Rao puts the finishing touches on the food. The mood is relaxed and congenial, so Sandy asks, "By the way, what's your name, Mrs. Rao?"

Coolly, the hostess answers, "Mrs. Rao."

The tone and response stun Sandy. She falls silent, feeling embarrassed and rebuffed. For her, the visit has lost its flavor. She can hardly wait for the evening to end.

Americans pride themselves on their informality, but people from Asia and most other places in the world do not see this as a virtue. Instead, informality often equals disrespect. Mrs. Rao believed that Sandy was impertinent. The major issue was age differences. Since Sandy was younger, she should not have taken liberties by wanting to call the older woman by her first name. In many parts of the world, even when they are well acquainted, young people must show their respect by addressing older persons as "Aunt" or "Uncle." This tradition, popular throughout West Africa, is still observed by many African Americans. It is common in the Middle East as well as Europe. Furthermore, in some Chinese families, the members themselves may not address each other by their first names and must call each other by their family relationship, for example, "Sister" or "Brother."

In some cultures, people avoid using names entirely and describe the social relationships instead. Fay tells how annoyed she used to become when Zuhayra, a Palestinian friend of her daughter, used to call on the phone and address her, "Hello, Karen's mother?"

Fay incorrectly assumed that the girl couldn't remember her last name. She was surprised when she learned that according to Palestinian tradition, Zuhayra was paying proper respect to Fay by doing this.

• People from most other cultures believe it is disrespectful to be addressed by their first name. Younger persons should be especially careful to address older persons by their titles or as custom dictates.

Naming Traditions

President Bill Clinton travels to South Korea to visit with President Kim Young Sam. While speaking publicly, the American president repeatedly refers to the Korean president's wife as Mrs. Kim. The South Korean officials are embarrassed.

In error, President Clinton's advisers assumed that Koreans had the same naming traditions as the Japanese. President Clinton had not been informed that in Korea, wives retain their maiden names. President Kim Young Sam's wife was named Sohn Myong Suk. Therefore, her correct name was Mrs. Sohn. In Korea, the family name comes before the given name.

President Clinton arrived in Korea directly after leaving Japan and had not shifted cultural gears. His failure to follow Korean protocol gave the impression that Korea was not as important as Japan.

In addition to Koreans, other Asian husbands and wives do not share the same surnames: Cambodians, Chinese, Hmong, Mien, and Vietnamese. This practice often puzzles teachers when interacting with a pupil's parents. They become perplexed about the student's "correct" last name. Also, the number of names a person has varies with the culture. Koreans and Chinese use three names; Vietnamese can use up to four.

Placing the family name (or surname) first is found among a number of Asian cultures, for example, Vietnamese, Mien, Hmong, Cambodian, and Chinese. Often this reversal from the American system of placing the family name last causes confusion.

Mexican naming customs differ as well. When a woman marries, she keeps her maiden name and adds her husband's name after the word *de* (of): After marrying Tino Martinez, María Gonzales becomes María Gonzales de Martinez. When children are born, the name order is as follows: given name, father's family name, mother's family name. Tino and María's child Anita is named Anita Martinez Gonzales. This affects how they fill out forms in this country.

Mexican applicants usually write their mother's family name in the last-name slot. When requested to fill in a middle name, they generally write the father's family name. This conforms to the sequence used at home. Consequently, in the United States, Mexicans are addressed by the last name written—the family name of the mother. For men, this is not the last name they would ordinarily use. Instead, they would rather be called by their father's family name. This often causes consternation.

- Don't assume a married woman has her husband's last name.
- In many Asian traditions, the order of first and last names is reversed.
- In Myanmar, a person doesn't have a family name. Names are based on the day a person was born, for example, Thein means "Friday-born." Women do not take their husband's name after marriage.

- In Latino traditions, males prefer to use their father's family name, which frequently is filled in on forms as the middle name.
- To avoid offense, ask which names a person would prefer to use. If the name is difficult to pronounce, admit it and ask the person to help you say it correctly.

Idioms

(See also: *"No Molesta,"* p. 192.)

Sean Seward crams all night for his medical school exams. At 3:00 A.M., he gets hungry and drives to a supermarket to pick up some snacks. Tae-Soon, a Korean man, is the only other shopper in the market. Sean walks down the aisle, where Tae-Soon seems absorbed in studying a canned soup label. Since Sean is a friendly fellow, he says to Tae-Soon as he passes, "Hey, how's it going?"

Tae-Soon looks at Sean bewilderedly, then turns away and ignores him.

Tae-Soon didn't understand the expression "How's it going?" because he didn't know what "it" referred to. Many immigrants share Tae-Soon's confusion about this common American greeting.

Another Korean newcomer, Ji Young, described what happened to him when he didn't understand the expression and also chose to ignore his classmate's query of "How's it going?" The classmate became so exasperated by Ji Young's lack of response to the question that he finally yelled, "How's it going?" to which a nonplussed Ji Young answered, "My house is not going." This brought jeers from the other students.

"What's up?" is similarly confusing. New English speakers have no idea what "what" refers to, nor what would be "up."

Although it is difficult, when speaking with new English speakers, it is best to avoid idiomatic language. However, people use idioms so frequently and unconsciously that they are difficult to recognize—let alone eliminate from the vocabulary.

Furthermore, new speakers of English are very literal in their understanding of the language. This explains the behavior of the immigrant who turned down a job on the "graveyard shift" because he thought it meant working in a cemetery.

- If you receive a blank look or seem to be ignored when speaking with a new English speaker, consider that you might be using an idiom that the other person does not understand. Try phrasing your message another way.

"No Molesta"

(See also: "Stupid!" p. 41; Idioms, p. 191.)

Each workday morning, several moms on the block happily drop off their toddlers at the home of their Colombian babysitter. She takes excellent care of the children.

One afternoon, the sitter's thirteen-year-old son, Ernesto, accompanies her as she walks the children back to their homes. When they arrive at Isa's house, her father, Fred, greets them. It is the first time he has met Ernesto.

In halting English, Ernesto says, "Your daughter is very beautiful." Fred thanks him, and Ernesto says, "*No molesta.*" A strange look crosses Fred's face. Then, when he sees his daughter kiss Ernesto good-bye, Fred becomes enraged.

With heightened consciousness about sexual abuse, Fred had jumped to the conclusion that Ernesto meant "I didn't molest her" when he said, *"No molesta."* Although Fred's wife challenged her husband about his Spanish language skills, Fred insisted that he understood Spanish very well.

Later, the wife told the other parents what had happened—that Ernesto said he would not molest Isa. One of the fathers was Puerto Rican. When he heard Ernesto's exact words, he roared with laughter, then explained: In Spanish, *molestar* also means "to disturb." All that Ernesto was trying to tell Fred was, "She's no trouble" or "She's no bother." There was no threat of sexual abuse.

- Even though a word in another language may be similar or identical to an English word, it may have a completely different meaning.

Compliments about Appearance

Cindy has always struggled with her weight. She experiments with the latest diets and enrolls in different weight-loss centers—but to no avail. She bounces up and down between different-sized clothing and has become extremely sensitive about her body. One day while crossing the university campus, she runs into a former classmate from Iran who greets her enthusiastically.

"Cindy, you look good. You gained weight!"

Cindy is crushed.

Contrary to how it seemed, the young man was praising her appearance. Americans who go to the extreme in promoting thinness forget that this is not a worldwide value. Standards of beauty vary with culture. In the Middle East, a beautiful woman is amply proportioned. In Farsi, they call it "*kopoly*" or "*topoly*." Wide hips signify that women can produce children; hence, they are considered appealing and good candidates for courtship and marriage. Even here in the United States, voluptuous women used to be appreciated. In the mid-to-late-nineteenth century, plumpness was fashionable. Large hips, bosoms, waists, and strong arms were "in." Believing that fat promoted health and beauty, women competed over their weight gains.

While most American women, like Cindy, are unhappy to have someone comment on their weight gain, there are others today who find it complimentary. Members of the AIDS community will say to each other with enthusiasm and appreciation, "You look good. You gained weight." For them, a weight gain affirms power over the deadly virus, life over death.

- A comment about a woman's weight gain may be a compliment.

Yes or No?

(See also: Heads Up, Down, or Sideways?, p. 11; Classroom Behavior, p. 37.)

Betty Woolf thinks of herself as a no-nonsense writing teacher. She is very direct in her interaction with her students, yet at the same time tries to be sensitive to their needs. To ensure their comprehension, she always asks, "Do you understand?" However, her new composition class confuses her. Whenever she asks them if they understand, they always answer yes; yet when she looks over their work, it is apparent that they haven't understood at all.

Most of Mrs. Woolf's new class came from Asian countries, where they are reluctant to admit that they don't understand something. From the students' point of view, that would be disrespectful to their teacher. It would indicate that she didn't do a good job of explaining.

Eventually, Mrs. Woolf discovered that she was more successful with her students if she avoided yes/no questions. Instead, she would say, "Tell me what you don't understand" or "What confuses you?" This brought effective results.

Asking yes/no questions of other immigrants can bring equally unsuccessful outcomes. An office manager reported that after explaining telephone procedures to her Armenian employees, she, like Betty Woolf, asked, "Do you understand?" The workers said yes but then demonstrated their lack of understanding by immediately botching up communications.

First, language limitations prevented the employees from comprehending the question. Second, the workers were embarrassed to admit their ignorance about the new technology. The manager found a solution. After explaining a new procedure, she would ask the workers to demonstrate how the equipment worked. In that way, how much the novice understood was readily apparent.

- Avoid asking yes/no questions, which often results in misleading answers.
- Demonstration of techniques is a more accurate way to assess comprehension. "Show me" is better than "Do you understand?"

Can't Say No

The college has an active faculty-and-student exchange program in Japan, administered by Mark Sterling. Sterling needs to change a faculty member's schedule. He writes to Mr. Masuoka, his Japanese counterpart, and explains the reason for the request. At the end of his letter, he writes, "Please feel free to say no."

Mr. Masuoka never answers.

Mr. Masuoka was so put off by Mark's letter, he turned to a non-Japanese intermediary for help. Eventually, the intermediary contacted Sterling, made the schedule adjustment, and informed him about the problem his letter had caused. It was the phrase "Please feel free to say no" that caused Masuoka's predicament.

Japanese *never* feel free to say no. They avoid saying no because it creates ill feelings. Instead, they prefer harmony and ordinarily use indirect communication to achieve that goal. Sterling's comment placed Masuoka in such an uncomfortable position that Masuoka had to find someone else to answer the letter.

When Mark discovered how his one sentence had undermined communication, he carefully avoided any future situation that might place his Japanese colleagues in a position of having to answer in the negative.

• Some Asian cultures consider it rude to say no and will go to extremes to avoid doing so.

Bargaining

(See also: Sealing a Deal, p. 158.)

All the parties have assembled in the bank conference room to close the multimillion-dollar deal: Bevins, the broker who has put the package together; Adams, the bank vice president who is handling the flow of funds; Morady, the borrower; and Green, the lender.

As Morady is about to sign, he unexpectedly announces, "I don't want to pay Bevins's commission. Green should pay it."

At first the others sit in stunned silence; then Bevins retorts, "If you don't pay the commission, you don't get the money."

Morady acquiesces. "Okay. Okay. I'll pay the commission."

They sign the papers. A check is turned over to Morady, another to Bevins. Smiling as if no unpleasantries had taken place, Morady turns to Bevins and says, "Let me take you to dinner to celebrate."

Bevins is incredulous. He abruptly replies, "No, thanks."

Morady came from the Middle East, where a deal is not done even after the terms have been agreed upon. Negotiation continues until the signing of the contract. This is part of the Middle Eastern cultural style of doing business. Although Morady happened to be Iranian, this bargaining mode applies to others from that part of the world, as well.

Part of this has to do with differing styles of commerce. Americans come from a fixed-price society. Except for automobiles, the price tag on merchandise is rarely challenged. Likewise, conditions are rarely adjusted or questioned once a contract has been signed.

In other parts of the world, bargaining is the mode of doing business and it continues until the last moment. American travelers have learned about shopping customs in Mexico, for example; one shouldn't pay the originally asked-for price. Tourists make an offer far lower than the worth of the product, then negotiate with the seller toward a realistic middle price. Sometimes the shopper will say no and leave, and the seller will chase the buyer and close the deal on the street.

The Middle East is similar to Mexico. Morady tried until the last moment to gain an extra advantage. He did not see this as a betrayal of the contract or of his agreement with Bevins, merely an acceptable means of trying to obtain an extra point. Even though Morady's last-second attempt was rejected, he saw nothing inconsistent about going out to celebrate with Bevins. According to Sondra Thiederman, international business consultant, Morady was merely exhibiting his negotiating skills by trying to obtain a last-minute concession.

Bevins, on the other hand, took Morady's ploy personally, as a double-dealing move. They had made a prior agreement, and Bevins expected Morady to live up to it. Bevins would not forgive Morady, and they never did business again.

- In Middle Eastern styles of doing business, negotiation continues until the contract is signed.

- Retailers report that while most Americans accept a fixed price on merchandise, many Asians or Middle Easterners try to negotiate for a lower price, using convincing arguments like "But I'm a good customer . . ."

Believing What They Say

(See also: Offering Food, p. 73; Refusing a Gift, p. 98.)

Shortly after arriving from Beirut, Mrs. Berberian breaks her ankle and goes to a doctor who expresses interest in her Middle Eastern background. Consequently, on her next appointment, she brings him homemade Armenian pastries. He falls in love with her cooking, so on subsequent visits, she brings him more treats.

One day he asks her if she would be willing to make three hundred spinach *bouraks* (spinach-filled pastries) for a party he is hosting. "I'll pay you for your costs," he says.

Flattered, Mrs. Berberian agrees. She labors many hours, spends a lot of money on the ingredients, and even buys a special tray to display the finished delicacies.

When the doctor comes to pick them up, he is delighted and asks, "How much do I owe you?"

"Oh, nothing," demurs an exhausted Mrs. Berberian.

Surprised, the doctor says, "Why, thank you," and leaves with the three hundred pastries.

Mrs. Berberian weeps bitterly.

Even though she had said "nothing," that's not what Mrs. Berberian meant. She was certain that after she rejected his first offer the doctor would insist upon paying. She expected him to ask her *at least* one more time, and then she would have reluctantly told him what he owed her. That's how all transactions were handled at home. That's what she expected here and why she felt so crushed with the results.

Since Americans tend to be direct in communication style, they may accept or reject a first offer that was intended merely as an opening formality.

- When interacting with people from many other cultures, do not accept the first response as being the real answer.

2

Clearing Cultural Confusions

A Quick Reference Guide

People and places that we once considered exotic and confined to *National Geographic* have now become staples of our evening news. Accordingly, our need to know more about them grows more critical, especially as the United States increasingly involves itself in global affairs.

"Clearing Cultural Confusions" is a brief comparative guide for learning about these people and their ethnicity, language, religion, and customs.

Obviously, there is not enough space to cover the entire world, so I have concentrated on the countries that figure most prominently in the news: parts of Africa, especially in the north; Asia; the Balkans; the independent countries that were formerly part of the USSR; and the Middle East. I have included a map to help readers' orientation. (See pages 202–203.)

I have only focused on official countries as of the writing of this book. I have not included entities where borders, which often arouse passion and bloodshed, are in dispute or where independence has not yet been realized. Chechnya, Kashmir, Kurdistan, Palestine, the Gaza Strip, and the West Bank are territories that are currently involved in such disputes. Since borders are merely fictional lines dividing people, they are also porous. Despite official regulations and dangers, people shift back and forth across them.

Each country is classified by ethnicities, languages, religions, and customs. These data make us realize how multicultural/multitribal the world is. Homogeneity in any nation today is practically a fantasy. In addition, political and economic upheavals in those countries have driven their refugees to our shores, so I have included information about their most populous settlements in the United States—some have lived here for generations.

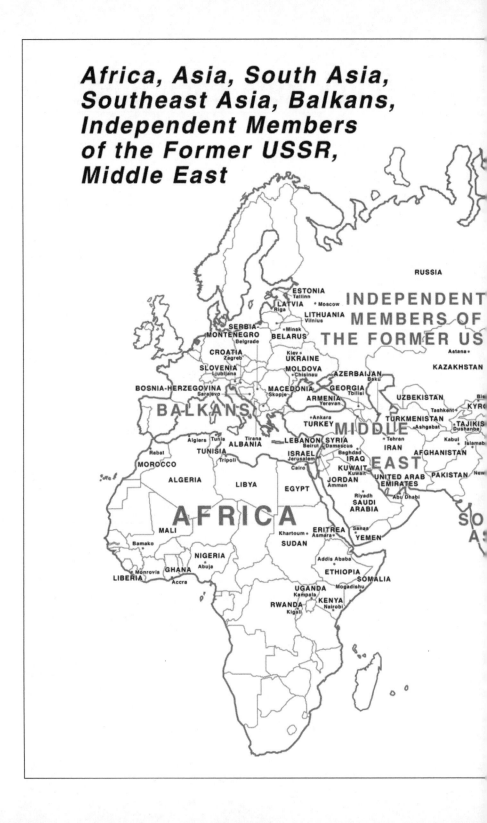

Africa, Asia, South Asia, Southeast Asia, Balkans, Independent Members of the Former USSR, Middle East

RUSSIA

ESTONIA
Tallinn
LATVIA
Riga
• Moscow
LITHUANIA
Vilnius

INDEPENDENT
MEMBERS OF
THE FORMER US

SERBIA-
MONTENEGRO
Belgrade
• Minsk
BELARUS

Astana •

CROATIA
Zagreb
Kiev •
UKRAINE

KAZAKHSTAN

SLOVENIA
Ljubljana
MOLDOVA
• Chisinau
AZERBAIJAN
Baku

BOSNIA-HERZEGOVINA
Sarajevo
MACEDONIA
Skopje
GEORGIA
Tbilisi
UZBEKISTAN
Bis

ARMENIA
Yerevan
Tashkent •
KYRC

BALKANS
• Ankara
TURKEY
TURKMENISTAN
Ashgabat
TAJIKIS
Dushanbe

MIDDLE
Kabul
Islamab

• Tehran
IRAN

Algiers Tunis Tirana
ALBANIA
LEBANON SYRIA
Beirut • Damascus
AFGHANISTAN

Rabat
TUNISIA
ISRAEL
Jerusalem
Baghdad
IRAQ
EAST

MOROCCO
Tripoli
Cairo
KUWAIT
Kuwait
PAKISTAN New

ALGERIA
LIBYA
EGYPT
JORDAN
Amman
UNITED ARAB
EMIRATES

Riyadh
SAUDI
ARABIA
Abu Dhabi

SO
A

AFRICA

MALI
Khartoum •
ERITREA
Asmara •
Sanaa •
YEMEN

Bamako
SUDAN

NIGERIA
Abuja
Addis Ababa •

GHANA
ETHIOPIA
SOMALIA

Monrovia
LIBERIA
Accra
UGANDA
Kampala •
Mogadishu

RWANDA
Kigali
KENYA
Nairobi

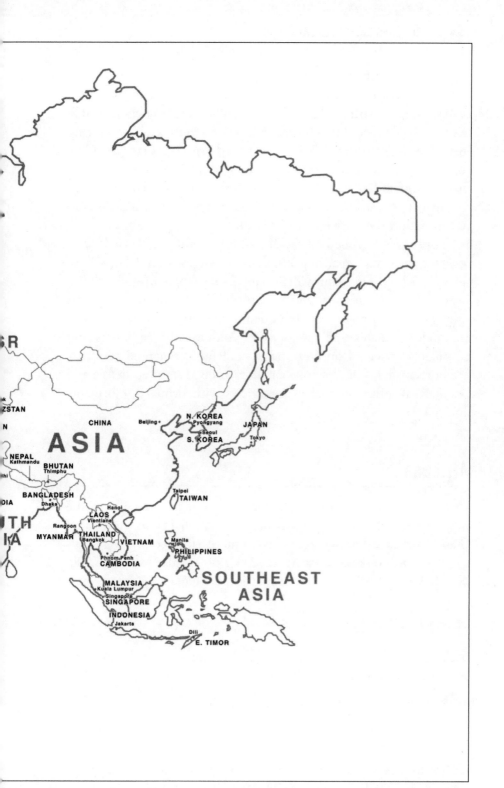

For each cultural group I have added brief descriptions of customs, whittling them down to a few as practiced in their own countries. Since space is limited, I have omitted references to highly controversial practices such as female genital mutilation, preferring instead to focus on more widely accepted aspects of culture. Customs practiced in one region or by one ethnicity within a country may be unfamiliar elsewhere within the same boundaries. I have excluded the history and politics of each region because they do not fit within the purview of this book.

For sources, I relied on the 2004 edition of the *CIA World Factbook* for statistics regarding ethnicities, religions, and languages. The 2000 U.S. census provided numbers of people of each ethnicity living here. Ancestry and birthplace are the major categories used by the Census Bureau, but one must assume that the numbers are underestimates and out of date. Additionally, embassies and consulates provided only estimates, and undocumented residents are unrecorded. For descriptions of customs, I used academic and popular resources as well as interviews with primary informants and scholars.

Africans

Only those countries that have been featured prominently in the news have been selected. Regarding Africans living in the United States, the 2000 Census figures combine African countries, lumping them into regions: East Africa, 213,299; Middle Africa, 26,900; North Africa, 190,491; Southern Africa, 66,496.

Algerians

Background: Capital: Algiers, Algeria; Population: 32,129,324; Ethnicities: Arab-Berber 99%, European less than 1%.

Languages: Arabic (official), French, Berber dialects.

Religions: Sunni Muslim (state religion) 99%, Christian and Jewish 1%.

U.S. Populations: No official numbers. Unofficially, there are approximately 20,000 living in Chicago, Los Angeles, Houston, New

Jersey, Pennsylvania, Washington, D.C., Massachusetts, and Cupertino, California.

Customs: The groom is responsible for the costs of the marriage celebration. After days of singing and eating, participants carry off the bride to her groom and the union is followed by another week of celebration.

Couscous, yellow granules of semolina made from durum wheat, is their national dish. It is precooked and then dried before use. Couscous is indigenous to North Africa and was probably invented by Muslim Berbers in the tenth or eleventh century, then later introduced elsewhere by the Portuguese. In Morocco, Tunisia, Libya, and Egypt, it is also a staple. Couscous is served with chicken, lamb, and vegetables and spiced with cumin, coriander, and cinnamon.

Egyptians

Background: Capital: Cairo, Egypt; Population: 76,117,421; Ethnicities: Eastern Hamitic stock (Egyptians, Bedouins, and Berbers) 99%, Greek, Nubian, Armenian, and other European (primarily Italian and French) 1%.

Languages: Arabic (official), English and French widely understood by educated classes.

Religions: Muslim (mostly Sunni) 94%, Coptic Christian and other 6%.

U.S. Populations: Census 2000: 142,832 (ancestry). Copts number 265,000. Southern California has 40% to 50%; others are in New York, New Jersey, Washington, D.C., Chicago, New York, and Los Angeles. The majority are Christians (Copts). Egyptian Muslims are generally diffuse, but communities live in Washington, D.C., Chicago, New York, and Los Angeles.

Customs: Seventy-five percent of all Muslim and Coptic Christian males are circumcised, generally at birth but sometimes when the child is older. They celebrate the baby's birth on the seventh day.

Muslim men greet each other by grasping the other's right hand, placing the left hand on the other's right shoulder, and exchanging kisses on each cheek, but kisses are always between members of the same sex.

As in the rest of the Arab world, the left hand is considered unclean. The right hand is always used for eating and gesturing.

Eritreans

Background: Capital: Asmara, Eritrea; Population: 4,447,307; Ethnicities: Tigrinya 50%, Tigre and Kunama 40%, Afar 4%, Saho (Red Sea coast dwellers) 3%, other 3%.

Languages: Afar, Amharic, Arabic, Tigre and Kunama, Tigrinya, other Cushitic languages.

Religions: Sunni Muslim 50%, Coptic Christian 40%, Roman Catholic 5%, Protestants 2%, Indigenous religions 2%, Seventh-Day Adventists and Jehovah's Witnesses, less than 1%.

U.S. Populations: Combined with Ethiopians, 100,000 (1995). Washington, D.C., has the largest concentration. Others live in Los Angeles, Dallas, New York City, Maryland, and Virginia.

Customs: Women traditionally wear the *kidan habesha*, a large piece of cloth wrapped around the body to form a dresslike garment, with part used as a shawl that falls down on her back.

Many Christians from the Highlands have crosses tattooed on their foreheads.

Both Coptic Christians and Muslims forbid eating the meat of wild animals, wild fowl, snakes, wild and domestic pigs, dogs, horses, and shellfish. They eat with *injera*, a spongy pancake-like bread that becomes a utensil for scooping up stews and sauces.

Ethiopians

Background: Capital: Addis Ababa, Ethiopia; Population: 67,851,281; Ethnicities: Oromo 40%, Amhara and Tigre 32%, Sidamo 9%, Shankella 6%, Somali 6%, Afar 4%, Gurage 2%, other 1%.

Languages: Amharic, Tigrinya, Oromigna, Guaragigna, Somali, Arabic, other local languages, English (major foreign language taught in schools).

Religions: Muslim 45% to 50%, Ethiopian Orthodox 35% to 40%, animist 12%, other 3% to 8%.

U.S. Populations: Census 2000: 86,918 (ancestry). Combined with Eritreans, 100,000 (1995). Washington, D.C. has the largest concentration. Others live in Los Angeles, Dallas, New York City, Maryland, and Virginia. Combined with Ethiopians, approximately 10,000 live in the San Francisco Bay area.

Customs: Traditional female garb is the *shämma*, a large piece of cloth wrapped around the body to form a dresslike garment, with a smaller piece of the same fabric for a head scarf or hood.

On Janurary 7 they celebrate Christmas, called Genna. Coptic Church services begin at 3:00 A.M. and end at 9:00 A.M. Priests wear ceremonial robes and carry long prayer sticks and church rattles as they walk in procession. After the service, Christmas meals and festivities ensue. Then the men and older boys play genna, a hockeylike game with two competing teams. The winning team celebrates by visiting each house. Households honor them with refreshments and gifts.

Ghanaians

Background: Capital: Accra, Ghana; Population: 20,757,032; Ethnicities: Black African 98.5% (major tribes—Akan 44%, Moshi-Dagomba 16%, Ewe 13%, Ga 8%, Gurma 3%, Yoruba 1%), European and other 1.5%.

Languages: English (official), African languages (including Akan, Moshi-Dagomba, Ewe, and Ga).

Religions: Indigenous beliefs 21%, Muslim 16%, Christian 63%.

U.S. Populations: Census 2000: 49,944 (ancestry), 65,572 (birthplace). Most live in urban areas: 40.3% in Mid-Atlantic States, 75% of those in New York; others live in California, Maryland, Virginia, and Washington, D.C.

Customs: *Homowo* means "hooting at hunger." It is an annual harvest festival of the Ga people, referring to their early migration to the west coast of Ghana. En route they experienced famine, but because they helped each other, they survived. Later, when harvests were bountiful, they held a feast where they jeered at the hunger and hard times of their past. They believe that any Ga person who fails to celebrate Homowo will incur the wrath of ancestors and will die.

Activities during this festival include the opening of the fishing season for bream; special meals of a palm oil fish stew of steamed corn dough, bream, and okra; the sprinkling of libations to ancestors; and special dances.

In modern-day Accra, Ghanaians are being buried in fantastic wooden-shaped coffins appropriate to the lives of the deceased: fish, crab, and lobster shapes for fishermen; a big chicken for a mother who took great care of many children; a car for a taxi driver; an eagle for a chief.

Kenyans

Background: Capital: Nairobi, Kenya; Population: 32,021,856; Ethnicities: Kikuyu 22%, Luhya 14%, Luo 13%, Kalenjin 12%, Kamba 11%, Kisii 6%, Meru 6%, other African 15%, non-African (Asian, European, and Arab) 1%.

Languages: English (official), Kiswahili (official), numerous indigenous languages.

Religions: Protestant 45%, Roman Catholic 33%, indigenous beliefs 10%, Muslim 10%, other 2%.

U.S. Populations: Census 2000: 17,336 (ancestry). Unofficially, 25,000. Kenya has the largest number of African students in the United States, approximately 5,000 per year. They settle in Texas, Atlanta, Boston, the Washington, D.C., metro area, New Jersey, Missouri, and Minnesota.

Customs: At Christmas it is common for people who still live in traditional mud-walled houses with thatched roofs to give the outer walls a new coat of clay whitewash and paint them with holiday greetings, such as "Merry Christmas" and "Happy New Year."

During Kikuyu coming-of-age ceremonies for boys and girls, their parents wear brass earrings to symbolize that their child has been reborn as a child of the community.

Harambee is their concept of self-help. Communities, without government aid, come together to build secondary schools and raise money to aid students who desire to go overseas for higher education.

Liberians

Background: Capital: Monrovia, Liberia; Population: 3,390,635; Ethnicities: indigenous African tribes 95% (including Kpelle, Bassa, Gio, Kru, Grebo, Mano, Krahn, Gola, Gbandi, Loma, Kissi, Vai, Dei, Bella, Mandingo, and Mende), Americo-Liberians 2.5% (descendants of immigrants from the United States who had been slaves), Congo People 2.5% (descendants of immigrants from the Caribbean who had been slaves).

Languages: English 20% (official), some 20 ethnic group languages, of which a few can be written and are used in correspondence.

Religions: Indigenous beliefs 40%, Christian 40%, Muslim 20%.

U.S. Populations: Census 2000: 25,575 (ancestry). Unofficially, there are hundreds of thousands in pockets in Rhode Island, Minnesota, Pennsylvania, and Massachusetts. One official disputes that number, claiming it is under 20,000.

Customs: When shaking hands, they grasp the middle finger of the other person in the right hand between the thumb and third finger, then bring it up quickly with an audible snap. Freed slaves considered this greeting a sign of their liberation, as it was not uncommon for slave owners to indicate bondage by breaking slaves' fingers.

Goat soup is their "national soup," eaten with *foo-foo*, a special bread made from cassava and served with palm butter. Tables are set with inverted plates and glasses, with napkins placed atop the plates. They eat with their fingers. Ginger beer and palm wine are the preferred beverages.

Libyans

Background: Capital: Tripoli, Libya; Population: 5,631,585; Ethnicities: Berber and Arab 97%, Greeks, Maltese, Italians, Egyptians, Pakistanis, Turks, Indians, Tunisians.

Languages: Arabic, Italian, English.

Religions: Sunni Muslim 97%.

U.S. Populations: No official figures.

Customs: Most meals are eaten with kasrah, a flat round nonyeast bread. They eat the kasrah with dips, for example, babaghanouj (roasted eggplant mixed with lemon, tahina, and salt). Dates are a favorite snack. They roast the pits and grind them to make date coffee.

Berber wedding feasts may last up to seven days, during which the bride and groom are not seen together. The wedding celebration finishes up with at least three days of dancing.

The Italians introduced polenta (porridge of cornmeal) into the Berber diet. In the Sahara, the staple foods are dates, butter, the meat of camels, goats, and sheep, and camel and goat milk.

Malians

Background: Capital: Bamako, Mali; Population: 11,956,788; Ethnicities: Mande 50% (Bambara, Malinke, Soninke), Peul 17%, Voltaic 12%, Songhai 6%, Tuareg and Moor 10%, other 5%.

Languages: French (official), Bambara 80%, numerous African languages.

Religions: Muslim 90%, indigenous beliefs 9%, Christian 1%.

U.S. Populations: No official numbers living here permanently. There are a few hundred students and some in New York working in imports and exports. Students come to Louisiana for agricultural training since the climate and crops (cotton, rice, sugarcane) are similar to Mali's. Musicians travel back and forth for music festivals.

Customs: Among the Mande, *griots*, skilled musician/singers, serve as oral historians conserving and transmitting traditions to succeeding generations. As an accompaniment to singing, married women play the *gita*, a calabash/gourd turned upside down on a piece of heavy cloth and struck with two wooden chopsticklike batons.

Among the Bambara (3.5 million), when a non-Muslim old woman or man dies, they celebrate the person's life, especially if she or he has left behind children and grandchildren.

Moroccans

Background: Capital: Rabat, Morocco; Population: 32,209,101; Ethnicities: Arab-Berber 99.1%, other 0.7%, Jewish 0.2%.

Languages: Arabic (official), Berber dialects, French often the language of business, government, and diplomacy.

Religions: Muslim 98.7%, Christian 1.1%, Jewish 0.2%.

U.S. Populations: 2000 Census: 38,923 (ancestry).

Customs: They usually eat out of a common dish set on a knee-high round table using no utensils. Food is taken with the fingers or scooped up with bread. The main course is generally *tajin*, a stew of meat and vegetables in a rich broth. Diners eat from the portion of the bowl closest to them.

Circumcision takes place generally between the ages of three and four, performed at home by a barber.

Each autumn, Berber families barter wares and arrange and hold marriages for daughters between the ages of ten and eighteen. After a five-day celebration, the girls may divorce their selected husbands in order to marry someone else.

Nigerians

Background: Capital: Abuja, Nigeria; Population: 137,253,133; Ethnicities: Nigeria is the most populous African country, with more than 250 ethnic groups. The most populous and politically influential are the Hausa and Fulani 29%, Yoruba 21%, Igbo (Ibo) 18%, Ijaw 10%, Kanuri 4%, Ibibia 3.5%, Tiv 2.5%.

Languages: English (official), Hausa, Yoruba, Igbo (Ibo), Fulani.

Religions: Muslim 50%, Christian 40%, indigenous beliefs 10%.

U.S. Populations: Census 2000: 165,481 (ancestry), 134,940 (birthplace). According to the Nigerian Peoples Forum, one million live in the United States, of which 500,000 are U.S. citizens. Many are Igbo. The largest Nigerian settlements are in New York and Washington, D.C. They are mostly Christians. Large Yoruba groups live in New York City, Newark, Washington, D.C., Atlanta, and Los Angeles.

Customs: Hausa men wear large flowing gowns with elaborate embroidery around the neck and sometimes down the front. They also wear colorful embroidered caps. Hausa women wear a wrapper made of colorful cloth with matching blouse, head tie, and shawl. Some of these cloths are extremely expensive and women collect them, together with gold jewelry, as a sign of status and wealth.

For the Igbo of South Nigeria, circumcision takes place eight days after the birth of a boy and is performed by a skilled woman in the village. They bury the umbilical cord at the foot of the most fruitful oil palm tree.

Rwandans

Background: Capital: Kigali, Rwanda; Population: 7,954,013; Ethnicities: Hutu 84%, Tutsi 15%, Twa (Pygmoid) 1%.

Languages: Kinyarwanda (official), universal Bantu vernacular, French (official), English (official), Kiswahili (Swahili) used in commercial centers.

Religions: Roman Catholic 56%, Protestant 26%, Adventist 11.1%, Muslim 4.6%, indigenous beliefs 0.1%, none 1.7%. Note: After their 1994 massacre, increasing numbers are turning to Islam and the new unofficial number of Muslims is over one million, or 15% of the population.

U.S. Populations: Unofficially, there are approximately 2,000 in the United States and 5,000 in Canada, particularly in Toronto and Montreal.

Customs: Among the Hutu, the groom's family legitimizes a marriage through the transfer of bridewealth to the bride's family. Payment is in cattle, goats, and home-brewed beer. They purify the bride by smearing her with herbs and milk, which is a highly valued food source, as is cattle meat.

Bridewealth among the Tutsi (some of whom live in Burundi) usually consists of a cow and other gifts. Milk, butter, and meat are the most highly valued foods. Tutsi women used to wear numerous copper bracelets and anklets that were often so heavy that the elite were unable to do much work. Not being able to perform agricultural tasks distinguished them from ordinary women who worked in the fields.

Somalis

Background: Capital: Mogadishu, Somalia; Population: 8,304,601; Ethnicities: Somali 85%, Bantu and other non-Somali 15% (including Arabs, 30,000).

Languages: Somali (official), Arabic, Italian, English.

Religions: Sunni Muslim.

U.S. Populations: Census 2000: 36,313 (ancestry). Between 100,000 and 150,000 migrated to Canada and the United States in 1980 and their numbers increased after their 1991 civil war, with 80,000 in Toronto. The Twin Cities of Minnesota have the largest numbers, from 10,000 to 30,000, drawn by available work at the Heartland Foods turkey factory, where no work experience or English-language skills are needed for assembly-line jobs. Other settlements include Columbus, Ohio; Seattle, Washington; Atlanta, Georgia; and San Diego, California, where approximately 4,500 refugees live in a two-mile stretch called "Little Mogadishu." (See also: Traffic Violations, p. 151.)

Customs: According to historian Charles Geshekter, genealogy is to Somalis what an address is to Americans, as exemplified by their asking "Whom are you from?" instead of "Where are you from?"

Spaghetti, *baasto*, a common food, reflects an Italian colonial influence. They use *canjeero* (bread) to scoop up their staples of rice, meat, and vegetables. At traditional meals they employ *canjeero*, utensils, and fingers. To clean one's plate indicates that the diner desires more food.

Newborn care includes warm water baths, sesame oil massages, and passive stretching of the baby's limbs. They burn myrrh incense twice a day to protect the baby from ordinary smells of the world, believing that they can make the baby sick.

Sudanese

Background: Capital: Khartoum, Sudan; Population: 39,148,162; Ethnicities: Black 52%, Arab 39%, Beja 6%, foreigners 2%, other 1%.

Languages: Arabic (official), Nubian, Ta Bedawie, diverse dialects of Nilotic, Nilo-Hamitic, Sudanic languages, English.

Religions: Sunni Muslim 70% (in the north), indigenous beliefs 25%, Christian 5% (mostly in the south and Khartoum).

U.S. Populations: Census 2000: 14,936 (ancestry). A small community lives in San Diego.

Customs: In the south's largest black tribe, Dinka adult males decorate initiated boys' heads with deep gashes that form lifetime scars. The Dinka have more than 400 words to refer to cattle alone—differentiating their movement, diseases, varieties of color, and form.

Among the Nuer, the next largest tribe in the south, scarification consists of six horizontal lines across the entire forehead as a sign of achieving manhood.

At the end of the Ramadan fast, children wear new clothing. (See also: Ramadan, p. 115.) They give special sweets and red candy dolls holding paper fans to children. Hand-operated Ferris wheels and merry-go-rounds appear in public squares for the children's enjoyment. They visit friends and relatives during this holiday.

Tunisians

Background: Capital: Tunis, Tunisia; Population: 9,974,722; Ethnicities: Arabic 98%, European 1%, Jewish and other 1%.

Languages: Arabic (official and one of the languages of commerce), French (commerce).

Religions: Muslim 98%, Christian 1%, Jewish and other 1%.

U.S. Populations: No figures available.

Customs: *Shisha* is another name for the *hookah* (water pipe), which is popular in coffeehouses. Using sweet tobacco, smokers pass the pipe around and each takes a few puffs. This activity stimulates conversation.

Each spring thousands of Jews of North African descent attend a two-day festival on the Tunisian island of Djerba, which considers itself the oldest Jewish community in the diaspora. The festival is called El Ghriba (the marvelous one), referring to the cornerstone of the synagogue, which, according to legend, came from King Solomon's Temple. They claim it has healing powers.

Ugandans

Background: Capital: Kampala, Uganda; Population: 26,404,543; Ethnicities: Baganda 17%, Ankole 8%, Basoga 8%, Iteso 8%, Bakiga 7%, Langi 6%, Rwandan 6%, Bagisu 5%, Acholi 4%, Lugbara 4%, Batoro 3%, Bunyoro 3%, Alur 2%, Bagwere 2%, Bakonjo 2%, Jopodhola 2%, Karamojong 2%, Rundi 2%, non-African (European, Asian, Arab) 1%, other 8%.

Languages: English (official national language), Ganda, also called Luganda (the most widely used of the Niger-Congo languages, it is preferred for native-language publications in the capital and may be taught in school), other Niger-Congo languages, Nilo-Saharan languages, Swahili, Arabic.

Religions: Roman Catholic 33%, Protestant 33%, Muslim 16%, indigenous beliefs 18%.

U.S. Populations: No official numbers, but probably less than 1,000, mostly graduate students here on a temporary basis studying at schools in the Washington, D.C., area and Boston, working toward Ph.D.s and MBAs.

Customs: The staple food is *matooke*, a plantain of which there are over 40 varieties. They steam or boil them and commonly serve them with groundnut sauce or meat soups. Two or three meals of plantains per day are customary.

Mubende, 90 miles west of Kampala, is the site of Boma Hill. Here the Nakaima tree has been attracting worshipers for more than 500 years. It is dedicated to the first ruler of the Muchwezi people, who no longer exist. People still believe his spirit dwells here, and they flock to this site to consult him regarding sickness, wealth, and politics. People make offerings in exchange for luck and blessings.

Asians

For ease of comprehending relationships, I am using a tripartite view of Asian cultures. Asia includes China, Japan, and Korea, while Southeast Asia refers in part to those countries that became prominent during the Vietnam War: Vietnam, Laos, Cambodia, and Thailand. South Asia includes Afghanistan, Bangladesh, India, and Pakistan. Technically, however, all these places are part of Asia.

Bhutanese

Background: Capital: Thimphu, Bhutan; Population: 2,185,569; Ethnicities: Bhote 50%, ethnic Nepalese 35% (includes Lhotsampas, one of several Nepalese ethnic groups), indigenous or migrant tribes 15%.

Languages: Dzongkha (official); the Bhotes speak various Tibetan dialects; the Nepalese speak various Nepalese dialects.

Religions: Lamaistic Buddist 75%, Indian- and Nepalese-influenced Hinduism 25%.

U.S. Populations: Unofficially, there are less than 500, with the majority in New York and some in California.

Customs: Archery is their national sport, and the most popular form is *Cho-dha*. Villages or regions compete. Dancers and cheerleaders provide praise as well as jeers, but good humor prevails. Opposing teams mock each other when shots are missed. In preparation for competitions, participants give up the comforts of home and wives. To enhance their chances, archers consult astrological charts before competitions and carry items that have been blessed by deities.

Traditional food features chilies, and their most popular dish is *ema datse*, made with large green hot chilies in a cheese sauce. They eat a slightly nutty red variety of rice and several Tibetan-style dishes of dumplings and noodles.

Chinese

Background: Capital: Beijing, China; Population: 1,298,847,624; Ethnicities: Han Chinese 91.9%, Zhuang, Uygur, Hui, Yi, Tibetan, Miao, Manchu, Mongol, Buyi, Korean, and other nationalities 8.1%.

Languages: Standard Chinese or Mandarin (Putonghua, based on the Beijing dialect), Yue (Cantonese), Wu (Shanghainese), Minbei (Fuzhou), Minnan (Kokkien-Taiwanese), Xiang, Gan, Hakka dialects.

Religions: Daoist (Taoist), Buddhist, Muslim 1% to 2%, Christian 3% to 4%. *Note:* officially atheist (as of 2002).

U.S. Populations: Census 2000: 1,518,652 (birthplace). Total: 2.4 million including ancestry. These are a combination of Chinese from Hong Kong, Taiwan, mainland China, and Singapore. The first Chinese came to work on the railroads, then later as part of the gold rush. Half of the total Chinese population lives on the West Coast, including Hawaii. New York City has the largest urban numbers, 352,079, followed by San Francisco with 151,151. The total Chinese population in Los Angeles County is 245,000.

Customs: On a person's birthday, they eat noodles, symbolic of long life, which is considered a blessing. On New Year's Eve, children must be obedient and stay awake to welcome the new year. Some believe that the longer they stay awake, the longer their parents will live and the children themselves will also live long lives.

In Harbin, where the temperature reaches 40 below and stays freezing half the year, they hold annual snow and ice sculpture displays going back to the Manchu era. The ice sculptures are mostly architectural, such as the Great Wall, while the snow sculptures are realistic or abstract forms. Since 1985, teams have come from all over the world to compete.

Japanese

Background: Capital: Tokyo, Japan; Population: 127,333,002; Ethnicities: Japanese 99%, others 1% (Korean 511,262, Chinese 244,241, Brazilian 182,232, Filipino 89,851, other 237,914) (as of 2002).

Languages: Japanese.

Religions: Shinto and Buddhist 84%, other 16% (including Christian 0.7%).

U.S. Populations: Census 2000: 347,539 (birthplace). Total: 787,724. Most are located in California, Hawaii, and New York. Honolulu has 85,954.

Customs (see also: Physical Contact, p. 13; Gender Expectations, p. 141): *Setsubun* is a bean-throwing ritual on February 3, when they throw beans at shrines to drive away evil spirits.

At weddings, the bride and groom exchange cups of sake three times, taking three sips at a time.

In public baths, they wash with soap and completely rinse before entering the pool. They may use a towel to cover themselves or place on their heads while soaking.

Maneki Neko is a ceramic replica of a cat with an uplifted paw that signifies prosperity. Tied to a nineteenth-century legend, cats with upright left paws are placed inside businesses facing the front door, beckoning customers. Cats with upright right paws are used in homes for good fortune.

Koreans, North

Background: Capital: Pyongyang, North Korea; Population: 22,697,553; Ethnicities: racially homogeneous; there is a small Chinese community and a few ethnic Japanese.

Languages: Korean.

Religions: Traditionally Buddhist and Confucianist, some Christian and syncretic Chondogyo (Religion of the Heavenly Way). Note: Autonomous religious activities are now almost nonexistent; government-sponsored religious groups exist to provide the illusion of religious freedom.

U.S. Populations: North and South Koreans are counted together, but the majority are from the South. Los Angeles County has the largest numbers with 200,000, primarily from South Korea.

Customs: See: South Korean Customs (below).

Koreans, South

Background: Capital: Seoul, South Korea; Population: 48,289,037; Ethnicities: homogeneous (except for about 20,000 Chinese).

Languages: Korean; English widely taught in junior and senior high schools.

Religions: Christian 49%, Buddhist 47%, Confucianist 3%, Shamanist, Chondogyo (Religion of the Heavenly Way), and other 1%.

U.S. Populations: Census 2000: 864,125 (birthplace). See North Korean U.S. Populations (above). From South Korea, the majority of Korean churches are Presbyterian or other Protestant denominations.

Customs: Brides decorate their faces with large dots made of fabric and placed on the cheekbones.

A happily married man makes two small wooden ducks as a good-luck charm for the groom because ducks mate for life.

On Shampoo Day (*Yoodoonal*), the fifteenth day of the sixth month, villagers bathe and shampoo in streams and waterfalls to protect themselves from heat or fever during the coming year. They offer macaroni and wheat flour cakes, melons, and other fruits at family shrines.

On New Year's Day, they play *yoot*, a competitive team game of throwing sticks in the air. They yell and cheer. Food and alcohol add to the festivities.

Taiwanese

Background: Capital: Taipei, Taiwan; Population: 22,749,838; Ethnicities: Taiwanese (including Hakka) 84%, mainland Chinese 14%, aborigine 2%.

Languages: Mandarin Chinese (official), Taiwanese (Min), Hakka dialects.

Religions: Mixture of Buddhist, Confucian, and Taoist 93%, Christian 4.5%, other 2.5%.

U.S. Populations: Census 2000: 326,215 (birthplace). One to 1.5 million. Most live in California—in Monterey Park, Alhambra, Rosemead, Hacienda Heights, and San Gabriel, plus a large settlement in Flushing, New York.

Customs: On Double Fifth Day (5th month, 5th day), they make sweet rice dumplings to throw into the water to honor an honest official who threw himself into the river in ancient times. To celebrate, they have dragon boat races and burn incense to ward off wall lizards, toads, centipedes, spiders, and snakes.

The Yami, an aboriginal people, have a Flying Fish Ceremony during March (per the solar calendar). They kill a chicken or piglet on the beach and collect its blood. Each male wets his finger with the blood, smears it on a pebble around the tide line, and prays for a year of good health and good harvest. Then they begin nighttime fishing by torchlight.

South Asians

Afghans

Background: Capital: Kabul, Afghanistan; Population: 28,513,677; Ethnicities: Pashtun 44%, Tajik 25%, Hazara 10%, minor ethnic groups (Aimaks, Turkmen, Baloch, and others) 13%, Uzbek 8%. Note: The people call themselves Afghans, not Afghanis, which is a unit of their money.

Languages: Pashtu (official) (also called Pushto) 35%, Afghan Persian (Dari) 50%, Turkic languages (primarily Uzbek and Turkmen) 11%, 30 minor languages (primarily Balochi and Pashai) 4%, much bilingualism.

Religions: Sunni Muslim 84%, Shi'a Muslim 15%, other 1%.

U.S. Populations: Census 2000: 45,195 (birthplace). By 1985 more than 40,000 lived in the United States and Canada. The largest concentrations are in Fremont, California, New York, Washington, D.C., and Toronto.

Customs: Vehicular art is popular, especially on large trucks (also found in India and Pakistan). They may paint eyes over the radiator grille, paste mirrors to the doors, hammer brass and chrome to the exterior, and paint murals on the sides with depictions of wild animals or jet aircraft or ocean liners. Sometimes they depict the mosque in Medina or verses from the *Qur'an*.

At weddings, the groom's family gives money to the bride's family for the costs of raising her, outfitting her for the wedding, and the wedding feast, and a stipulated amount in cash or kind promised in case she is divorced without cause.

Bangladeshis

Background: Capital: Dhaka, Bangladesh; Population: 141,340,476; Ethnicities: Bengali 98%, tribal groups and non-Bengali Muslims 2%.

Languages: Bangla (official, also known as Bengali), English.

Religions: Muslim 83%, Hindu 16%, other 1%.

U.S. Populations: Census 2000: 95,294 (birthplace). Unofficially, 100,000 to 150,000 in 1995. More than 50,000 live in New York City.

Customs: The Bengalis engage in verbal dueling, with performances held at festivals and wedding ceremonies. Performers can be professional poets as well as villagers, including women.

Ricksha art is popular. The three-wheeled pedicabs have elaborately decorated upholstered seats, armrests, and footrests. Cabs are covered with colorful images of movie posters, tigers, astronauts, and movie stars.

Rice is their staple, served at lunch and dinner, and sometimes breakfast. In most middle-class homes, cooking is done by wives and mothers. In urban areas, families sit together to eat, but in villages and less well-to-do families, the women serve the food and eat after everyone has finished.

Indians

Background: Capital: New Delhi, India; Population: 1,065,070,607; Ethnicities: Indo-Aryan 72%, Dravidian 25%, Mongoloid and others 3%.

Languages: English is the most important for national, political, and commercial communication; Hindi is the national language and primary tongue of 30%; the other fourteen official languages are Bengali, Telugu, Marathi, Tamil, Urdu, Gujarati, Malayalam, Kannada, Oriya, Punjabi, Assamese, Kashmiri, Sindhi, and Sanskrit. Hindustani is a variant of Hindi/Urdu spoken throughout the north, but it is not an official language.

Religions: Hindu 81.3%, Muslim 12%, Christian 2.3%, Sikh 1.9%, other groups including Buddhist, Jain, and Parsi 2.5%.

U.S. Populations: Census 2000: 1,022,552 (birthplace). Unofficially: 1,678,765 total, with most in California (314,819), New York (251,724), New Jersey (169,180), Texas (129,365), and Illinois (124,723). Punjabis, people from a region in Northern India and the east side of Pakistan, include Pakistanis, Indians, Hindus, Sikhs, Christians, and Muslims. They were the first group of people from South Asia to start migrating to the United States more than a century ago. Primarily working on the Western Pacific Railways in northern California, they moved on to farming, currently playing a vital role in the agricultural industry of the Central and Sacramento valleys. Today many are in the hotel industry, so a popular saying circulates: "Hotel, Motel, Patel" (a common Gujurati name).

There are 40,000 Jains, with 35% in New Jersey and New York and 15% in California.

Customs: In July/August the Snake Festival occurs, showing respect for snakes, *nagas*. *Nagas* can bring wealth and rain, but if displeased can cause famine or the collapse of one's home.

Punjabis wear the *salwar kameez*, a long tunic top over baggy drawstring trousers. Men wear turbans and women a length of cloth draped over the head and shoulders.

During the Sacred Thread Festival (July/August, full moon), Brahmans and Chetri men change the sacred thread wound around the neck and underarm. Buddhist and Hindu men, women, and children of all castes have a thread tied around their wrists and keep it there for three months until the priest blesses and removes it.

Myanmar/Burmese

Background: Capital: Rangoon, Myanmar; Population: 42,720,196; Ethnicities: Burman 68%, Shan 9%, Karen 7%, Rakhine 4%, Chinese 3%, Indian 2%, Mon 2%, other 5%. The name of the country is still controversial. Burma is its former name, but it has not been approved by the legislature in Burma, nor has it been adopted by the United States. Myanmar is the name that most natives here prefer.

Languages: Burmese; minority ethnic groups have their own languages.

Religions: Buddhist 89%, Christian 4% (Baptist 3%, Roman Catholic 1%), Muslim 4%, animist 1%, other 2%.

U.S. Populations: Unofficial in the 1990s: 7,000. Southern California has one of the largest centers residing outside of Myanmar. Other settlements are in Chicago, New York, Washington, D.C., and Maryland.

Customs: During the Buddhist holiday *Thingyan*, held in the last month of the lunar calendar (January/February), people throw clear or fragrant water on each other to cool one another and wash away the grime of the previous year. They wash the hair of their elders and cut their nails, clean pagodas and icons, and set free cattle and fish to grant life.

During the Kason Festival (full moon in May), women carry pots of scented water on their heads in procession to the banyan trees. Devotees chant prayers for happiness and peace of mankind, then throw the blessed water on the root of the sacred Bo tree.

Nepalese

Background: Capital: Kathmandu, Nepal; Population: 27,070,666; Ethnicities: Brahman, Chetri, Newar, Gurung, Magar, Tamang, Rai, Limbu, Sherpa, Tharu.

Languages: Nepali (official; spoken by 90% of the population), about a dozen other languages and about 30 major dialects. Many in government and business also speak English.

Religions: Hinduism 86.2%, Buddhism 7.8%, Islam 3.8%, other 2.2%.

U.S. Populations: In 1995, 3,000 in the United States were permanent residents or naturalized citizens. Forty-five percent are of the Chetri subgroup. The Newar community is from Kathmandu. They are scattered in residence and are mostly first-generation. They live in New York City, Washington, D.C., California, and Florida.

Customs (see also: What Makes a Meal?, p. 76): Limbu mothers name babies immediately after birth. Sherpa women give birth in their parents' home. The father's family comes to name the baby several days after the birth. His party brings a prayer flag and some beer. Naming is done by a kinsman or friend of the father who smears butter on the baby's head and mouth and ties a scarf to the central house post.

They say that to sneeze while eating means you've been touched by an untouchable. To nullify that, someone must immediately sprinkle the person with water before resuming the meal.

Pakistanis

Background: Capital: Islamabad, Pakistan; Population: 159,196,336; Ethnicities: Punjabi, Sindhi, Pashtun (Pathan), Baloch, Muhajir (immigrants from India at the time of partition and their descendants).

Languages: Punjabi 48%, Sindhi 12%, Siraiki (a Punjabi variant) 10%, Pashtu (also called Pushto) 8%, Urdu (official) 8%, Balochi 3%, Hindko 2%, Brahui 1%, English (official and lingua franca of Pakistani elite and most government ministries), Burushaski, and other 8%.

Religions: Muslim 97% (Sunni 77%, Shi'a 20%), Christian, Hindu, and other 3%.

U.S. Populations: Census 2000: 223,477 (birthplace). Census 1990 reports 100,000, but the unofficial count is 500,000 to 750,000. New York, California, and Illinois have the largest settlements. New York City has an annual Pakistan parade.

Customs: Up until the 1980s in the Peshawar region, they practiced *baithak*, an exorcism rite for women. Used mostly for mental illness, it was held in a cleaned room with new and freshly washed coverings. The patient bathed and donned clean clothing. A female singer sang songs to put the patient into a healing trance, causing her to sway back and forth. The swaying movement healed her. Afterward, they served food and gave gifts to the singer and all attendees.

When a child loses a tooth, she wraps it in cotton and at sunset throws it in the water to receive good luck. If there is no water, she throws it into a garden.

Sri Lankans

Background: Formerly Ceylon. Capital: Colombo, Sri Lanka; Population: 19,905,165; Ethnicities: Sinhalese 74%, Tamil 18%, Moor 7%, Burgher, Malay, and Vedda 1%.

Languages: Sinhala (official and national language) 75%, Tamil (national language) 18%, other 8%. English is commonly used in government and is spoken competently by about 10% of the population.

Religions: Buddhist 70%, Hindu 15%, Christian 8%, Muslim 7%.

U.S. Populations: 100,000, with 40,000 in California, 24,000 in New York, others in Washington, D.C., Chicago, and Florida. Of the total, 49% are Sinhalese (Buddhists) with eight temples, five in Los Angeles, and 50% Tamils, who are Hindu.

Customs: Firewalking over a bed of hot coals is practiced by both Hindus and Buddhists to fulfill vows and gain protection. Among the Tamil in the Batticaloa district, the number of firewalkers has dramatically increased since the occupation by Sri Lankan security forces in the mid-1980s.

Since 1775, in July/August, according to the lunar calendar, they honor the Sacred Tooth of Lord Buddha. The tooth is carried in a procession in a golden casket on top of an elephant.

When a child loses a tooth, she closes her eyes and says, "Squirrel, Squirrel, take this tooth and give me a new one." She throws it on the roof and runs into the house without looking.

Southeast Asians

Cambodians

Background: Capital: Phnom Penh, Cambodia; Population: 13,363,421; Ethnicities: Khmer 90%, Vietnamese 5%, Chinese 1%, other 4%.

Languages: Khmer (official) 95%, French, English.

Religions: Theravada Buddhist 95%, other 5%.

U.S. Populations: Census 2000: 136,978 (birthplace). This is a highly underreported population. Immigration began in 1979. Unofficially, by 2000, 200,000 lived in the United States. California has 70,000, primarily in Long Beach, others in Stockton. Also in Lowell, Massachusetts, Colorado, and Texas.

Customs: When children lose a tooth, they throw a lower tooth on the roof and place an upper tooth under the bed in hopes that the new tooth will grow in straight toward the old one.

At weddings, the Buddhist monk cuts a lock of hair from the bride and groom to symbolize the sharing of lives.

Souls from the underworld visit the living during *Prachum Ben*, a fifteen-day ritual. If these souls do not find proper offerings at shrines, they might cause ill to their families. As offerings, they make *ben*, balls of glutinous rice mixed with coconut and arranged on a platter, sitting on a pedestal and decorated with flowers, flags, and joss sticks.

East Timorese

Background: Capital: Diu, East Timor (Timor-Leste); Population: 1,019,252; Ethnicities: Austronesian (Malayo-Polynesian), Papuan, small Chinese minority. Officially gained independence from Indonesia in 2002.

Languages: Tetum (official), Portuguese (official), Indonesian, English. *Note:* There are about sixteen indigenous languages: Tetum, Galole, Mambae, and Kemak are spoken by significant numbers of people.

Religions: Roman Catholic 90%, Muslim 4%, Protestant 3%, Hindu 0.5%, Buddhist, animist.

U.S. Populations: No census figures available, and it is doubtful if many live here.

Customs: They create and wear batik fabrics, found throughout Indonesia. East Timor produces one of the best waxes for batik, consisting of a mixture of beeswax and paraffin. Typical patterns are colorful rainbow stripes.

Men use large flat cloths (*selimut*) as loincloth skirts, often worn with a belt. They wear another cloth of the same size tossed over the shoulder. Traditionally, no shirt is worn, but today villagers often wear a T-shirt or collared cotton shirt. Women wear sarongs, pulled up to the waist or underarms.

Filipinos

Background: Capital: Manila, Philippines; Population: 86,241,697; Ethnicities: Christian Malay 91.5%, Muslim Malay 4%, Chinese 1.5%, other 3%.

Languages: Two official—Filipino (based on Tagalog) and English; eight major dialects—Tagalog, Cebuano, Ilocan, Hiligaynon or Ilonggo, Bicol, Waray, Pampango, and Pangasinense.

Religion: Roman Catholic 83%; Protestant 9%, Muslim 5%, Buddhist and other 3%.

U.S. Populations: Census 2000: 1,369,070 (birthplace). Unofficially: 1,850,300. Filipinos are the second-largest Asian group in the United States after Chinese. California has the largest settlements, in Los Angeles and San Francisco: 918,678 in the two cities. Hawaii has 170,635, followed by Illinois, New York, Washington, Texas, Florida, Virginia, and Nevada.

Customs: In rural areas during wedding receptions, they release caged doves and pin peso bills to the newlyweds.

They enjoy *balut*, a fertilized egg from a native Filipino duck called *itik*. The egg contains a half-incubated duckling. They boil it for twenty minutes and it tastes crunchy and tart. A nutritious snack food, it is sold everywhere on the streets and seasoned with a pinch of rock salt.

Jeepneys, originally old American Jeeps left over after World War II, are the most common form of cheap public transportation. The Filipinos added two meters to the size and two long seats, and colorfully paint and decorate the vehicles, attaching ornaments to the hoods, tops, and fronts, sometimes using glittering ornaments and extra lights mounted everywhere.

Indonesians

(See also: Giving Praise, p. 185.)

Background: Capital: Jakarta, Indonesia; Population: 238,452,952; Ethnicities: Javanese 45%, Sundanese 14%, Madurese 7.5%, coastal Malays 7.5%, other 26%. The world's largest archipelago, it includes Java, Sumatra, Bali, and Borneo. It is the fourth most populous nation in the world.

Languages: Bahasa Indonesia (official, modified form of Malay), English, Dutch, local dialects, the most widely spoken of which is Javanese.

Religions: Muslim 88%, Protestant 5%, Roman Catholic 3%, Hindu 2%, Buddhist 1%, other 1%.

U.S. Populations: Census 2000: 72,552 (birthplace). Unofficial: 100,000. Los Angeles has the largest population, mostly from Java.

Customs: Shadow puppet plays, *wayang kulit*, are important forms of theater, usually depicting stories from the *Ramayana*. These events may last all night long, ending at sunrise.

In Bali, pubescent boys and girls undergo teeth-filing rituals. Front incisors and canines are filed down to decrease passion, lust, anger, greed, stupidity, intoxication, and jealousy and to increase physical and spiritual beauty.

Balinese cremation ceremonies include zigzagging en route to the cremation site to keep spirits from finding their way back home.

After Javanese wedding ceremonies, the newlyweds mix together a bowl of yellow rice and a bowl of white rice. The bride and groom eat from each other's plates.

Lao

Background: Capital: Vientiane, Laos; Population: 6,068,117; Ethnicities: Lao Loum (lowland) 68%, Lao Theung (upland) 22%, Lao Soung (highland) including the Hmong ("Meo") and the Yao (Mien) 9%, ethnic Vietnamese/Chinese 1%.

Languages: Lao (official), French, English, and various ethnic languages.

Religions: Buddhist 60%, animist and other 40% (including various Christian denominations 1.5%).

U.S. Populations: Census 2000: 204,284 (birthplace). Unofficial in 1990: 250,000, with 45% in California. Others in Wisconsin, Minnesota, Texas, Washington, and Massachusetts. St. Paul, Minnesota, has the largest urban concentration of Hmong, 24,000.

Customs: Upon the death of a parent, the son becomes a temporary monk. In the United States they continue the bride price tradition, where the groom's family gives money and valuables to the bride's family.

They celebrate New Year's in mid-April. During birth, death, marriage, and sickness, they tie strings around their wrists to bind the person's spirit to the body. They must be left on for three days.

The Hmong practice sewing arts. In Lao villages the women handstitched the family's garments for work and ceremonial occasions, and while living in Thai refugee camps in the 1970s, they created "story cloths" for export depicting village life as well as their escape from Laos.

Malaysians

Background: Capital: Kuala Lumpur, Malaysia; Population: 23,522,482; Ethnicities: Malay and other indigenous 58%, Chinese 24%, Indian 8%, others 10% (2000).

Languages: Bahasa Melayu (official), English, Chinese dialects (Cantonese, Mandarin, Hokkien, Hakka, Hainan, Foochow), Tamil, Telugu, Malayalam, Panjabi, Thai; in addition, in East Malaysia several indigenous languages are spoken, mainly Iban and Kadazan.

Religions: Muslim, Buddhist, Daoist, Hindu, Christian, Sikh; in addition, shamanism is practiced in East Malaysia.

U.S. Populations: Census 2000: 49,459 (birthplace). Unofficial: 60,000 to 70,000. The largest population centers are in New York and Los Angeles.

Customs: When children lose their teeth, they bury the old tooth because it is a part of the body and needs to be returned to the earth.

In Kelantan, they have been flying kites for 1,500 years. Called Wau, the kites are beautifully decorated with colored paper. The most popular form has a tail bent in the shape of a crescent moon.

Thaipusam is the Hindu Day of Atonement. Outside Kuala Lumpur at the Batu Caves they decorate the grounds with lights. Penitents carry *kavadis*, huge decorated canopies of wood and steel, up 272 steep steps to the sacred cave. As a sign of their faith, many penitents pierce their bodies with skewers.

Singaporeans

Background: Capital: Singapore, Singapore; Population: 4,608,595; Ethnicities: Chinese 76.7%, Malay 14%, Indian 7.9%, other 1.4%.

Languages: Chinese (official), Malay (official and national), Tamil (official), English (official).

Religions: Buddhist (Chinese), Muslim (Malays), Christian, Hindu, Sikh, Taoist, Confucianist.

U.S. Populations: Not possible to assess because they identify themselves as either Chinese or Malay.

Customs: Malay hosts place a dish of salt on the table. When the host offers some to a guest, the guest dips the forefinger of the right hand into the bowl and tastes it. This act cements friendship.

On Buddha's birthday, Vasak Day (April/May on the lunar calendar), the Chinese release caged birds to symbolize the setting free of captive souls.

Some Chinese call their children nicknames like "little dog" or "little pig" to fool the spirits into thinking their children are not beautiful, fat, or healthy. This protects the children from envy.

Thai

Background: Capital: Bangkok, Thailand; Population: 64,865,523; Ethnicities: Thai 75%, Chinese 14%, other 11%.

Languages: Thai, English (secondary language of the elite), ethnic and regional dialects.

Religions: Theravada Buddhist 95%, Muslim 3.8%, Christian 0.5%, Hindu 0.1%, other 0.6%.

U.S. Populations: Census 2000: 169,801 (birthplace). Los Angeles and San Francisco have the largest settlements, with 36,525 in the two cities. California has 200 Thai restaurants as of 2000. Other settlements are in New York, Texas, Florida, Illinois, and Virginia.

Customs: They excel in fruit and vegetable carving, creating flowers, birds, swans, rabbits, and other animals. This was originally a fourteenth-century palace art, but now people of all classes create it.

Sitting on the floor is the norm. Although monks sit cross-legged, ordinary people sit with their legs tucked underneath their bodies. They always step over thresholds and never on them.

In eastern Thailand, the Suay people have the Surin Elephant Roundup the third weekend in November. Elephants compete in games of soccer, dance to rock music, lift huge logs, and have a tug-of-war with a single elephant against two hundred Thai soldiers. They end with a parade of elephants and mahouts (elephant trainers) dressed in historic battle costume.

Vietnamese

Background: Capital: Hanoi, Vietnam; Population: 82,689,518; Ethnicities: Vietnamese 85% to 90%, Chinese, Hmong, Thai, Khmer, Cham, mountain groups. The Kinh are the ethnic majority and the Hoa are the Chinese Vietnamese. There are fifty officially recognized ethnic groups.

Languages: Vietnamese (official), English (increasingly favored as a second language), some French, Chinese, and Khmer, mountain-area languages (Mon-Khmer and Malayo-Polynesian). More than fifty languages are spoken.

Religions: Buddhist, Hoa Hao, Cao Dai, Christian (predominantly Roman Catholic, some Protestant), indigenous beliefs, Muslim.

U.S. Populations: Census 2000: 988,174 (birthplace). 2000, unofficial: 1,122,528. The largest settlements are in California with 477,032, especially Westminster, Santa Ana, Los Angeles, San Francisco, and San Jose. Texas has 134,961, with sizeable other settlements, in descending numbers, in Washington, Virginia, Massachusetts, Florida, Pennsylvania, Georgia, Louisiana, and New York.

Customs: Guests at mourners' homes say that they have come to "divide the sadness." Families place a tray with lit incense sticks and bowls of rice porridge outdoors. When funerals don't meet the deceased's expectations, they become angry. The porridge appeases their hunger and keeps them from entering the house.

Wandering Souls Day (July/August on the lunar calendar) is not only a Buddhist holiday but is celebrated by all who believe in God and good and evil. On this day the gates of hell are said to be opened at sunset and unclothed hungry souls fly out. Families prepare food for the souls: three kinds of meat, boiled chicken, roast pork, crabs, and five fruits. They also burn votive papers that look like money and clothes.

The Balkans

This section addresses the issue of "Whatever happened to Yugoslavia?" I exclude Greece, Bulgaria, and Romania because they offer less confusion and have had more stability—borderwise, that is.

Albanians

Background: Capital: Tirana, Albania; Population: 3,544,808; Ethnicities: Albanian 95%, Greek 3%, other 2% (Vlach, Gypsy, Serb, and Bulgarian).

Languages: Albanian (Tosk is the official dialect), Greek.

Religions: Muslim 70%, Albanian Orthodox 20%, Roman Catholic 10%.

U.S. Populations: Census 2000: 113,661 (ancestry). Early immigrants settled in New York and Boston. In 1990, 47,710 Americans claimed at least one Albanian ancestor. The total may range from 75,000 to 150,000. There are thirteen Albanian Orthodox parishes in the United States, including Worcester, Massachusetts; Farmington Hills, Michigan; and Trumbull, Connecticut. Albanian Americans founded their first society in Biddeford, Maine, in 1915. Other Albanian American Muslim societies are in Detroit; Waterbury, Connecticut; Chicago; Brooklyn; and the Bronx.

Customs (see also: Heads Up, Down, or Sideways?, p. 11): Both Muslims and Christians observe the New Year's January First custom requiring the first person who steps over the threshold to bring a log for the fire. They put a coin inside the New Year's cake, and the person who discovers it will prosper for the year. On New Year's Day, they exchange hankies.

Mothers use amulets to protect their babies from the evil eye. Christians use crosses and Muslims use triangular pieces of silver called *hajmali*. When someone compliments a Muslim baby, they touch it and say "*Mashalla*" to keep away the evil eye.

Bosnians and Herzegovinans

Background: Capital: Sarajevo, Bosnia-Herzegovina; Population: 4,007,608; Ethnicities: Serb 37.1%, Bosniak 48%, Croat 14.3%, other 0.6%. Note: *Bosniak* has replaced *Muslim* as an ethnic term, in part to avoid confusion with the religious term Muslim.

Languages: Croatian, Serbian, Bosnian.

Religions: Muslim 40%, Orthodox 31%, Roman Catholic 15%, Protestant 4%, other 10%.

U.S. Populations: Census 2000: 98,766 (birthplace). Chicago has 75% of the population; most of the rest is in Milwaukee and Gary, Indiana. Others are in Detroit, San Francisco, Cleveland, San Jose, and Santa Clara.

Customs: The Muslim population avoids using the left hand as much as possible. They shake hands firmly. Lunch is the primary meal of the day. They observe Friday noon prayers in the mosque and the ritual washing ceremony beforehand.

Godparents sponsor the cutting of a newborn's dried umbilical cord five to seven days after birth.

They celebrate their 1998 Independence from Yugoslavia on March 3.

Muslim women wear a *feredza*, a kind of dark, thick cloak made of wool that covers the body and head.

Croats

Background: Capital: Zagreb, Croatia; Population: 4,496,869; Ethnicities: Croat 89.6%; Serb 4.5%, Bosniak 0.5%, Hungarian 0.4%,

Slovene 0.3%, Czech 0.2%, Roma 0.2%, Albanian 0.1%, Montenegrin 0.1%, others 4.1%.

Languages: Croatian 96%, other 4% (including Italian, Hungarian, Czech, Slovak, and German).

Religions: Roman Catholic 87.8%, Orthodox 4.4%, Muslim 1.3%, Protestant 0.3%, others and unknown 6.2%.

U.S. Populations: Census 2000: 374,241 (ancestry). Unofficially, there are 1.5 to 2.5 million, the third-largest Slavic group after the Poles and the Czechs. Pennsylvania has nearly 250,000, the largest number in the country. Other concentrations are found in Chicago; New York City; Cleveland; Kansas City, Missouri; and Gary, Indiana. Those from Dalmatia came to California to pan for gold in 1849; others came for fishing in San Pedro, California, and Washington State.

Customs: The origin of men's neckties has its roots in Croatia. Some say that wearing a *kravata* (tie) was originally part of fashion. Others say that it was part of the Croatian soldier's uniform that was subsequently adopted by the French in the seventeenth century. The word *cravat* evolved from *Croat*.

Licitar are red cakes of honey dough/gingerbread, often heart-shaped, with colorful icing decorations. Sweethearts exchange them, especially on St. Valentine's Day.

During Christmas, choral groups sing *koleda*, secular songs that date back to Slavic pagan winter solstice festivities. During this time young people visited homes and sang songs in return for food and drink.

Macedonians

Background: Capital: Skopje, Macedonia; Population: 2,071,210; Ethnicities: Macedonian 66.6%, Albanian 22.7%, Turkish 4%, Roma 2.2%, Serb 2.1%, other 2.4%.

Languages: Macedonian 70%, Albanian 21%, Turkish 3%, Serbo-Croatian 3%, other 3%.

Religions: Macedonian Orthodox 67%, Muslim 30%, other 3%.

U.S. Populations: Census 2000: 38,051 (ancestry).

Customs: On Cheese Sunday, the Sunday before Lent, younger members visit elders begging for forgiveness and blessings. The women bring an orange or lemon cake as an offering. Before dining, they kneel and receive absolution from their elders. Later they play "gaping" by attaching a piece of pastry or boiled egg to the end of a long thread hanging from a stick. The person holding the stick swings it toward others sitting in a ring holding their mouths wide open. They try to catch the morsel with their mouths.

Coffee is important. Prospective husbands may judge a future wife based on the taste of her coffee.

Serbians and Montenegrans

Background: Capital: Belgrade, Serbia-Montenegro; Population: 10,825,900; Ethnicities: Serbian 62.6%, Albanian 16.5%, Montenegran 5%, Hungarian 3.3%, other 12%.

Languages: Serbian 95%, Albanian 5%. Montenegrans speak the *Jekavski* dialect of Serbo-Croatian. Serbs speak *Ekavski*.

Religions: Serbian Orthodox 65%, Muslim 19%, Roman Catholic 4%, Protestant 1%, other 11%.

U.S. Populations: Census 2000: 140,337 (ancestry). In the 1880s, Serbs came to California and settled in the Mother Lode country to mine. By the end of the nineteenth century, they were working in the Gulf Coast, in the steel mills of Pittsburgh and Youngstown, Pennsylvania, and other industrial jobs in Detroit; South Chicago; Gary, Indiana; and Milwaukee. After World War II, 50,000 Serbs came, while many Montenegrans immigrated to Serbian centers in Milwaukee, Chicago, Detroit, Cleveland, and New York. In the United States, they consider themselves Serbs. Today tens of thousands of Americans consider themselves of Montenegran descent.

Customs: *Krsna Slava* is a unique Serbian custom honoring the patron saint of each Orthodox family, observed in Serbia the same as in the United States. It pays tribute to the first family who embraced Christianity after paganism. Each family has its own patron saint, and they celebrate annually on that particular saint's day. The most popular saints are St. Michael, St. Nicholas, St. John, St. George, and St. Steven.

Families place the following items on an east-facing table where the icon of the family patron saint is located: burning candle, red wine, Slava's bread (*kolach*), and boiled sweet wheat. The priest cuts a cross into the round bread. When possible, the priest comes to the homes of his parishioners. Others celebrate in church.

Slovenians/Slovenes

Background: Capital: Ljubljana, Slovenia; Population: 2,011,473; Ethnicities: Slovene 88%, Croat 3%, Serb 2%, Bosniak 1%, Yugoslav 0.6%, Hungarian 0.4%, other 5%.

Languages: Slovenian 91%, Serbo-Croatian 6%, other 3%.

Religions: Roman Catholic 70.8% (Uniate Catholics 2%), Lutheran 1%, Muslim 1%, atheist 4.3%, other 22.9%.

U.S. Populations: Census 2000: 176,691 (ancestry). During the early 1900s, Cleveland became the largest settlement outside of Slovenia. Others lived in Milwaukee, Waukegan, and North Chicago. Many worked in the coal mines of Pennsylvania and West Virginia, where they were not allowed into the coal miners' union until 1905. Others settled in Fly Creek, New York, where they became farmers; some became coal miners in Colorado. Traunik, Michigan, was founded by Slovenian immigrants in 1923, where they continue their traditions at the Traunik Slovenian Club.

Customs: On the last Sunday before Shrove Tuesday, mythical Carnival figures, Kurents, chase away winter and welcome spring. Groups of men masquerading as Kurents dress in sheepskins with cowbells dangling from their belts or chains. They wear leather face masks with eyeholes outlined in red, and enormous red tongues hang down to their chests. Hair is made from horsetails, and they wear huge furry caps decorated with feathers, sticks or horns, and colored streamers. Girls offer hankies to them and housewives break clay pots at their feet for good luck and good health.

Independent Members of the Former USSR

With the 1991 final dissolution of the Union of Soviet Socialist Republics, we have had to learn new names and try to understand the distinctions between the countries, now allowed to pursue their freedom. Described customs refer to those taking place in the countries of origin. The republics fall into two categories: the Baltic States (Lithuania, Latvia, and Estonia) along the eastern coast of the Baltic Sea and those of Central Asia, many along the old Silk Road.

Armenians

Background: Capital: Yerevan, Armenia; Population: 2,991,360; Ethnicities: Armenian 93%, Azeri 1%, Russian 2%, other (mostly Yezidid Kurd) 4%.

Languages: Armenian 96%, Russian 2%, other 2%.

Religions: Armenian Apostolic 94%, other Christian 4%, Yezidid (Zoroastrian/animist) 2%. Armenians were the first Christians, even before the Romans.

U.S. Population: Census 2000: 385,488 (ancestry), 65,208 (birthplace). Over one million live in the United States, with half in California, especially Glendale, Fresno, Los Angeles, and San Francisco. Early migrants settled in California's Central Valley, becoming leaders in agriculture, especially in producing grapes, raisins, figs, and bulghur (cracked wheat). Subsequent large numbers arrived following a 1988 earthquake that damaged 40 percent of Armenia. Los Angeles County contains the largest Armenian population outside Armenia.

Customs: Last names end in "*ian*" or "*yan*," meaning "of" or "from."

Armenian Martyrs Day, April 24, commemorates the 1915 genocide perpetrated by the Turkish Ottoman Empire, when one and one-half million perished. To date, the Turkish government has neither acknowledged nor apologized for this tragedy.

When a baby's first tooth appears, they have a party where babies predict their own future based on the first object they select from an array placed before them: a book means a scholar; money means a rich person; a knife means a surgeon; a hammer means the building trades.

Azerbaijanis

Background: Capital: Baku, Azerbaijan; Population: 7,868,385; Ethnicities: Azeri 90%, Dagestani 3.2%, Russian 2.5%, Armenian 2%, other 2.3%.

Languages: Azerbaijani (Azeri) 89%, Russian 3%, Armenian 2%, other 6%. From 1910 to 1930, they used the Arabic alphabet; from 1929 to 1939, they used the Latin alphabet, and from 1939 to 1991 they used the Cyrillic alphabet. Since the collapse of the Soviet Union in 1991, they have used a modified Latin alphabet.

Religions: Muslim 93.4%, Russian Orthodox 2.5%, Armenian Orthodox 2.3%, other 1.8%.

U.S. Populations: Although there are no official figures, many of those identified as Iranians are of Azerbaijani descent. They are found in California, New York, and the Washington, D.C. area.

Customs (see also: Refusing Food, p. 72): Before leaving on an important journey, a person will toss a ladle of water after the traveler to symbolically cleanse the way and make the journey smooth. They may also say, "May your way be as clear as water" (*Yolun su kimi ayden olsun*).

Gift-giving is important. When visiting someone's home, they bring a box of candy or flowers, but they never give an even number of flowers. Even numbers are associated with death, presented at funerals or laid on the graves. (See also: Odd or Even?, p. 135.) When they travel they bring many souvenirs to friends at home.

Belarusians

Background: Capital: Minsk, Belarus; Population: 10,310,520; Ethnicities: Belarusian 81.2%; Russian 11.4%; Polish, Ukrainian, and other, 7.4%. Of all the republics of the former Soviet Union,

Belarus had the most nuclear contamination from the Chernobyl disaster of 1986.

Belarus means "White Russia," with various name explanations referring to either their fair complexions, their white folk costumes, or perhaps their maintenance of ethnic identities despite the Mongolian conquest.

Languages: Belarusian (official) 66%, but 90% also have fluency in Russian, reflecting earlier Soviet rule. In 1995, the people voted to give the more familiar Russian equal official status.

Religions: Eastern Orthodox 80%, other (including Roman Catholic, Protestant, Jewish, and Muslim) 20%.

U.S. Populations: Census 2000: 38,504 (birthplace). Between 600,000 to 650,000 arrived between the end of the nineteenth century and World War I. The biggest settlements are in the states between Illinois and New York, especially industrial cities and mining regions.

Customs: *Rushnik*, richly embroidered ornamental towels, are used for baptisms, funerals, weddings, calendar rituals, and religious head scarves.

They consider the following behaviors rude: sitting on one's coat at a concert or restaurant (it's acceptable at the movies); wearing an overcoat in a public building, concert hall, restaurant, or theater (it should be checked in the coatroom); standing with hands in pockets, raising one's voice, or laughing loudly in public buildings, subways, or on the street. Good-luck gestures include knocking on wood three times and sitting a minute before leaving home.

Estonians

Background: Capital: Tallinn, Estonia; Population: 1,341,664; Ethnicities: Estonian 65.3%, Russian 28.1%, Ukrainian 2.5%, Belarusian 1.5%, Finn 1%.

Languages: Estonian (official), Russian, Ukrainian, Finnish, other. The Estonian language belongs to the Balto-Finnic section of the Finno-Ugric language group because the two largest tribes to inhabit the country were the Finns and Hungarians.

Religions: Evangelical Lutheran, Russian Orthodox, Estonian Orthodox, Baptist Methodist, Seventh-Day Adventist, Roman Catholic, Pentecostal, Word of Life, Jewish.

U.S. Populations: Census 2000: 25,034 (ancestry). In the 1990 census more than 25,000 identified themselves as being of Estonian ancestry. The heaviest concentrations are in New Jersey, New York, and California.

Customs: Historically, St. George's Day, April 23, has been one of their most popular festivals, when they release the poisons of the earth through magic powers. Before or on St. George's Day, they cleaned their faces with snow or birch sap or took special baths to acquire a fair, clean, and unfreckled complexion and to avoid skin diseases.

Folk arts include the decorating of costumes, blankets, and household tools with ornamental patterns believed to possess magical powers. These symbols identify and protect objects. Symbolic designs in knitted mittens, wristbands, and neckbands are supposed to protect against the evil eye, and those in belts against snake bites.

Georgians

Background: Capital: Tbilisi, Georgia; Population: 4,693,892; Ethnicities: Georgian 70.1%, Armenian 8.1%, Russian 6.3%, Azeri 5.7%, Ossetian 3%, Abkhaz 1.8%, other 5%.

Languages: Georgian 71% (official), Russian 9%, Armenian 7%, Azeri 6%, other 7%. *Note:* Abkhaz is the official language in Abkhazia.

Religions: Georgian Orthodox 65%, Muslim 11%, Russian Orthodox 10%, Armenian Apostolic 8%, unknown 6%.

U.S. Populations: Unofficially, there are approximately 45,000, most located in New York, New Jersey, the Washington, D.C., area, and California. The first to arrive came in the 1890s as horsemen who toured for twenty years with the Buffalo Bill Cody and Wild West Congress of Ruff Riders. In 1900 the Ringling Brothers Circus signed on thirty more and called them the Cossacks. Today,

California and New York have large settlements. Large Georgian Jewish populations live in Queens, Philadelphia, Baltimore, and Washington, D.C.

Customs: When children lose their baby teeth, they throw the tooth high on a rooftop and ask a mouse to take it away and send back a strong, healthy one.

After a wedding, when crossing the threshold, the couple stomps on an upside-down ceramic plate. Whoever breaks it will rule the marriage. The number of broken pieces indicates how many troubles will face the couple. Those who wish to marry next place a piece of the plate under their pillow. One family member is deliberately not invited. This designated person arrives late and brings two doves to set free for good luck.

Kazakhs

Background: Capital: Astana, Kazakhstan; Population: 15,143,704; Ethnicities: Kazakh (Qazaq) 53.4%, Russian 30%, Ukrainian 3.7%, Uzbek 2.5%, German 2.4%, Uighur 1.4%, other 6.6%.

Languages: Kazakh (Qazaq, state language) 64.4%, Russian (official, used in everyday business, designated the "language of inter-ethnic communication") 95%.

Religions: Muslim 47%, Russian Orthodox 44%, Protestant 2%, other 7%.

U.S. Populations: Unofficially there are approximately 5,000 who live in New York, Houston, and the Washington, D.C., area. Most are professionals, especially scientists and biologists. Since Kazakhstan is rich in oil and gas, there is an exchange of personnel between the countries.

Customs: Ethnic Kazakhs arrange marriages through a process that may last up to forty days. Families exchange gifts of livestock. Fathers and other men of the family eat sheep's liver to bind promises and forge bonds.

Horsemanship is key; festivals feature horse races. The Kazakhs originated stirrups and chariots and perfected the art of shooting arrows while mounted on a galloping horse. They also eat horse meat and drink mare's milk, *koumyss*.

Brides wear conical hats, a celebratory symbol of Buddhist origin.

When a child loses a tooth, she asks a mouse to bring her a new one.

Kyrgyz

Background: Capital: Bishkek, Kyrgyzstan; Population: 5,081,429; Ethnicities: Kyrgyz 64.9%, Russian 12.5%, Uzbek 13.8%, Ukrainian 1%, Uygar 1%, other 5.7%.

Languages: Kyrgyz (official language); Russian (official language). The two languages are of equal status.

Religions: Muslim 75%, Russian Orthodox 20%, other 5%.

U.S. Populations: No official figures.

Customs: *Kymyz*, made from fresh mare's milk, is their favorite drink. They invented the *yurt (yurta)*, an easily assembled and reassembled dome-shaped house of felt made from boiled camel's wool. Originally used by their nomads, today they are popular with shepherds who spend summers in the high pastures. Layout rules exist: the door faces south or southeast; they keep blankets, trunks, and chests with family valuables opposite the door; the fire and a low table are in the center; household utensils and children's items are on the right-hand side; saddles and bridles are stored on the left-hand side.

Latvians

Background: Capital: Riga, Latvia; Population: 2,306,306; Ethnicities: Latvian 57.7%, Russian 29.6%, Belarusian 4.1%, Ukrainian 2.7%, Polish 2.5%, Lithuanian 1.4%.

Languages: Latvian (official), Lithuanian, Russian.

Religions: Lutheran, Roman Catholic, Russian Orthodox.

U.S. Populations: Census 2000: 87,564 (ancestry). In the 1960s the largest cities with settlements were New York, Chicago, Boston, Milwaukee, Cleveland, Minneapolis, and St. Paul. By 2004, younger Latvian Americans had settled in Kalamazoo, Michigan; Washington, D.C.; and Seattle, Washington, where the University of Washington offers the only Latvian language program in the United States.

Customs: Because of the extreme cold, knitted wool mittens are critical. Girls learn to knit as early as four, and in the past they would knit one hundred pairs before they were married for use during the ceremony and for gifts.

St. John's Day, held on the summer solstice, is their greatest festival, celebrating the longest day and shortest night. It features singing, dancing, cheese-making, and beer-brewing.

For more than 125 years, the Latvian Song Festival, held in Riga every four years, has attracted thousands of singers and tens of thousands of attendees. The song festival symbolizes the re-awakening and unity of the nation.

Lithuanians

Background: Capital: Vilnius, Lithuania; Population: 3,607,899; Ethnicities: Lithuanian 80.6%, Russian 8.7%, Polish 7%, Belarusian 1.6%.

Languages: Lithuanian (official), Polish, Russian.

Religions: Roman Catholic (mainly), Lutheran, Russian Orthodox, Protestant, Evangelical Christian Baptist, Muslim, Jewish.

U.S. Populations: Census 2000: 659,992 (ancestry). According to the 1990 census, 526,089 claimed Lithuanian ancestry. Most live in the Northeast, Midwest, and California.

Customs: A child's birthday or name day is special. The celebrant sits in a decorated chair and is lifted up three times to signify that all will go well for him/her next year and the child will be healthy and happy. If the ceremony is not observed, children will become sickly. They do the same for adults, providing there are enough sturdy men to hoist the chair.

St. Casimir's Day, March 4, celebrates the only Lithuanian saint. The most popular part is the Kaziukas Fair, featuring handcrafts such as the Vilniaus verbos, various dried flowers and grasses braided together, tied to short sticks, and taken to church on Palm Sunday.

Moldovans

Background: Capital: Chisinau, Moldova; Population: 4,446,455; Ethnicities: Moldovan/Romanian 64.5%, Ukrainian 13.8%, Russian 13%, Jewish 1.5%, Bulgarian 2%, Gagauz and other 5.2%.

Languages: Moldovan (official, virtually the same as the Romanian language), Russian (official), Gagauz (a Turkish dialect).

Religions: Eastern Orthodox 98%, Jewish 1.5%, Baptist and other 0.5%.

U.S. Populations: No official numbers.

Customs: A unique food specialty is *tochitura Moldoveneasca*, pan-fried pork in a spicy pepper sauce served with soft cornmeal mush (*mamaliga*) and topped with a fried egg.

On Christmas Eve they have a food exchange called *lichie*. It can consist of flat cakes, biscuits, or small loaves of yeast-free wheat bread.

Modern wedding ceremonies include the old custom of bowing to the parents. After the wedding ceremony, the bride holds someone's child to foretell having many children of her own. Before the couple enters their home for the first time, others shower them with grain for prosperity.

Russians

Background: Capital: Moscow, Russia; Population: 143,782,338; the largest ethnic groups are Russian 81.5%, Tatar 3.8%, and Ukrainian 3%.

Languages: Russian.

Religions: Russian Orthodox and Muslim.

U.S. Populations: Census 2000: 2,652,214 (ancestry), 340,177 (birthplace). According to the 2000 census, 2,980,776 live here. Approximately 85% to 90% are Russian-speaking Jews. The rest are minority Christian groups. The largest populations are in New York, California, Florida, Pennsylvania, New Jersey, and Illinois. Pentecostal Christians have settled in the Seattle region. Old Believers reside in Oregon, Alaska, and Canada. (See: Sign of the Cross, p. 14.)

Customs: Grandfather Frost arrives on New Year's Eve and delivers gifts to children. For a fee he can be hired to drop by one's home. Over 1,000 Grandfather Frosts are in service on New Year's Eve. Snegourka, the Snow Maiden, often accompanies him.

One week before Lent they celebrate Pancake Week, feasting on hot, golden sun-shaped pancakes (*blini*). Gorging on these delicacies is a good way to use up butter and eggs before Lenten diet restrictions. Pancakes symbolize the heat and color of the sun and the advent of Spring. Russians top them with honey or caviar.

Tajiks

Background: Capital: Dushanbe, Tajikistan; Population: 7,011,556; Ethnicities: Tajik 64%, Uzbek 25%, Russian 3.5%, other 6.6%.

Languages: Tajik (official), Russian widely used in government and business.

Religions: Sunni Muslim 85%, Shi'a Muslim 5%, other 10%.

U.S. Populations: No official numbers, but 51,000 Jews came from the Bukhara area, which included Tajikistan, Uzbekistan, Kyrghystan, and Kazakhstan, and settled in New York City.

Customs: Because of the cold climate, their clothes are cotton-padded. Women prefer bright-colored long skirts. Outdoors they wear kerchiefs: white for older women, yellow or green for younger women. Men wear caps lined with black lambskin, shaped like barrels, with the lower brim turned up.

On the Pamir Plateau, brides and grooms hold separate three-day banquets, each side dining with its own families. On the fifth day, the groom goes to his bride's home. An imam (*priest*) asks each for their opinions. If they both agree, they drink a cup of water and eat some meat, cake, and salt. Only then are they allowed to be together. A big celebration follows.

Turkmens

Background: Capital: Ashgabat, Turkmenistan; Population: 4,863,169; Ethnicities: Turkmen 77%, Uzbek 9.2%, Russian 6.7%, Kazakh 2%, other 5.1%.

Languages: Turkmen 72%, Russian 12%, Uzbek 9%, other 7%.

Religions: Muslim 89%, Eastern Orthodox 9%, unknown 2%.

U.S. Populations: No official numbers, 1,000 to 2,000 maximum. Most in New York and California, but there is no community.

Customs: They are known for their carpets that serve as both floor covering and decorative wall hangings that insulate the yurt. Although woven by the Turkmen, they are called Bukhara rugs because they are mostly sold there. Primarily red, they have geometric designs, and each tribe has its own pattern. Carpet designs are so key that their national flag includes five traditional designs.

Women wear heavy, ankle-length silk dresses of wine red and maroon over spangled, striped trousers. They tie their hair back tucked under a scarf. Young unmarried women wear two braids covered by a small scarf. Married women wear one braid and cover their heads with a big kerchief.

Ukrainians

Background: Capital: Kiev, Ukraine; Population: 47,732,079; Ethnicities: Ukrainian 77.8%, Russian 17.3%, Belarusian 0.6%, Crimean Tatar 0.5%, Bulgarian 0.4%, Hungarian 0.3%, Romanian 0.3%, Polish 0.3%, Jewish 0.2%.

Languages: Ukrainian, Russian, Romanian, Polish, Hungarian.

Religions: Ukrainian Orthodox—Moscow Patriarchate, Ukrainian Orthodox—Kiev Patriarchate, Ukrainina Autocephalous Orthodox, Ukrainian Catholic, Protestant, Jewish.

U.S. Populations: Census 2000: 892,922 (ancestry), 275,153 (birthplace). Most in the United States are Ukrainian Catholics. The first wave of 500,000 ended in 1914. From 1920 until 1939, 15,000 more arrived. After World War II, 85,000 displaced persons arrived. Current cities with large populations include Chicago; Philadelphia; Los Angeles; New York City; Cleveland, Ohio; Jersey City, New Jersey; and Glastonbury and Bridgeport, Connecticut.

Customs: *Pysanky* are whole raw eggs that have been decorated with a wax-resistant method for drawing on eggs. They are made as gifts for family and respected outsiders. They represent life, and the designs are chosen to match the character of the person to whom the *pysank* is to be given. Made during the last week of Lent, they are taken to church on Easter Sunday to be blessed, then given away, after which they are proudly displayed in homes.

Vesillia refers to family and community wedding rituals such as the making of wedding wreaths for the bridal couple to wear during the marriage ceremony. Made of myrtle and periwinkle, they symbolize eternal love, purity, and fertility.

Uzbeks

Background: Capital: Tashkent, Uzbekistan; Population: 26,410,416; Ethnicities: Uzbek 80%, Russian 5.5%, Tajik 5%, Kazakh 3%, Karakalpak 2.5%.

Languages: Uzbek 74.3%, Russian 14.2%, Tajik 4.4%, other 7.1%.

Religions: Muslim 88% (mostly Sunnis), Eastern Orthodox 9%, other 3%.

U.S. Populations: No official numbers, but there are approximately 85,000 living in New York, New Jersey, Pennsylvania, Washington, D.C., Virginia, and California. A large settlement of Bukharan Jews live in New York.

Customs (see also: Cracked Eggs, p. 71.): When they serve tea they first pour it into the cup, then pour it back into the pot. They do this three times before they finally let the tea remain in the cup. The first time they say the Uzbeki word for "dirt," the second time, "oil," the third time, "tea" ("*Loi, Moi, Choi*"). When guests have had enough tea, they turn their cups upside-down on the table. This occurs more frequently in rural areas.

Nearly all men wear the *dopy*, a black, four-sided skullcap embroidered in white. Married women wear one or two braids while single women wear more braids.

Middle Easterners

With the exception of Israel, Middle Eastern countries are primarily Islamic, with two main divisions. The Shi'ites are a smaller branch of Islam than the Sunni. Shi'ite Muslims share the fundamental beliefs of the Sunni but differ as to who should be the successor to Mohammad. The Shi'ites also give clerics more power over interpretation of the law, educational institutions, and the administration of justice.

Iranians

Background: Capital: Tehran, Iran; Population: 69,018,924; Ethnicities: Persian 51%, Azeri 24%, Gilaki and Mazandarani 8%, Kurd 7%, Arab 3%, Lur 2%, Baloch 2%, Turkmen 2%, other 1%. *Note*: Although they use the Arabic alphabet and practice Islam, Iranians are not Arabs. They are ethnically diverse, categorized as Indo-Euopean and Aryan, meaning "Man from Iran." Persia was the country's original name, changed to Iran in 1934.

Languages: Farsi (Persian and Persian dialects) 58%, Turkic and Turkic dialects 26%, Kurdish 9%, Luri 2%, Balochi 1%, Arabic 1%, Turkish 1%, other 2%.

Religions: Shi'a Muslim 89%, Sunni Muslim 10%, Zoroastrian, Jewish, Christian, and Baha'i 1%.

U.S. Populations: Census 2000: 283,226 (birthplace). Over one million, with approximately 400,000 in California. Los Angeles has the largest concentration of Iranians outside of Iran. Those who came during the Shah's reign and after were mostly secular, highly educated professionals and entrepreneurs. In 1980, 40 percent had Bachelor of Arts degrees or higher.

Customs: Nouruz is their New Year's holiday, observed by all religions. Taking place at the Vernal Equinox, March 20/21, it lasts for thirteen days. (See also: Jumping over Fires, p. 117.) A unique feature is a *haft seen* table set with seven traditional items beginning with the equivalent letter of "s" in Farsi. Items include sweet wheat pudding, dried crushed tart berries (sumac), vinegar, an apple, a gold coin, flowers, and garlic. Other items on the table are a bowl of goldfish and the *Qur'an*. On the thirteenth day, they attend picnics and everyone sprinkles sprouted wheat and lentils they have grown for this ritual into a body of water.

Iraqis

(See also: The *Qur'an*, p. 153.)

Background: Capital: Baghdad, Iraq; Population: 25,374,691; Ethnicities: Arab 75% to 80%, Kurdish 15% to 20%, Turkoman, Assyrian, or other 5%.

Languages: Arabic, Kurdish (official in Kurdish regions), Assyrian, Armenian.

Religions: Muslim 97% (Shi'a 60% to 65%, Sunni 32% to 37%), Christian or other 3%.

U.S. Populations: Census 2000: 37,714 (ancestry), 89,892 (birthplace). Chaldeans (part of the Roman Catholic Church) came to the Detroit area in 1910 to work in the auto industry. Large numbers reside in San Diego and Phoenix, Arizona. The largest concentration of Muslims, 300,000, lives in the Detroit/Dearborn, Michigan, area. Others live in Chicago and Los Angeles. In Southern California there are 40,000, a mixture of Catholics, Kurds, and Muslims.

Customs: Each year during Muharam, the first month of the Islamic calendar, Shi'ites celebrate the martyrdom of Imam Al Hussein in the seventh century A.D. On this occasion they make food and invite others to eat to remind everyone that Imam Al Hussein and his fellows died hungry and thirsty after being deprived of water and food rather than surrender to the dictator Yazid Ben Mawya.

Since Saddam Hussein has been deposed, hundreds of thousands of residents now descend upon the shrine city of Karbala on this holy day. Lamentations, chest beatings, and whipping chains over their shoulders are attendant rituals.

Israelis

Background: Capital: Jerusalem, Israel; Population: 6,199,008; Ethnicities: Jewish 80.1% (European/American–born 32.1%, Israel-born 20.8%, Africa-born 14.6%, Asia-born 12.6%), non-Jewish 19.9% (mostly Arabic, 1.2 million).

Languages: Hebrew (official), Arabic used officially for Arab minority, English most commonly used foreign language.

Religions: Jewish 80.1%, Muslim 14.6% (mostly Sunni Muslim), Christian 2.1%, other 3.2%.

U.S. Populations: Census 2000: 15,723,355 (Israeli ancestry), 109,719 (birthplace). There are 30,000 in metropolitan New York City, 15,000 in Los Angeles.

Customs: For their Sabbath meal, religiously observant Jews eat *cholent*, a one-pot meal of meat, beans or lentils, carrots, and potatoes placed in a slow oven on Friday to cook overnight. Slow cooking avoids breaking the Sabbath taboo of turning the stove off and on. It is ready to serve at the midday meal on Saturday.

Sometime in May they celebrate *Lag B'Omer*, when the Orthodox gather at the Tomb of Simon for three-year-old boys to have their first haircut by a rabbi. After the rabbi's first snip, other relatives follow suit. A celebration follows.

Jordanians

Background: Capital: Amman, Jordan; Population: 5,611,202; Ethnicities: Arab 98%, Circassian 1%, Armenian 1%.

Languages: Arabic (official), English widely understood among upper and middle classes.

Religions: Sunni Muslim 92%, Christian 6% (majority Greek Orthodox, but some Greek and Roman Catholics, Syrian Orthodox, Coptic Orthodox, Armenian Orthodox, and Protestant denominations), other 2% (several small Shi'a Muslim and Druze populations).

U.S. Populations: Census 2000: 39,734 (ancestry), 46,794 (birthplace). Detroit has a large concentration.

Customs: Chartered ships carry pilgrims to Mecca each Id Al-Kabir (February/March). In several days of ritual, the pilgrims circle the Kaaba (square building in the center) and run between the two holy hills at the site. They travel to Mount Arafat, twelve miles east of Mecca, to sacrifice sheep and camels. Upon their return to Jordan, friends and family greet them and decorate their homes with palm-leaf arches, carpets, and colored lights. Feasting and thanksgiving follow.

Their coffee is thick, syrupy, and strong. If they want no more coffee, they tip the cup back and forth a few times. Generally, they refuse offers of food two times before accepting it.

Kuwaitis

Background: Capital: Kuwait, Kuwait; Population: 2,257,549; Ethnicities: Kuwaiti 45%, other Arab 35%, South Asian 9%, Iranian 4%, other 7%.

Languages: Arabic (official), English widely spoken.

Religions: Muslim 85% (Sunni 70%, Shi'a 30%), Christian, Hindu, Parsi, and other 15%.

U.S. Populations: No census figures available.

Customs: When a newcomer enters a room, everyone rises to greet him. Each person introduces himself as the new arrival proceeds around the room, usually beginning on the right. Often the host will perfume his guests with a sandalwood incense that is wafted into the hair and sprinkle rosewater onto the hands.

They serve tea in small glass cups and saucers. The cup is filled to the rim with the spoon resting on the saucer. If hosts want the guests to depart quickly, they put the spoon in the glass. They serve coffee as a sign that the evening is over and guests should leave. The proper host will try to dissuade his guests from leaving, but polite guests decline.

Lebanese

Background: Capital: Beirut, Lebanon; Population: 3,777,218; Ethnicities: Arab 95%, Armenian 4%, other 1%.

Languages: Arabic (official), French, English, Armenian.

Religions: Muslim 59% (including Shi'a, Sunni, Druze, Isma'ilite, Alawite, and Nusayri), Christian 39% (including Armenian Orthodox, Roman Catholic, Armenian Catholic, Maronite Catholic, Melkite Catholic, Syrian Catholic, Protestant), other 1.3%. *Note:* Seventeen religious sects are recognized.

U.S. Populations: Census 2000: 440,279 (ancestry), 105,910 (birthplace). Four hundred thousand Christians are spread evenly in the Northeast, Midwest, and South. Muslims, mostly Shi'a, are concentrated in Detroit, Pittsburgh, and Michigan City, Indiana. Lebanese in Detroit number 32,942 (as of 1990).

Customs: Men commonly carry worry beads. Although they resemble rosary beads, they have no religious significance. Instead, they relieve stress. While walking on the streets, sitting, or visiting, the men finger and twist the beads, traditionally made of amber.

Upon greeting, family members kiss three times, alternating cheeks. They call their maternal uncle *Khalo* and their paternal uncle *Yammo*, terms also used as a sign of respect for older male friends of the family.

When children lose their baby teeth, they throw the tooth into the sea or a field and ask the sun to exchange it for a gold one.

Saudis

Background: Capital: Riyadh, Saudi Arabia; Population: 25,795,938; Ethnicities: Arab 90%, Afro-Asian 10%.

Languages: Arabic.

Religions: Muslim 100%.

U.S. Populations: Census 2000: 205,822 (ancestry). The majority of current Saudi-born residents are students.

Customs: On a daily basis they follow strict Muslim rules of praying five times a day. Men may even take a twenty-minute break and leave a business meeting with Westerners to do this. More than two million people converge annually at the Grand Mosque in the holy city of Mecca for the *hajj*, a Muslim pilgrimage.

Crossing legs is disrespectful, as is showing the soles of the shoes. They say yes by swiveling their heads side to side. To indicate no, they tip their heads backwards and click their tongues. They consider the American A-OK gesture to be a curse.

Syrians

Background: Capital: Damascus, Syria; Population: 18,016,874; *Note:* In addition, 40,000 people live in the Israeli-occupied Golan Heights—20,000 Arabs (18,000 Druze and 2,000 Alawites) and about 20,000 Israeli settlers. Ethnicities: Arab 90.3%, Kurds, Armenians, and other 9.7%.

Languages: Arabic (official), Kurdish, Armenian, Aramaic, Circassian widely understood, French, English somewhat understood.

Religions: Sunni Muslim 74%, Alawite, Druze, and other Muslim sects 16%, Christian (various sects) 10%, Jewish (tiny communities in Damascus, Al Qamishli, and Aleppo).

U.S. Populations: Census 2000: 142,897 (ancestry). By the mid-1990s, two million lived here, with the largest settlements in New York, Detroit, Chicago, Dallas, Houston, Seattle, San Francisco, and Los Angeles. The Druze settled in Detroit. The earliest Muslim immigrants went to Detroit and Ross, North Dakota, and also to Cedar Rapids, Iowa, where they established the first U.S. mosque.

Customs: September 14 is Holy Cross Day, commemorating the discovery of the cross on which Christ died. Villagers enter their vineyards, cut the grapes, dip them into a mixture of alkali and olive oil, and spread them out to dry. At the end of the day, the families gather in the vineyards for feasting and dancing. Bedouins and the neighborhood poor help themselves to the grapes left on the vines.

At the wedding ceremony, the bride and groom try to step on each other's toes. The one to succeed will be the boss of the marriage.

Turks

Background: Capital: Ankara, Turkey; Population: 68,893,918; Ethnicities: Turkish 80%, Kurdish 20%.

Languages: Turkish (official), Kurdish, Arabic, Armenian, Greek.

Religions: Muslim 99.8% (mostly Sunni), other 0.2% (mostly Christians and Jews).

U.S. Populations: Census 2000: 117,575 (ancestry), 78,378 (birthplace). The largest numbers live in New York City, Washington, D.C., and Detroit.

Customs: Since the Ottoman Empire, Turkish coffee has played an important role, involved in betrothal, gender customs, and hospitality. Turkish coffeehouses are social institutions. The coffee is spiced with cardamom and served with no spoon. After drinking it, they turn the cup upside down on the saucer and allow it to cool. Fortunes can be told based on the shape of the coffee grounds.

Ritual circumcision for boys, *summet*, generally occurs between ages seven and eight. The day before, the boys wear white clothes with red ribbons and parade through town in decorated cars. Afterward, they lie on large richly decorated beds. Guests bring gifts and compliment the boys on their bravery.

United Arab Emirates

Background: Capital: Abu Dhabi; Population: 2,523,915; Ethnicities: Emirati 19%, other Arab and Iranian 23%, South Asian 50%, other expatriates (includes Westerners and East Asians) 8%. *Note:* Less than 20% are UAE citizens (as of 1982). Abu Dhabi is the seat of the federal government and a major oil industry center. Dubai is the main commercial center, with trading and business ties extending beyond the Middle East to all corners of the world.

Languages: Arabic (official), Farsi, English, Hindi, Urdu.

Religions: Muslim 96% (Shi'a 16%), Christian, Hindu, other 4%.

U.S. Populations: No figures available.

Customs: Women wear a long-sleeved full-length dress called a *kandoura*, embroidered in gold, silver, or colored thread and covered entirely by a black *abayah*. They cover their hair with a *shayla*, a thin black veil. Men wear a white ankle-length loose-fitting garment called a *kandoura* or *dishdasha*, which is usually white cotton. Heavier, darker materials may be seen in winter. They cover their heads to protect them from the sand and the midday sun.

Arabic coffee is a sign of welcome, poured from a long spouted Arabian coffeepot into small cups with no handles. It is considered polite to accept one to three cups. They shake the cup gently from side to side to indicate they've had enough.

Yemenis

Background: Capital: Sanaa, Yemen; Population: 20,024,867; Ethnicities: mostly Arab, but also Afro-Arab, South Asians, Europeans.

Languages: Arabic.

Religions: Muslim including Sunni and Shi'a, small numbers of Jewish, Christian, and Hindu.

U.S. Populations: No census figures are available. An estimated 5,000 live in the United States, with the largest numbers in South Dearborn, Michigan, working in the auto industry; Oakland, California, working in farming; New York, working in steel factories; Queens and Brooklyn, New York, and Detroit had 1,624 in 1990.

Customs: Brides wear long woolen braids as an expression of strength and fertility. Wedding guests eat sweet fritters to symbolize the sweet life the newlyweds will have with each other. Before weddings, they have henna parties where young women stain each other's hands, feet, arms, toes, and calves with intricate patterns using the dried, crushed leaves of the henna bush, mixed with water and a little lime juice. Henna parties occur in Yemen and in the United States as well, and take place before weddings, before the birth of babies, or before a potential groom arrives for a visit from Yemen.

Bibliography

Abraham, Nabeel, and Andrew Shryock, eds. 2000. *Arab Detroit: From Margin to Mainstream*. Detroit, MI: Wayne State University Press.

Allen, James Paul, and Eugene James Turner. 1988. *We the People: Atlas of America's Ethnic Diversity*. New York: Macmillan.

al-Qaradawi, Yusuf. 1989. *The Lawful and the Prohibited in Islam*. Kuwait: Al Faisal Press, International Islamic Federation of Student Organizations.

Anderson, June. 1998. *Return to Tradition: The Revitalization of Turkish Village Carpets*. San Francisco: The California Academy of Sciences in association with the University of Washington Press, Seattle and London.

Arax, Mark. 1994. Cancer Case Ignites Culture Clash. *Los Angeles Times*, 21 November, A3, 19.

Armour, Monica, Paula Knudson, and Jeffrey Meeks, eds. 1983. *The Indochinese: New Americans*. Provo, UT: Brigham Young University Language Research Center.

Avoian, Samuel D. 1992. *Training College Football Coaches to Recruit across Cultures*. Master's thesis, Central Missouri State University. Warrensburg: University Microfilms, Inc.

Axtell, Roger E. 1990. *Do's and Taboos around the World*. New York: John Wiley & Sons.

———. 1990. *Do's and Taboos of Hosting International Visitors*. New York: John Wiley & Sons.

———. 1991. *Gestures: The Do's and Taboos of Body Language around the World*. New York: John Wiley & Sons.

Banner, Lois W. 1983. *American Beauty*. New York: Alfred A. Knopf.

Barrie-Anthony, Steven. 2004. "Home Is Where His Heart Was." *Los Angeles Times*, 8 June, E1, 10.

Beeler, Selby B. 1998. *Throw Your Tooth on the Roof: Traditions from Around the World*. Boston: Houghton Mifflin.

Belarusian Traditional Embroidered Towels—Rushniks. 2003. http://www .belarusguide.com/culture1/visual_arts/Belarusion_rushn.

Belkin, Lisa. 1992. Battling Contagions of Superstition and Ignorance. *New York Times*, 11 August, B1, 2 (L).

Berger, Leslie. 1994. Learning to Tell Custom from Abuse. *Los Angeles Times*, 24 August, A1, 16–17.

Bertelsen, Cynthia, and Kathleen G. Auerbach. 1987. *Nutrition & Breast-feeding: The Cultural Connection*. Franklin Park, IL: La Leche League International.

Beyene, Yewoubdar. 1992. Medical Disclosure and Refugees: Telling Bad News to Ethiopian Patients. *Western Journal of Medicine* 157 (September): 328–332.

Bloomberg News. 2004. An Auspicious Date for Park. *Los Angeles Times*, 23 November, C2.

Brodkin, Margaret, and Coleman Advocates for Children and Youth. 1993. *Every Kid Counts*. San Francisco: Harper Publishing.

Brody, Jane E. 1993. Keeping Your Wits in the Jungle of Cold Remedies. *New York Times*, 20 January, C14 (L).

Brown, Karen McCarthy. 1991. *Mama Lola: A Voodoo Priestess in Brooklyn*. Berkeley: University of California Press.

———. 1987. The Power to Heal: Reflections on Women, Religion, and Medicine. In *Shaping New Visions: Gender and Values in American Culture*, eds. Clarissa W. Atkinson, Constance H. Buchanan, and Margaret R. Miles. Ann Arbor, MI: Harvard Women's Studies in Religion Series; UMI Research Press.

Buchwald, Dedra, Sanjiv Panwala, and Thomas M. Hooton. 1992. Use of Traditional Health Practices by Southeast Asian Refugees in a Primary Care Clinic. *Western Journal of Medicine* 156 (May): 507–511.

Buonadonna, Paola. 1994. Acupuncture for Unhappy Homes. *The European* (London), 11–17 February, Elan: 26.

Carey, Benedict. 2001. When a "Good Death" Isn't for Everyone. *Los Angeles Times*, 20 August, S1, S6.

Carpenter, Mackenzie. 2003. Sikh's Turban a "No-No" at Clubs. *Post Gazette* (Pennsylvania), 30 July. http://www.sikhmediawatch.org/news/newsdetail.asp?newsid=524

Carr, Teresa. 1993. Patient, Treat Thyself: Home Remedies. *American Health* (June): 56–62.

Cereal? They'll Pass. 1994. *Los Angeles Times*, Westside Supplement, 31 March, 2.

Chassiakos, Linda Reid. 2003. What the Doctor Ordered and What the Patient Heard. *Los Angeles Times*, 25 August, F3.

Childs, Robert B., and Patricia B. Altman. 1982. *Vive Tu Recuerdo* (Monograph Series No. 17). Los Angeles: UCLA Museum of Cultural History.

Choi, Elizabeth C. 1986. Unique Aspects of Korean-American Mothers. *JOGN Nursing* 15 (September/October): 394–400.

Clinton's Flair Turns to Flubs. 1993. *Los Angeles Times*, 11 July, A10.

Coates, Mary-Margaret. 1990. *The Lactation Consultant's Topical Review and Bibliography of the Literature on Breastfeeding*. Franklin Park, IL: La Leche League International.

Cofer, Judith Ortiz. 1992. Don't Misread My Signals. *Glamour*, January, 136.

Cohen, David. 1991. *The Circle of Life: Rituals from the Human Family Album*. New York: Harper San Francisco.

Cohen, Henig, and Tristram Potter Coffin. 1991. *America Celebrates!* Detroit: Visible Ink.

Cooper, Robert, and Nanthapa. 1990. *Culture Shock: Thailand*. Portland, OR: Graphic Arts Center Publishing Company.

Craig, JoAnn. 1979. *Culture Shock! What Not to Do in Malaysia and Singapore, How and Why Not to Do It*. Singapore: Times Books International.

Culture and Tradition in the Arab Countries. http://www.habiba.org/culture.html

Dalton, Rex. 1994. Health or Tradition? *San Diego Union-Tribune*, 27 July, E1, 6.

Deinard, Amos S., and Timothy Dunnigan. 1987. Hmong Health Care—Reflections on a Six-Year Experience. *International Migration Review* 21 (Fall): 857–865.

de Lys, Claudia. 1948. *A Treasure of American Superstitions*. New York: Philosophical Library.

Diaz, Joseph O. Prewitt. 1991. The Factors That Affect the Educational Performance of Migrant Children. *Education* 111 (4): 483–486.

Donin, Rabbi Hayim Halevy. 1972. *To Be a Jew*. New York: Basic Books.

Dresser, Norine. 1994. *I Felt Like I Was from Another Planet*. Menlo Park, CA: Addison-Wesley, The Alternative Publishing Group.

————. 1996. The "M" Word: The 1994 Archer Taylor Memorial Lecture. *Western Folklore* 55 (Spring): 95–111.

————. 1991. Marriage Customs in Early California. *The Californians*, 9 (3): 46–49.

————. 1999. *Multicultural Celebrations: Today's Rules of Etiquette for Life's Special Occasions*. New York: Three Rivers Press.

————. 1993. *Our Own Stories*. New York: Longman Publishing Co.

Dunn, Ashley. 1994. Ancient Chinese Craft Shifts Building Designs in the U.S. *New York Times*, 22 September, A1, B4.

Eck, Diana. 2001. *A New Religious America: How a "Christian Country" Has Become the World's Most Religiously Diverse Nation*. New York: Harper San Francisco.

Ethnic Influences on Gift-Giving. 1993. *National KAGRO* (Korean American Grocers) *Journal* (Holiday): 44–45, 47.

Exploring Culture: Cultural Overviews and Insights. 2002. North Hollywood, CA: Erlich Transcultural Consultants.

Fentress, Debbie. 1993. Educating Special Citizens. *The Social Studies* 84 (5): 218–223.

Fishman, Claudia, Robin Evans, and Eloise Jenks. 1988. Warm Bodies, Cool Milk: Conflicts in Postpartum Food Choice for Indochinese Women in California. *Social Science Medicine* 26 (11): 1125–1132.

Gale Encyclopedia of Multicultural America: Primary Documents. 1999. Farmington Hills, MI: Vols. 1–3.

Gardenswartz, Lee, and Anita Rowe. 1990. The ABC's of Culture: A Blueprint for Cooperation in a Diverse Environment. *Working World*, 4 June, 28–30.

Garibova, Jala, and Betty Blair. 2000. International Relationships: Some Do's and Don'ts: Sociolinguistically Speaking: Part 8. *Azerbaijan International.* http://www.azeri.org/Azeri/az_learn/az_socio/articles/az_socio_84/84_socio.html

———. 1996. Names: History in a Nutshell: 20th Century Personal Naming Practices in Azerbaijan. *Azerbaijan International* 4.3 (Autumn): 54–59, 63, 82.

Gayne, Carrie. 2004. Bridging Cultural Gap Helps Heal Temple Fire. *The Palladium Times*: Online Edition. 11 February. http://www.pall-times.com/articles/2004/02/11/news/news1.txt

Getlin, Josh. 2004. Celebrating Immigration's New Face. *Los Angeles Times.* 17 April, A16.

Gilman, Stuart C., Judith Justice, Kaota Saepharn, and Gerald Charles. 1992. Use of Traditional and Modern Health Services by Laotian Refugees. *Western Journal of Medicine* 157 (September): 310–315.

Goode, Erica. 1993. The Cultures of Illness. *U.S. News & World Report*, 15 February, 74–76.

———. 2004. More and More Autism Cases, Yet Causes Are Much Debated. *New York Times*, 26 January. http://www.nytimes.com/2004/01/26/national/26AUTI.html

Greenhouse, Linda. 1993. Court, Citing Religious Freedom, Voids a Ban on Animal Sacrifice. *New York Times*, 12 June, 1, 9.

Griffin, Robert H., and Ann H. Shurgin, eds. 1998. *The Folklore of World Holidays*, 2nd ed. Detroit/London: Gale Publications.

Hall, Edward T. 1977. *Beyond Culture*. New York: Anchor Press.

Hamidullah, Muhammad. 1990. *Islam in a Nutshell*. Philadelphia, PA: Hyderabad House.

Hargraves, Orin. 2001. *Culture Shock! Morocco*. Portland, OR: Graphic Arts Center Publishing Company.

Hayes-Bautista, David E., and Roberto Chiprut. 1998. *Healing Latinos: Realidad y Fantasía*. Los Angeles: Center for the Study of Latino Health/UCLA and the Cedars-Sinai Health System.

Hilts, Philip J. 1993. Ban on H.I.V.-Infected Immigrants Is Retained in Final Capitol Test. *New York Times*, 25 May, A18 (L).

Himelstein, Shmuel. 1990. *The Jewish Primer*. New York: Facts on File.

Hofmeister, Sallie. 2004. Want a Corner Office? First Check the *Chi. Los Angeles Times*, 21 March, C1, 5.

Holley, David. 2004. Russians Flip Out Over Flapjacks as Lent Nears. *Los Angeles Times*, 22 February, A5.

Home Remedies. 1994. *Natural Health* (May/June): 54.

Hughes, Mary Kay. 1993. You Must Not Spank Your Children in America: Hmong Parenting Values, Corporal Punishment, and Early Childhood Intervention Programs. Paper presented at the Annual Northwest Anthropology Conference, Bellingham, WA.

Hur, Sonja Vegdahl, and Ben Seunghwa Hur. 2000. *Culture Shock! Korea*. Portland, OR: Graphic Arts Center Publishing Company.

Huy, Nguyen Van, and Laurel Kendall, eds. 2003. *Vietnam: Journeys of Body, Mind, and Spirit*. Berkeley, Los Angeles; London: University of California Press in association with the American Museum of Natural History, New York, and the Vietnam Museum of Ethnology, Hanoi.

I Tried to Ignore the Pain. 1994. *Newsweek*, 4 July, 36.

Ito, Robert. 2004. The Phantom Chaser. *Los Angeles*, April, 50–57.

Jacinto, Leela. 2001. Bias Fallout: How One Sikh-American Learned a Hard Lesson in Identity Politics. *ABCNEWS.com*, 30 October. www .abcnews.go.com/sections/us/DailyNews/sikh011030_hair.html

Jacobs, Bruce. 2000. *Race Manners: Navigating the Minefield Between Black and White Americans*. New York: Arcade Publishing.

Jacobs, Deborah L. 1990. Japanese-American Cultural Clash. *New York Times* (Sec. 3, Pt. 2) 9 September, 25.

Janis, Pam. 1998. Do Cells Remember? *USA Weekend.com*, 22–24 May. http://www.usaweekend.com/98_issues/980524/980524cells.html

Jenkins, Kathie. 1993. Want to Eat *Haute Cuisine*? Join the Club. *Los Angeles Times*, 29 May, Calendar 77.

Kamen, Mara. 1997. Georgian Wedding Traditions. http://www.frua.org/ waiting/wedding.html

Kamsler, Harold M. 1938. Hebrew Menstrual Taboos. *Journal of American Folkore* 51 (199): 76–82.

Kang, K. Connie. 1994. Forum to Focus on Spouse Abuse among Asians. *Los Angeles Times*, 27 August, B3, 8.

———. 2002. Indian Americans Will Honor a Hero. *Los Angeles Times*, 1 December, B4.

———. 1994. Rescue of Boy, 2, Played like Thriller. *Los Angeles Times*, 5 September, A1, 26.

———. 1994. "Smile, You're in America." *Los Angeles Times*, 22 October, A1, 20.

———. 1994. When East Meets West within the Same Person. *Los Angeles Times*, 22 October, A20, 21.

Kasbarian, Lucine. 1998. *Armenia: A Rugged Land, An Enduring People*. New York: Dillon Press.

Keiter, John J. 1990. *The Recruitment and Retention of Minority Trainees in University Affiliated Programs*. Madison, WI: Waisman Center University Affiliated Program.

Kelley, Ron, ed. 1993. *Irangeles: Iranians in Los Angeles*. Berkeley: University of California Press.

Kirkpatrick, Joanna. 2004. The Ricksha Arts of Bangladesh: Conveying the Dreams and Desires of the Man in the Street. http://www.persimmon-mag.com/winter2004/feature2.htm

Kolatch, Alfred J. 1981. *The Jewish Book of Why*. Middle Village, NY: Jonathan David Publishers, Inc.

Kraut, Alan M. Healers and Strangers. 1990. *Journal of the American Medical Association* 263 (13): 1807–1811.

———. 1994. *Silent Travelers: Germs, Genes, and the "Immigrant Menace."* New York: Basic Books.

Lagatree, Kirsten M. 1993. Fixing "Bad" *Feng Shui*. *Los Angeles Times*, 18 July, K6.

———. 1993. The Power of Place. *Los Angeles Times*, 18 July, K1, K6.

Langdon, Philip. 1991. Lucky Houses. *Atlantic*, November, 146.

Lebowitz, Larry. 2003. Santería Powder Making Mess at Money-Laundering Trial Site. *The Miami Herald. Herald.com*, 16 December. http://www.miami.com/mld/miamiherald/news/7503584.htm?lc

Lehrer, Warren, and Judith Sloan. 2003. *Crossing the Blvd: Strangers, Neighbors, and Aliens in a New America*. New York: W.W. Norton.

Leonelli, Laura. 1993. Adaptive Variations: Examples from the Hmong and Mien Communities of Sacramento. Unpublished paper delivered at the Southwestern Anthropology Association meeting, April, San Diego, CA.

Levenson, David, and Melvin Ember, eds. 1997. *Immigrant Cultures: Builders of a Nation*. New York: Macmillan Reference, Vols. 1, 2.

Liberia in Perspective: An Orientation Guide. 2003. Defense Language Institute Foreign Language Center. August. http://www.lingnet.org/areaStudies/perspectives/liberia/libera.pdf

Liberia: Menus & Recipes from Africa. http://www.sas.upenn.edu/African_Studies/Cookbook/Liberia.html

Linton, Kate Ruth. 2003. Knowing by Heart: Cellular Memory in Heart Transplants. *Montgomery College Student Journal of Science & Mathematics* 2, September. http://www.montgomerycollege.edu/Departments/StudentJournal/volume2/Kate.pdf

Lip, Evelyn. 1985. *Chinese Beliefs and Superstitions.* Singapore: Graham Brash.
——— . 1985. Feng Shui *for the Home.* Union City, CA: Heian International, Inc.

Mammad, Galib. 1994. When Words Fail: The Notion of "Refugee" and the Theory of Translation. *Azerbaijan International*, Spring, 2.1. http://www.azer.com/aiweb/categories/magazine/21_folder/21_articles/21_refuge_e.html

Manderson, Lenore, and Megan Mathews. 1981. Vietnamese Attitudes towards Maternal and Infant Health. *Medical Journal of Australia* 1 (24 January): 69–72.

Maple, Eric. 1971. *Superstition and the Superstitious.* New York: A. S. Barnes and Co.

Massara, Emily B. 1989. *¡Que Gordita! A Study of Weight among Women in a Puerto Rican Community.* New York: AMS Press.

McCarthy, Shawn. 2003. No Smiling! We're Canadian. *Globe and Mail*, 27 August. http://www.theglobeandmail.com/servlet/story/RTGAM.20030827

McKenzie, Joan L., and Joel J. Chrisman. 1977. Healing Herbs, Gods, and Magic: Folk Health Beliefs Among Filipino-Americans. *Nursing Outlook* 25 (5): 326–329.

Mena, Jennifer. 2004. Virgin of Guadalupe Is in Fashion, to Many of the Faithful's Dismay. *Los Angeles Times*, 12 December, B1, 8.

Mills, Margaret, Peter J. Claus, and Sarah Diamond, eds. 2003. *South Asian Folklore: An Encyclopedia.* New York, London: Routledge.

Moore-Howard, Patricia. 1992. *The Ethnic Lao—Who Are They?* Sacramento City Unified School District.
——— . 1982. *The Hmong—Yesterday and Today.* Lansing, MI: Collection of MSU Museum.

Morrison, Terri, Wayne A. Conaway, and George A. Borden. 1994. *Kiss, Bow, or Shake Hands.* Holbrook, MA: Adams Media Corporation.

Mull, J. Dennis. 1993. Cross-cultural Communication in the Physician's Office. *Western Journal of Medicine* 159 (November): 609–613.

Müller, Klaus E., and Ute Ritz-Müller. 2000. *Soul of Africa: Magical Rites and Traditions*. Cologne, Germany: Könemann Verlagsgesellschaft mbH.

Nakayama, Takeshi. 1994. Domestic Violence Revealed a Hidden Problem in Asian Pacific Communities. *Rafu Shimpo*, 10 August, A1.

Newman, Andy. 2004. On Brooklyn's Avenue of Babel, Cultures Entwine. *nytimes.com*, 26 March.

Newsletter of the Slovenian Genealogy Society. 1993. Volume 7, Issues 1–4: 1 January, 1 April, 1 July, 1 October. http://www.sloveniangenealogy .org/onlineresources/sgs1993.htm

Ni, Ching-Ching. 2004. China's Moms Get Postnatal Reprieve. *Los Angeles Times*, 21 May, A3.

Nine-Curt, Carmen Judith. 1984. *Non-Verbal Communication in Puerto Rico* 2nd ed. Cambridge, MA: Evaluation, Dissemination and Assessment Center for Bilingual Education.

Ovalle, David. 2003. Animal Sacrifice All in a Day's Work: Police Get Lessons in Religious Rituals. *Miami Herald*, 17 April. http://www.rickross .com/reference/santeria/santeria3.html

Pachter, Lee M. 1994. Culture and Clinical Care. *Journal of the American Medical Association* 271 (2 March): 690–694.

Paddock, Richard C. 2004. Solace in a Box of Rocks. *Los Angeles Times*, 25 March, A1, 10, 11.

Peng, Tan Huay. 1991. *Fun with Chinese Festivals*. Union City, CA: Heian International Publishing Co.

Peoples and Cultures of Cambodia, Laos, and Vietnam. 1981. Washington, DC: Refugee Service Center-Center for Applied Linguistics.

Perry, Tony. 2004. Marines Returning to Iraq Consult Old Standby. *Los Angeles Times*, 8 March, A5.

Potter, Carole. 1983. *Knock on Wood*. New York: Beaufort Books, Inc.

Punch, Jeff. 1996. Cellular Memory (the Transfer of Characteristics and Behaviors from the Donor to the Recipient Via the Cells of the Transplanted Organ). http://www.transweb.org/qa/asktw/answers/ answers9701/96030807

Radford, Edwin, and Mona A. Radford. 1975. *The Encyclopedia of Superstitions*. Rev. ed. Ed. Christina Hole. London: Hutchinson & Co.

Rafi, Mohamed M., Bret C. Vastano, et al. 2002. Novel Polyphenol Molecule Isolated from Licorice Root (Glycrrhiza Glabra) Induces Apoptosis, G2/M Cell Cycle Arrest, and Bcl-2 Phosphorylation in Tumor Cell Lines. *Journal of Agricultural and Food Chemistry* 50:4 (13 February): 677–684.

Randall-David, Elizabeth. 1989. *Strategies for Working with Culturally Diverse Communities and Clients*. Washington, DC: Association for the Care of Children's Health.

Reitman, Valerie. 1999. Learning to Grin and Bear It. *Los Angeles Times*, 22 February, A1, 9.

Rise in Hispanics and Asian-Americans Is Predicted. 2004. *New York Times*, 18 March. http://www.nytimes.com/2004/03/18/national/18CENS .html

Robinson, James H. 1988. Linguistic, Cultural and Educational Contexts of Korea. Paper presented at the Advanced Professional Development Symposium on the Educational System of Korea, in conjunction with the NAFSA Region VI Conference, October, Columbus, OH.

Rosen, Nir. 2004. Beware of Iraq's Whipping Boys. *Asia Times Online*, 19 February. http://www.atimes.com/atimes/Middle_East/FB19Ak02 .html

Rosenblatt, Gary. 1998. Journey to a Jewish Past: On a Small Island off Tunisia, Reveling in a Springtime Rite. *Jewish World Review*, 20 July. http://www.jewishworldreview.com/cols/rosenblatt1.html

Rossbach, Sarah. 1987. *Interior Design with* Feng Shui. New York: Arkana.

Rotella, Sebastian. Taking Iraqi Customs to Heart. *Los Angeles Times*, 27 March, A8.

Sachs, Susan. 2002. In Chinatown, the Thanksgiving Refrain Becomes I Do, I Do, I Do, I Do, I Do. *New York Times*, 29 November. http:// www.nytimes.com

Sackner, Marvin A., Kiumars Saketkhoo, and Adolph Januszkiewicz. October 1978. Effects of Drinking Hot Water, Cold Water, and Chicken Soup on Nasal Mucus Velocity and Nasal Airflow Resistance. *Chest* 74 (4): 408–410.

"*Salah*": *The Muslim Prayer*. 1989. Durban, Republic of South Africa: Islamic Propagation Centre International.

Samolsky, Susan, Karen Dunker, and Mary Therese Hynak-Hankinson. 1990. Feeding the Hispanic Hospital Patient: Cultural Considerations. *Journal of the American Dietetic Association* 90 (12): 1707–1709.

Sandoval, Mercedes S. 1993. Santería. *Journal of the Florida Medical Association* 70 (8): 620–628.

Saylor, Lucinda. 1985. *Indochinese Refugees: An Administrator's Handbook*. Columbia, SC: South Carolina State Department of Education.

Scalora, Sal. 1993. A Salute to the Spirits. *Américas* 45 (2): 26–33.

Schwartz, Hillel. 1986. *Never Satisfied: A Cultural History of Diets, Fantasies and Fat*. New York: The Free Press.

Sheehan, Susan. 2003. The Autism Fight. *The New Yorker*, 1 December, 76–87.

Sherman, Josepha. 1992. *A Sampler of Jewish American Folklore*. Little Rock, AR: August House Publishers, Inc.

Sherman, Spencer. 1988. The Hmong in America. *National Geographic* (October): 586–610.

Sidibé, Samuel. 2003. Mali: A Rich and Diverse Culture. *37th Annual Smithsonian Folklife Festival*. Washington, DC: Smithsonian Institution, 43–45.

Silverman, Carol. 1991. Strategies of Ethnic Adaptation: The Case of Gypsies in the United States. In *Creative Ethnicity*, eds. Stephen Stern and John Allan Cicala, 107–121. Logan, UT: Utah State University Press.

Sing, Bill. 1989. *Asian Pacific Americans*. Los Angeles: National Conference of Christians and Jews.

Smith, Jane I. 1999. *Islam in America*. New York: Columbia University Press.

Sosnoski, Daniel, ed. 1996. *Introduction to Japanese Culture*. Rutland, VT and Tokyo, Japan: Charles E. Tuttle Company.

Spector, Rachel E. 1991. *Cultural Diversity in Health and Illness*. 3rd ed. Norwalk, CT: Appleton & Lange.

Stepanchuk, Carol. 1994. *Red Eggs and Dragon Boats: Celebrating Chinese Festivals*. Berkeley, CA: Pacific View Press.

Suro, Federico. 1991. Shopping for Witches' Brew. *Américas*: 43 (5): 84–88.

Tawa, Renee. 1994. Multicultural Medicine. *Los Angeles Times*, 27 January (San Gabriel Valley), 10.

Taylor, Meredith Mann. 1985. *Transcultural Aspects of Breastfeeding—USA*. Franklin Park, IL: La Leche League International.

Te, Huynh Dinh. 1991. *The Indochinese and Their Cultures*. San Diego, CA: Multifunctional Resource Center Policy Studies Department, College of Education, San Diego State University.

Thiederman, Sondra. 1991. *Profiting in America's Multicultural Marketplace*. New York: Lexington Books.

Thomas, James D. 1985. Gypsies and American Medical Care. *Annals of Internal Medicine* 102 (June): 842–845.

Thompson, C. J. S. 1989. *The Hand of Destiny: Folklore and Superstition for Everyday Life*. New York: Bell Publishing Co.

Thompson, Sue Ellen, ed. 1997. *Holidays, Festivals, and Celebrations of the World Dictionary*, 2nd ed. Detroit, MI: Omnigraphics, Inc.

Toelken, Barre. 2003. *The Anguish of Snails: Native American Folklore in the West*. Logan, UT: Utah State University Press.

Tom, K. S. 1989. *Echoes from Old China*. Honolulu: Hawaii Chinese History Center.

Toor, Frances. 1967. *A Treasury of Mexican Folkways*. New York: Crown Publishing Co.

Trager, James. 1972. *The Food Book*. New York: Flare Books.

Trepp, Leo. 1980. *The Complete Book of Jewish Observance*. New York: Behrman House, Inc./Summit Books.

Tsuchida, John Nobuya. 1991. *A Guide on Asian & Pacific Islander American Students*. Washington, DC: National Education Association.

U.S. Court Backs Sikh Pupils' Right to Wear Ceremonial Knives to School. 1994. *Los Angeles Times*, 3 September, A22.

Vecoli, Rudolph J. 1995. *Gale Encyclopedia of Multicultural America*, Vols. 1 and 2. New York: Gale Research.

Victoria's Secret Sorry for Buddha Bikinis. 2004. *Dhamma Times*, 30 July. http://www.dhammathai.org/e/news/m07/bnews30_2.php

Visser, Margaret. 1991. *The Rituals of Dinner*. New York: Grove Weidenfeld.

Wadd, Lois. 1983. Vietnamese Postpartum Practices: Implications for Nursing in the Hospital Setting. *JOGN Nursing* 4: 252–257.

Wagenhauser, Betsy. 1999. The Customs and Traditions of the Kazakh. *Washington Times*. http://www.internationalspecialreports.com/ciscentralasia/99/kazak

Warren, Jennifer. 1994. Schools Sued for Barring Sikhs Wearing Ceremonial Knives. *Los Angeles Times*, 16 April, A29.

Wedlan, Candace A. 2000. A More Mature Approach to Modeling. *Los Angeles Times*, 18 August, E2.

West, John O. 1988. *Mexican-American Folklore*. Little Rock, AR: August House.

When a "Weapon" Is a Sacred Symbol. 1994. *The Daily Review* (Oakland, CA), 16 February, A–14.

Wilgoren, Jodi. 2003. The End of the Road for "Devil's Highway." *New York Times*, 13 June. http://www.nytimes.com/2003/06/13/travel/Road .html?th-&p

Willcox, Don. 1986. *Hmong Folklife*. P.O. Box 1, Penland, NC 28765: Hmong Natural Association of North Carolina.

Wilson, Susan L. 2001. *Culture Shock!: Egypt*. Portland, OR: Graphic Arts Center Publishing Company.

Winton, Richard. 1993. Addressing Concerns about Unlucky Street Numbers. *Los Angeles Times* (Glendale), 30 September, J1, 4.

Wiscombe, Janet. 1994. The Boy from the Other Side. *Press-Telegram* (Long Beach, CA), 28 August, J1, 10.

Wolff, Craig. 1990. Parading into Fall to the Tempo of the Day. *New York Times*, 4 September, B1, 3.

Wong, Angi Ma. 1993. *Target: The U.S. Asian Market*. Palos Verdes, CA: Pacific Heritage Books.

World Factbook. 2004. Central Intelligence Agency. http://www.cia.gov/cia/publications/factbook

Yoffe, Emily. 1991. Ancient Art, Modern Fad. *Newsweek*, 23 December, 42.

Index

abrazo, 17
absenteeism, 49–50
accents, 187–188
affection, signs of, 18–19
Afghans, 220–221
  body language, 19
  colors, 66–67
  foodways, 72
  luck/supernatural forces, 129
African Americans, 204
  body language, 12, 22–24
  classroom behavior, 44
  race relations and, 169–170
  verbal expressions, 189
Africans, 204–216
  clothing/jewelry, 58
  foodways, 75, 79
  gifts, 95
  traffic violations, 151–152
  See also individual nationalities
age issues, 188–189
agusto, 30
AIDS, 101–102, 193
Alaskans, 171–172
Albanians, 11–12, 233–234
alcohol, 79, 115, 184
Algerians, 204–205
Al Hussein, Imam, 250–251
alternative healers, 107–108
Americans (United States)
  body contact, 23
  business practices, 155–157
  foodways, 78
  friendship, 161–162
  luck/supernatural forces,
    133–134
  male/female relations, 145, 149
  population, 2

verbal expression, 183–187, 191,
    193
  See also individual nationalities
Amish, 51
Anguish of Snails, The (Toelken), 152
appearance, importance of, 193
Arabs, 26, 79, 110. *See also individual
    nationalities*
archery, 216–217
Armenians, 238–239
  body language, 17, 24
  classroom behavior, 47
  gifts, 91–92
  luck/supernatural forces, 135
  male/female relations, 145
  time, 179–180
  verbal expression, 197
art
  folk arts, 241
  Ricksha, 222
  vehicular, 221
Asian Pacific American Legal
    Center, 144
Asians, 216–220
  body language, 13, 15–17, 21–22,
    22–24, 26
  child-rearing practices, 29–30, 35
  classroom behavior, 40–41, 43–44,
    46
  clothing/jewelry, 54, 56
  colors, 64–65, 65–66
  foodways, 73, 75, 78, 80–81
  friendship, 161–162
  gifts, 92–93
  health practices, 106–107
  male/female relations, 143–145
  physical contact, 15
  prejudice, 172–173

271

Asians *(continued)*
　temporary nuns, 156
　verbal expression, 189–191
　See also individual nationalities
Australia, 126–127
authority. *See* respect
autism, 38–39
Avoian, Samuel, 23
Azerbaijanis, 72, 184, 239

ba-gua, 130
baithak, 225
Bali, 229
Balkans, 233–237
balut, 228
bargaining, 195–197
baths, public, 218
batik, 227
beds, 29–30, 110–111, 130
Belarusians, 239–240
belching, 81
Bengali, 17, 221–222
Best Places to Kiss, The (Bykofsky), 18
Bhutanese, 216–217
birth control, 111–112
birthdays
　cakes, 99
　Chinese, 160–161, 217
　dates of, 151–152, 160–161
　Lithuanian, 244–245
black magic, 136
black wedding clothes, 67–68
blood, drawing, 105
blue, light, 65
body language
　affectionate displays, 18–19
　crooked finger gesture, 20
　eye contact, 22–24
　head, touching of, 15
　lining up, 24–25
　male/female, 12–13, 15–17, 18–19
　one-at-a-time interaction, 25–26
　physical contact, 12–13, 15–17
　smell, 26–27
　smiling, 20–22
　thumbs-up gesture, 19

　using ethnic gestures/jargon, 12
　yes/no head gestures, 11–12, 254
Bomse, Stephen V., 61
Bosnians and Herzegovinans, 72–73, 234
bowing, 16, 155–156, 245
boxes of food, 83
Brazilians, 108
breast feeding, 31–32
bribery, 94–95
Bridge Builders of Anchorage, 171–172
British, 119–120
Buddhists
　firewalking, 226
　holidays, 223, 231
　red ink, 64–65
　shoe removal, 54
　symbols of, 53–56
　temples, 155
Building Relationships Toward Racial Harmony (BRRH), 169–170
Bulgarians, 11–12
burial practices, 164, 208, 229.
　See also death
Burmese. *See* Myanmar/Burmese
business practices
　bargaining and, 196
　bribery, 94–95
　business cards, 155–156
　color and, 68–69
　consideration for customers' holidays and, 180–181
　establishing rapport, 156–157
　luck/supernatural forces, 130–131, 133–134
　Middle Eastern customs, 197–198
　Muslim business cards, 168
　one-at-a-time interactions, 26
Bykovsky, Sheree, 18

Cajuns, 108
cakes, birthday, 99
California State University–Fullerton, 163

Cambodians, 226–227
  body language, 23–24
  child-rearing practices, 31–32
  foodways, 80, 81–83, 88–89
  health practices, 108, 112
  verbal expression, 189–191
camouflage clothing, 52
Canadians, 22
Carey, Benedict, 112
Caribbean Islanders
  body language, 22
  classroom behavior, 48–49
  health practices, 108
  luck/supernatural forces, 127–128
  prejudice toward, 174–175
  See also individual nationalities
carpets, Turkmen, 247
cats, 218
cellular memory phenomenon, 103
Census, U.S., 2, 204
Central Americans, 39–40, 86
change, giving, 12–13
chaperones, 33
Chassiakos, Linda, 102–103
chastity, 147
cheating, in school, 44–45
Cheese Sunday, 236
chicken soup, 86
child custody, 149
child-rearing practices
  baby naming, 224
  bed sharing, 29–30
  birth attendants, 110
  breast feeding, 31–32
  chaperones, 33
  coining, 34–35
  complimenting babies, 183, 234
  ignoring newborn babies, 106–107
  independence, 32–33
  mother roasting, 88
  postpartum behavior, 29
  smell and, 27
  Somalian, 214
  white bonnets, 65–66
  See also birth control; *individual nationalities*

Chinese, 217–218
  birthday dates, 160–161, 217
  business practices, 156–157
  child-rearing practices, 29, 31–32
  clothing/jewelry, 54
  colors, 63–69
  foodways, 75–76, 80, 82, 83, 88–89
  gifts, 92–96
  health practices, 105, 110
  holidays, 116, 120–121, 181
  luck/supernatural forces, 125–126, 129–137
  nicknames for children, 231
  physical contact, 15–17
  verbal expression, 189–191
  weddings, 116
  See also Vietnamese
cholent, 251
chopsticks, 80, 105
Christians, secular holidays and, 117
Christmas, 208, 235, 245
Church of the Lukumi Babalu Aye v. Hialeah, 58
CIA World Factbook, 204
circumcision, 211, 212, 255–256
classroom behavior
  absenteeism, 49–50
  authority, fear of, 39–40
  authority, respect for, 46–49
  bribery, 94–95
  cheating, 44–45
  corporal punishment, 43–44
  enrichment activities, 38
  insulting language, 41–42
  left-handedness, 42–43
  modesty, 59–60
  special education, 38–39
  student participation, 40–41
  testing, 37–38
  See also schools
Clinton, Bill, 19, 189–191
clocks, as gifts, 96
clothing
  black worn by wedding guests, 67–68
  camouflage, 52

clothing (*continued*)
East Timorese, 227
feredza, 234
formality, 62
green hats, 63
hats, 51
Hmong sewing arts, 230
kandoura, 256
kidan habesha, 206
modesty in, 59–60
neckties, 235
Nigerian, 212
religious articles, 51, 56–57, 60–62
respect for teachers and, 47
salwar kameez, 223
shämma, 207
shoes, 54, 56
stereotypes and, 174
symbols, 55–56, 85
Tajik, 246
Turkmen, 247
white bonnets, 65–66
white worn by wedding guests,
66–67, 66–68
See also jewelry
coffee, 236, 252, 255, 256
coining, 34–35
coins
with gifts, 96
mourning customs, 97
cold foods, 87–89
collares, 58
Colombians, 32–33
colors
black worn by wedding guests,
67–68
green hats, 63
light blue, 63
red ink, 64–65
white appliances, 68
white bonnets, 65–66
white envelopes, 96–97
white worn by wedding guests,
66–68
yellow flowers, 91–92
yellow tags, 68–69

coming-of-age ceremonies, 209, 214,
229
communication, directness of,
183–184, 195. *See also* verbal
expression
competition, 185–186
"contagious magic," 127
contraception, 111–112
Cook Islanders, 83
corporal punishment, 43–44
Costa Ricans, 33
couscous, 205
Croats, 234–235
crooked finger gesture, 20
Cross, Sign of, 14
Crossing the BLVD (Lehrer, Sloan), 168
Cubans, 57–59, 108
cupping, 34

Daranaagama Kusaladhamma, 55
dating, 145–146, 149–150
deal-making
bargaining and, 195–197
completion of, 158
death
black worn to weddings, 67–68
funeral flowers, 93–94
Lao practices, 229
Prachum Ben, 226
red ink as sign of, 64–65
stones on graves, 139–140
Vietnamese customs, 232–233
wedding clothing and, 66–68
white bonnets, 65–66
white envelopes, 96–97
white flowers, 92–93
yellow flowers, 91–92
dietary laws, religious, 72–73, 77–79,
206
Dinka, 214
Discovery Channel, 103–104
"divide the sadness," 232
divorce, 149
dogs, 153
Dominicans, 33, 75–76
donkey beads, 56–57

Donna Karan International, 85
Double Fifth Day, 220
Dresser, Norine, 5–7
"Dutch treat," 76

East Africans, 151–152
Easter, 246
Eastern Europeans, 105. *See also individual nationalities*
Eastern Orthodox Church, 14
East Timorese, 227
Eck, Diana, 3, 4
Ecuadorans, 33, 149–150
eggs, 71, 248
Egyptians, 205–206
El Ghriba, 215
ema datse, 217
enrichment activities, for schools, 38
envelopes
    red, 97, 120, 136–137
    white, 96–97
envy, 98–99
Eritreans, 151–152, 206
Estonians, 240–241
Ethiopians, 151–152, 206–207
    friendliness and, 186–187
    student participation, 40–41
evil eye, 98, 99, 106–107, 138–139, 183, 234, 241
exorcism, 225
eye contact, 22–24, 52

facial expressions, smiling, 20–22
family, loyalty to, 49–50, 177–178
fast-food bag design, 84–85
feng shui, 111, 129–131
Filipinos, 227–228
    body language, 27
    child-rearing practices, 30
    clothing/jewelry, 54
    foodways, 74, 79, 80, 81, 82
    luck/supernatural forces, 129
    verbal expression, 186
    weddings, 228
fingers, eating with, 79, 80, 209, 213
Finkbeiner, Carty, 169

fire, jumping over, 117–118
firewalking, 226
first foot tradition, 119–120
fish, 79
flowers, 91–94, 135
Flying Fish Ceremony, 220
folk arts, 241
foodways, 78
    boxes of food, 83
    cleaning the plate, 81–83, 213
    eating noises, 80–81
    eating with utensils, 79–80
    eggs, 71
    fast-food bag design, 84–85
    habit changes, 72–73
    haft seen, 250
    heart transplants and licorice, 103–105
    hot/cold food, 87–89
    meal completeness, 76–77
    medicinal foods, 85–87
    milk intolerance, 74–75
    Moroccan, 211
    offering food, 73–74
    politics and, 83–84
    potluck style, 74–75
    refusing food, 72
    Romanian customs, 184
    taboos, 77–79
    See also holidays; *individual foods*
French
    body language, 14, 17
    colors, 69
    foodways, 78
friendliness, 186–187
friendship, 161–162, 231
fruit carving, 231–232
funeral flowers, 93–94

gangs, 53
garlic, 86
genealogy, 213
Genna, 207
Georgians, 241–242
Germans, 108
Geshekter, Charles, 213

Ghanaians, 207–208
gifts
    Azerbaijan customs, 239
    bribery and, 94–95
    bridewealth, 213
    envelopes, white, 96–97
    envy of, 99
    flowers, 91–94
    of food, 83
    refusal of, 98
    taboos, 95–96
gita, 211
gladioli, 93
glass-bead necklaces, 57–59
goat soup, 209
Greeks, 14
greetings, 27, 252–253, 253
    idioms, 191–192
    verbal expression, 184–185
    welcoming ceremonies, 158–159
    See also body language; *individual
        nationalities*
griots, 210–211
gris-gris, 123–124
Guatemalans, 162–163
gurdwara, 155
Gypsies. *See* Roms/Gypsies

hair, 167, 251
Haitians
    clothing/jewelry, 58
    foodways, 75–76
    health practices, 108
    luck/supernatural forces, 124
    See also voodoo *(voudun)*
Halloween, 116–117
hand-holding, 18–19
handshaking, 16, 209, 234
haole, 27
harambee, 209
hats
    dopy, 249
    green, 63
    religious, 51, 61, 167–169
    white bonnets, 65–66

Hawaiians, 27, 126–127, 183
head, 11, 15, 51, 61, 167–169.
    See also hats
Healing Latinos (Nuño), 103
health practices
    AIDS, stereotypes and, 101–102
    alternative healers, 107–108
    belief in evil spirits, 108–109
    birth attendants, 110
    birth control, 111
    coining, 34–35
    doctors' orders misunderstood,
        102–103, 111–112
    food as medicine, 85–87
    food temperature, 87–89
    hospital accommodations, 105–106,
        110–111
    ignoring babies, 106–107
    life support, 112–113
    physical examinations, 109–110
    transplants, 103–105
heart transplant, 103–105
henna parties, 257
Hindus
    dietary laws, 77–79
    firewalking, 226
    holidays, 230
    male/female relations, 164–165
    prayer scarves, 57
    swastika symbol, 53–54
    symbols in nonreligious items,
        55–56
    temples, 155
Hiroto Murasawa, 21
Hispanics, 68
Hmong, 1–2
    birthday dates, 160–161
    body language, 15
    foodways, 80
    health practices, 108–109, 112
    holidays, 116
    luck/supernatural forces,
        128–129
    sewing arts, 230
    verbal expression, 183, 189–191

holidays
  Armenian Martyrs Day, 238
  Cheese Sunday, 236
  Christmas, 208, 235, 245
  Double Fifth Day, 220
  Easter, 246
  El Ghriba, 215
  first foot tradition, 119–120
  Ganapati, 165
  Genna, 207
  Halloween, 116–117
  Hindus, 230
  Holy Cross Day, 255
  homowo, 207–208
  jumping over fires, 117–118
  Kason Festival, 224
  Krsna Slava, 236–237
  Lag B'Omer, 251
  New Year's offerings, 118–119
    (*See also* New Year customs)
  Passover, 77, 180
  Prachum Ben, 226
  Purim, 117
  Ramadan, 115, 214
  Setsubun, 218
  Shrove Tuesday, 237
  Snake Festival, 223
  St. Casimir's Day, 245
  St. George's Day, 241
  St. John's Day, 244
  Surin Elephant Roundup, 232
  sweeping away luck, 120–121
  Thanksgiving, 116
  Thingyan, 223
  Vasak Day, 231
  Wandering Souls Day, 233
  See also foodways
Holy Cross Day, 255
homosexuals, 65, 142
homowo, 207–208
honey, 85–87
Hong, Byung Sik, 21
hongi, 27
Hong Kong, 81. *See also* Chinese
Hopi Native Americans, 124, 153–154

horsemanship, 242–243
hospitality, 162–163, 179–180
hospitals, accommodations by,
    105–106, 110–111
hot foods, 87–89
Hutus, 212–213

ice sculptures, 217
idioms, 187–188, 191–192
immigration, misconceptions about,
    170–171
Indians, 222–223
  body language, 11–12, 17
  clothing/jewelry, 54, 57
  colors, 66–67
  foodways, 78, 79
  gifts, 98
  time and, 178–179
  verbal expression, 183, 188–189
  See also Roms/Gypsies
Indochine, 106
Indonesians, 228–229
  foodways, 76–77, 80
  verbal expression, 185
inequality, gender, 148
infidelity, 63
Iranians, 249–250
  birthday dates, 161
  classroom behavior, 43–44
  clothing/jewelry, 54, 56–57
  foodways, 85–87, 88
  gifts, 91–92, 98
  health practices, 113
  holidays, 117–118, 250
  luck/supernatural forces, 129,
    138–139
  male/female relations, 147
  prejudice and, 168
Iraqis, 52, 149, 250
Islam. *See* Muslims
Israelis, 60, 251
Italians, 14, 17

Jacobs, Bruce, 169–170
Jains, 53–54

Jamaicans, 47–49
Japanese, 218
    body language, 13, 16, 18, 20, 21,
        22
    business cards, 155–156
    clothing/jewelry, 54
    foodways, 81
    gifts, 96
    luck/supernatural forces, 132, 134
    male/female relations, 141, 148
    verbal expression, 195
jargon, 12
Javanese, 74
Jeepneys, 228
jewelry, 52–54, 55–59. *See also* clothing
Jews
    burial practices, 139–140, 164
    clothing/jewelry, 51–52, 52
    evil eye, 107
    foodways, 77–78
    holidays, 77, 117, 180, 215, 251
    Sabbath, 105–106, 251
    temples, 155
    time and, 180–181
    verbal expression, 183
    See also Orthodox Jews
Jordanians, 82, 251–252
jumping over fires, 117–118

Kason Festival, 224
Kazakhs, 242–243
Kenyans, 208–209
kidan habesha, 206
kirpan, 60–62
kissing, 18–19
kites, 230
knives, 60–62, 96
Koreans
    body language, 13, 21, 23
    business practices, 156–157
    clothing/jewelry, 54
    colors, 64–65
    foodways, 74, 78, 80, 82
    gifts, 94–95
    luck/supernatural forces, 132

    North, 218–219
    South, 219–220
    verbal expression, 189–191
Kosavars, 42
kosher, 77–78. *See also* dietary laws,
        religious
koufeih, 57
Krsna Slava, 236–237
Kuwaitis, 252–253
Kyrgyz, 243

lactose intolerance, 74–75
Lag B'Omer, 251
language. *See* verbal expression;
        individual nationalities
Lao, 80, 88, 229–230. *See also* Hmong
Latinos
    body language, 14, 15, 17, 22, 23,
        25–26
    business practices, 156–157
    child-rearing practices, 29–30,
        31–32, 33, 35
    classroom behavior, 37–38, 39–40,
        43–44, 44, 49–50
    clothing/jewelry, 57–59
    foodways, 88–89
    friendship, 161–162
    health practices, 103, 108, 111–112
    male/female relations, 143,
        144–145, 150
    prejudice toward, 170–171
    verbal expression, 190–191
    See also individual nationalities
Latter-Day Saints. *See* Mormons
Latvians, 243–244
lauk-pauk, 76
Lebanese, 253–254
left hand, hygiene and, 79, 206, 234
left-handedness, 42–43
Lehrer, Warren, 168
lesbians, 142
Liberians, 209
Libyans, 210
Lichtenstein, Mark, 168
licitar, 235

licorice, 103–105
life support medical practices,
    112–113
Limbu, 224
line forming, 24–25
lip smacking, 81
Lithuanians, 244–245
Liz Claiborne Inc., 85
luck and supernatural forces
    baby furniture delivery, 137–138
    black magic, 136
    complimenting babies, 183, 234
    cremated ashes, 124–125
    evil eye, 138–139
    feng shui, 111, 129–131
    gris-gris, 123–124
    knocking on wood, 240
    moving, timing of, 131–132
    numbers and, 132–135
    powder and, 127–128
    red envelopes, 136–137
    rocks and, 126–127, 139–140
    solar eclipse, 128–129
    sweeping away, 120–121
    washing, 125–126
    See also individual nationalities
Lucumi religion. *See* Santería religion

Macedonians, 235–236
mad-dogging, 23–24
Mahoney, Michael T., 2
Malaysians, 230
male/female relations
    birth attendants and, 110
    birth control, 111–112
    menstruation, separation of women
        during, 164–165
    physical contact, 12–19
    sexual education, 143, 187
    surnames, 189–191
Malian, 210–211
Maneki Neko, 218
Maoris, 27
map, 202–203
Martyrs Day, Armenian, 238

matooke, 215–216
McGrayne, Sharon Bertsch, 141
medicine
    alternative, 107–108
    food as, 85–87, 103–105
    misunderstandings about, 102–103
    See also health practices
Mediterranean culture, 15, 17, 34–35.
        See also individual nationalities
meishi, 155–156
menstruation, 164–165
Mexicans, 163
    body language, 22
    child-rearing practices, 29–30
    classroom behavior, 41–42, 49–50
    clothing/jewelry, 55–56
    colors, 64–65
    gifts, 91–92, 95
    health practices, 107–108, 110
    holidays, 118
    prejudice toward, 173–174
    verbal expression, 183, 189–191, 196
Middle Easterners, 249–257
    body language, 15, 17, 19
    business practices, 156–157
    child-rearing practices, 29–30,
        34–35
    classroom behavior, 44
    clothing/jewelry, 56–57
    foodways, 88–89
    friendship, 161–162
    gifts, 95, 98, 99
    male/female relations, 149
    verbal expression, 193, 196,
        197–198
    See also individual nationalities
Miens, 189–191
milk, 74–75
modesty, 59–60
Moldovans, 245
Mongolian spots, 35
Mormons
    foodways, 79
    luck/supernatural forces, 134
    temples, 154–155, 159

Moroccans, 211
mosques, 171
mother roasting, 88
Motorola, 130
Mountain Bible College, 134
"multiculturalism," 3
Multicultural Manners (Dresser), 5–7
Muslims, 252
    birthday dates, 161
    body language, 12–13, 17, 205–206
    classroom behavior, 42–43
    clothing/jewelry, 59–60
    foodways, 72–73, 78, 79, 85
    health practices, 105, 110–111
    holidays, 115, 214
    male/female relations, 143,
      145–147
    prejudice toward, 168
    Qur'an, 42–43, 85, 153
    Shi'ite, 249–251
    Sunni, 249
    traffic violations and, 151–153
Myanmar/Burmese, 156, 190,
    223–224
Mystrom, Rick, 172

Nakaima tree, worship at, 216
namaste, 17
name traditions, 189–191, 224, 231
National Centers for Disease Control,
    101
Native Americans
    business practices, 158
    child-rearing practices, 35
    foodways, 75
    generosity, 153–154
    luck/supernatural forces, 124–125,
      134
    prejudice toward, 171–172
    time and, 177–178
    visitors, 152–153
    welcoming ceremonies, 158–159
Navajo Native Americans
    foodways, 79
    generosity, 153–154

    luck/supernatural forces, 134
    visitors, 152–153
neckties, 235
Nepalese, 76–77, 224
New Year customs
    Albanian, 233–234
    Chinese, 116, 120–121, 181
    Iranian, 117–118, 250
    Jewish, 180
    Korean, 219
    Lao, 230
    Russian, 246
    Vietnamese, 117–121, 125–126,
      160–161
New York State Board of Regents, 181
Nigerians, 178–179, 211–212
Niño Fidencio, 136
Nobel Prize Women in Science
    (McGrayne), 141
Northern Europeans, 174–175. *See
    also individual nationalities*
Nuer, 214
numbers
    of addresses, 132–134
    on business cards of Muslims, 168
    gifts and, 135
    photos and, 134–135
Nuño, Ismael, 103
nuns, temporary, 156

Old Farmer's Almanac, 131
oral history, 210–211
Orisha religion. *See* Santería religion
Orthodox Jews
    body language, 13, 17
    clothing/jewelry, 51, 60
    foodways, 77–78
    health practices, 105–106, 110
    holidays, 116–117
    luck/supernatural forces, 137–139
    male/female relations, 165
    See also Jews

Pakistanis, 54, 168, 224–225
Palau people, 83

Palestinians, 161
Pancake Week, 246
Passover, 77, 180
Persians. *See* Iranians
Pert, Candace, 104
Peruvians, 91–92
physical abuse, 43–44
physical education, 59–60
pineapple, 78
Plains Native Americans, 158
plate, cleaning of, 81–83, 213
polenta, 210
Portugese, 17
postpartum behavior. *See* child-rearing
    practices; health practices
potluck meals, 75–76
Prachum Ben, 226
praise, 185–186, 193
prayer. *See individual religions*
prayer scarves, 57
pregnancy. *See* child-rearing practices;
    health practices
prejudice
    Bridge Builders of Anchorage,
        171–172
    fear and, 171
    immigration, 170–171
    race relations, 169–170
    September 11, 2001 attacks and,
        167–169
    stereotypes and, 172–175
Protestants, 79
Puerto Ricans
    body language, 21, 25–26
    foodways, 75–76, 78, 86
    health practices, 108
    luck/supernatural forces, 139
    prejudice toward, 174
    verbal expression, 192–193
Punch, Jeff, 104
Punjabis, 223
puppet plays, 229
Purim, 117

Qur'an (Koran), 42–43, 85, 153

Race Manners (Jacobs), 169–170
race relations, 169–170
radiation, 105
Rafi, Mohamed, 104
Ramadan, 115, 214
Reagan, Ronald, 134
red envelopes, 97, 120, 136–137
religion. *See individual nationalities;*
    individual religions
respect
    fear of authority and, 39–40,
        151–152
    formality, 62, 188–189
    for older males, Lebanese, 253
    for teachers, 46–49
    yes/no questions and, 193–195
rice, 76, 222
Ricksha art, 222
right hand, eating with, 80
right-handedness, 42–43
Roberts, Malcolm R., 172
Robinson, Don, 131
rocks, 126–127, 139–140
Roman Catholics, 14, 55–56, 77–79
Romanians, 183–184
Roms/Gypsies, 109–110, 177–178
roosters, sacrifice of, 108–109
Rossbach, Sarah, 130
Russian Orthodox Church, 14
Russians, 245–246
    clothing/jewelry, 62
    colors, 65
    health practices, 105
    See also USSR
Rwandans, 212–213

Sackner, Marvin, 86
sacrifice, 58, 108–109, 220
salaam, 17
salwar kameez, 223
San Diego Police Department, 2,
    151–152
Santería religion, 57–59, 127–128
Saudis, 81, 85, 254
Saund, Dalip Singh, 167

schools
accommodations by, 108–109
time and, 181
visiting students at home, 152–153
See also classroom behavior
"scratch the wind," 34
selimut, 227
September 11, 2001 attacks, 167–169
Serbians and Montenegrans, 236–237
Setsubun, 218
Seventh-Day Adventists, 78
sexual education, 143, 187
shadow puppet plays, 229
shämma, 207
Shampoo Day, 219
Sheehan, Susan, 39
Shi'ite Muslims, 249–251
shoes, 54, 55, 56, 254
Shrove Tuesday, 237
Sign of the Cross, 14
Sikh Mediawatch and Resource Task
Force (SMART), 51
Sikhs
clothing/jewelry, 51, 60–62
prejudice toward, 167–169
temples, 155
Singaporeans, 231
Sloan, Judith, 168
Slovenians/Slovenes, 237
slurping, while eating, 80–81
smell, 26–27
smiling, 20–22
smoking, 215
Snake Festival, 223
sneezing, 224
snow sculptures, 217–218
socioeconomic class, 48, 175
Somalians, 151–152, 213–214
South Americans, 32–33, 52.
See also individual nationalities
South Asians, 220–226. *See also*
Afghans; Asians; Bengali;
Indians; Myanmar/Burmese;
Nepalese; Pakistanis;
Sri Lankans

Southeast Asians, 226–233
foodways, 86
gifts, 95
health practices, 105, 112
See also Cambodians; East
Timorese; Filipinos; Indonesians;
Lao; Malaysians; Singaporeans;
Thai; Vietnamese
South Pacific Islanders, 11–12
Soviet Union. *See* USSR
Spaniards, 14, 17, 69
spanking, in school, 43–44
special education, 38–39
spousal abuse, 143–145
Sri Lankans, 17, 79, 225–226
St. Casimir's Day, 245
St. George's Day, 241
St. John's Day, 244
stars, six-pointed, 52–53
stereotypes, 1–2, 101–102
about academic skill, 172–173
of immigrants, 170–171
See also prejudice
students. *See* classroom behavior
Sudanese, 151–152, 214
sun, eclipse of, 128–129
sunglasses, 52
Sunni Muslims, 249
Surin Elephant Roundup, 232
surnames, 189–191
Sustaya, Paul, 55
symbols
Estonian, 241
religious, 52–53, 55–56, 60–62, 85
swastika, 53–54
synagogues, 155
Syrians, 254–255

Taiwanese, 220
classroom behavior, 43–44, 46–47
colors, 63
foodways, 84
luck/supernatural forces, 128–129
Tajiks, 246–247
tajin, 211

tattoos, 206
teachers. *See* classroom behavior
teeth, lost by children, 225, 226, 230, 238–239, 242, 243, 254
teeth-filing rituals, 229
temperature, of foods, 87–89
temples, 154–155
testing, in schools, 37–38
Tet, 117–120, 125–126, 160–161
Thai, 231–232
   body language, 17
   clothing/jewelry, 54
   foodways, 74, 80
   temples, 155
Thanksgiving, 116
theater, 229
Thingyan, 223
thumbs-up gesture, 19
time
   community obligations *vs.*, 177–178
   consideration about holidays and, 180–181
   timeliness, 178–179
   unannounced visitors and, 179–180
Toelken, Barre, 152
Tongans, 73–74
traffic violations, 151–152
Transplanting Memories (Discovery Channel), 103–104
transplants, 103–105
Tunisians, 214–215
Turkmens, 247
Turks, 255
Tutsis, 213

UCLA Archive of American Popular Beliefs and Superstitions, 131–132
Ugandans, 215–216
Ukrainians, 247–248
umbrellas, as gifts, 95–96
United Arab Emirates, 256
Universal Studios, 24
U.S. Bureau of the Census, 2, 204
U.S. Marine Corps, 2

USSR
   classroom behavior, 47
   members of, 238–249
   See also individual nationalities
utensils, for eating, 79–80, 105, 213
Uzbeks, 71, 248–249

Vasak Day, 231
vegetable carving, 231–232
vehicular art, 221
verbal expression
   comments on appearance, 193
   complimenting babies, 183
   direct communication and, 183–184
   formality, 188–189
   friendliness, 186–187
   greetings, 184–185
   idioms, 191–192
   misinterpreting language, 192–193
   name traditions, 189–191
   praise, 185–186
   understanding accents, 187–188
   yes/no questions, 193–195
Vietnamese, 232–233
   body language, 15–17
   child-rearing practices, 31–32, 34
   classroom behavior, 40–41
   clothing/jewelry, 60, 66
   foodways, 73, 80, 84, 88–89
   gifts, 96–97
   health practices, 106–107
   holidays, 117–121, 125–126, 160–161
   luck/supernatural forces, 125–126
   politics and, 163
   verbal expression, 189–191
"Voodoo Squad," 127–128
voodoo *(voudun)*, 58, 123–124

Walt Disney Company, 131
Wandering Souls Day, 233
wat, 155
weddings, 142
   Afghan, 220

weddings *(continued)*
  arranged marriage, 242
  Berber, 210
  black worn to weddings, 67–68
  bowing and, 245
  boxes of food at, 83
  bride capture, 205
  bride price, 229
  bridewealth, 212–213
  Cambodian, 226
  Chinese, 116
  Filipino, 228
  Georgian customs, 242
  Japanese, 218
  Javanese, 229
  Korean, 219
  Moroccan, 211
  Syrian, 255
  Tajik, 247
  Ukrainian, 248
  white worn to weddings, 66–68
  See also male/female relations
welcoming home ceremonies,
  158–159
white
  bonnets, 65–66

  envelopes, 96–97
  flowers, 92–93
  worn by wedding guests, 66–68
Wong, Angi Ma, 133
wood, knocking on, 240
worry beads, 253
worship, places of, 54, 154–155, 171,
  216

Yami, 220
yarmulke, 51, 61
yellow
  flowers, 91–92
  tags, 68–69
Yemenis, 256–257
  classroom behavior, 50
  foodways, 75–76
  male/female relations, 143
yes/no questions
  body language, 11–12, 254
  verbal expression, 193–195
yogurt, 73
Yoruba, 58
yurt/yurta, 243, 247

zuo yuezi, 29

About the Author

Cross-cultural customs and beliefs have fascinated folklorist Norine Dresser for over thirty years and have been the focus of her university teaching, research, and writing. The original *Multicultural Manners* book (Wiley, 1996) and her *Los Angeles Times* "Multicultural Manners" column (1993 to 2001) earned the 1998 John Anson Ford Award for contributions toward resolving intergroup conflict, conferred by the County of Los Angeles Commission on Human Relations.

Demystifying cross-cultural miscommunication has become her passion, and she frequently addresses this issue in venues such as the New York State Department of Health, Food Stamp and Nutrition Workers; the Institute for the Study of Cultural Diversity and Internationalization; the Children's Hospital of Los Angeles; Magnet Schools of America; the Levi-Strauss Corporate Center; and the Los Angeles County Museum of Art.

She has published on eclectic topics ranging from missing gerbils to horse bar mitzvahs to Jewish shopping habits to ESL books. Her book *American Vampires: Fans, Victims & Practitioners* (Vintage, 1990) transported her to Hungary, where she appeared in a scene with George Hamilton in a TV special, *Dracula—Live from Transylvania*. In 1995, she was a guest of the Romanian Ministry of Tourism and a presenter at the groundbreaking First World Dracula Congress in Romania.

Dresser taught for twenty years in the English and American Studies Department at California State University, Los Angeles. She received research grants from the Smithsonian Institution and the National Endowment for the Humanities. She has been interviewed on radio's Voice of America and television shows airing on HBO, The Learning Channel, Women's Entertainment Channel, KTLA, Fox Family TV, and KNBC. Visit her Web site: www.norinedresser.com